THE NAKED TEXT

Roof boss from Norwich Cathedral. Photo by Julia Hedgecoe, Cambridge, England.

THE NAKED TEXT

CHAUCER'S
LEGEND OF GOOD WOMEN

Sheila Delany

University of California Press
Berkeley · Los Angeles · London

University of California Press
Berkeley and Los Angeles, California

University of California Press, Ltd.
London, England

© 1994 by
The Regents of the University of California

Library of Congress Cataloging-in-Publication Data

Delany, Sheila.
    The naked text : Chaucer's Legend of good women /
Sheila Delany.
        p.   cm.
    Includes bibliographical references and index.
    ISBN 0-520-08119-6 (alk. paper)
    1. Chaucer, Geoffrey, d. 1400. Legend of good
women.   2. Chaucer, Geoffrey, d. 1400—Political and
social views.   3. Women and literature— England—
History.   4. Mythology, Classical, in literature.   5. Women
in literature.   I. Title.
    PR1882.D45   1994
    821'.1—dc20   92-21191
                                                              CIP

Printed in the United States of America

9 8 7 6 5 4 3 2

Permission is gratefully acknowledged for use of lyrics to
"Silver Dollar" on p. 90. Words and music by Jack Palmer
and Clarke Van Ness. TRO © Copyright 1939 (renewed),
1950 (renewed). Essex Music, Inc., New York, N.Y.

The paper used in this publication meets the minimum
requirements of American National Standard for
Information Sciences—Permanence of Paper for Printed
Library Materials, ANSI Z39.48-1984. ∞

*In memory of
my friend Dr. Phyllis Saifer
and
my comrade Martha Phillips—
two good women
who made a difference.*

Contents

Acknowledgments

Portions of this book have appeared, in different versions, in the following journals or books: "Rewriting Woman Good: Gender and the Anxiety of Influence in Two Late-Medieval Texts," in *Chaucer in the Eighties*, ed. Julian Wasserman and Robert J. Blanch (Syracuse, N.Y.: Syracuse University Press, 1986), and in *Medieval Literary Politics* (see below); "The Logic of Obscenity in Chaucer's *Legend of Good Women*," *Florilegium* 7 (1987): 189–205; "Geoffrey of Monmouth and Chaucer's *Legend of Good Women*," *Chaucer Review* 22 (1988): 170–74; "The Naked Text: Chaucer's 'Thisbe', the *Ovide moralisé*, and the Problem of *translatio studii* in the *Legend of Good Women*," *Mediaevalia* 13 (1989 for 1987): 275–94; "Women, Nature and Language: Chaucer's *Legend of Good Women*," in S. Delany, *Medieval Literary Politics: Shapes of Ideology* (Manchester: Manchester University Press/New York: St. Martin's Press, 1990); "Orientalism," in the inaugural issue of *Chaucer Yearbook* (1992): 1–32. Some of the material has also been presented at conferences: Chaucer at Albany II (1982), the New Chaucer Society Biennial Congress (1984, 1986, and 1992), the Philological Association of the Pacific Coast (1984), and the Binghamton Medieval Conference (1986).

The last phase of research and writing was helped by two release-time stipends from Canada's Social Sciences and Humanities Research Council (SSHRC) during the academic years 1987–88 and 1989–90, and by a President's Research Grant from Simon Fraser University, which enabled me to consult manuscripts and early printed material at the British Library and Cambridge University in 1989. I have much appreciated the energetic efficiency of my research assistants Barry Maxwell, Arlene Cook, and Barry Reid at the beginning and end phases of the work, the always reliable help of Anita Mahoney and other staff in the Dean of Arts office at SFU in producing the manuscript, and the tireless, good-natured assistance of the Interlibrary Loans and other library staff at SFU.

Among my SFU colleagues I want to thank Margret Jackson and Paul Dutton for help in clarifying points of Latin. Tom Grieve called my attention to the relevance of Ezra Pound; Harvey deRoo made available at crucial moments his intimate knowledge of DOS. Further afield, I am grateful to David Aers of the University of East Anglia, whose warm encouragement over the years has meant a lot to me. He and Tom Hahn of Rochester made me more aware of the general importance of Lollardy; Felicity Riddy at the University of York brought the irrepressible John Hardyng to my attention. Martial Rose of Dereham, East Anglia, enabled me to really see the roof bosses at Norwich Cathedral in an unforgettable clerestory tour; he directed me also to Julia Hedgecoe, whose photograph of one of the bosses graces the cover of this book. Tom Hahn, Laura Kendrick, and Charlie Blyth deserve special thanks for their willingness to comment on the manuscript at an early stage. Karma Lochrie's interest in my observations on Chaucerian Orientalism stimulated me to develop them into the present form, while my discussion of the balade has benefited from the input of audiences that have heard it as it evolved, in talks at York (England), Liège, Utrecht, Claremont (California), Ottawa, and New York. Juris Lidaka and Mary Jo Arn provided information on the "Suffolk" poems. I am indebted to Al Shoaf and John Ganim for their meticulously learned, helpful, and generous readings for the University of California Press. Throughout the process of writing, I have been constantly aware of my debt to more distant laborers in the same or allied fields, whose work is acknowledged in my notes.

Translations from Latin, Old French, and Middle English are mine unless otherwise noted, and Middle English yogh and thorn have been modernized. Chaucer quotations are from *The Riverside Chaucer*, ed. Larry D. Benson (Boston: Houghton Mifflin, 1987).

Abbreviations

ChR	*Chaucer Review*
EETS	Early English Text Society
GP	General Prologue, *Canterbury Tales*
HCQ	*History of Childhood Quarterly*
Her.	Ovid, *Heroides*
HF	*House of Fame*
JEGP	*Journal of English and Germanic Philology*
JMRS	*Journal of Medieval and Renaissance Studies*
MED	*Middle English Dictionary*. Edited by Hans Kurath and Sherman M. Kuhn. Ann Arbor: University of Michigan Press.
MerchT	*Merchant's Tale*
Met.	Ovid, *Metamorphoses*
MLT	*Man of Law's Tale*
OED	*Oxford English Dictionary*
OM	*Ovide moralisé*
Pat. Lat.	*Patrologiae cursus completus . . . Series Latina.* 221 vols. Edited by J.-P. Migne. Paris: Garnier frères.
PIMS	Pontifical Institute of Medieval Studies
RR	Guillaume de Lorris and Jean de Meun, *Roman de la rose*

Prolocutory

"Naked text": Chaucer wrote the phrase before I did, in the poem this book is about, and others had written it before he did. What it meant to him and to them has given me a way to write about the poem and its culture. Less centrally, what it means to us has also given me a way to write about modern scholarly attitudes and the ways they have constructed the idea of medieval poetry. The notion of nakedness has thus worked as a key, if you will—indeed a "key of remembraunce," to borrow another phrase from the *Legend*.

This is a book about a single poem by a single author: it is as stripped, topic-wise, as it could be. On the other hand, my treatment renders the topic as fully clothed as I have been able to make it: after all, we have learned to ask what a text is, and what an author is. My interest in the *Legend* began when I was writing about the *House of Fame* as a graduate student at Columbia University. The *Legend* seemed to extend some of the philosophical concerns of the earlier poem to questions that might best be brought into the challenging and then newly opening arena of gender studies. In writing about the *Legend* over the past decade, I found it did that; moreover it inscribed much more that emerged into visibility under the light of new or newly applied work in historicism, semiotics, and language theory.

In a sense, then, I might metaphorize this study as itself a "naked text," knowing full well, just as Chaucer knew, that there is no such thing as true nakedness whether of texts or of people or of ideas: no thing completely *an sich*. A philosophical position is thus addressed with the metaphor of nakedness, a position relevant to the idea of "Woman"—that is, to the construction of femininity—and to much else besides. In showing the impossibility of nakedness, Chaucer necessarily administers a realistic corrective to the utopian impulse, wherever that impulse surfaces. This corrective is, at bottom, a theological gesture, indebted largely to St. Augustine, who hovers

1

as a kind of éminence grise in the background of the *Legend*. It is a theme Chaucer returned to again and again: the necessary dialectic of utopian desire and objective conditions. Dorigen and January exemplify it in its relatively innocent and its malevolent versions respectively, in connection with marriage; the *House of Fame* stages it as an adventure in epistemology; "Lak of Stedfastnesse" opens with a fairy-tale glance backward at the sociolinguistic "once upon a time" when

> the world was so stedfast and stable
> That mannes word was obligacioun;

"The Former Age" presents a full-fledged, if conventional, portrait of the time before "men first dide hir swety bysinesse" (28)—the reference is to mining—and before greed and "doublenesse" (62) entered the world; *Boece* 2. m. 5 offers a nostalgic evocation of the first age. Broadly speaking, then, the *Legend* is about ideals and realities—the title says as much, with its hagiographical parody— and nakedness was one means available to a medieval rhetor to represent that theme.

I have in mind also another use for nakedness: to metaphorize the poet's aesthetic procedure in his *Legend*. For Chaucer too chose a minimalism of topos (the woman faithful in love) but went on to clothe this bare plot in as varied costume as he could, producing a many-layered meditation on many things: on sex and gender, on language and nature, on philosophy and theology, on reading and writing, on hagiography and classical literature, on English intellectual life and English foreign policy. Some of this clothing is woven of rhetorical devices, particularly wordplay, which is attended to throughout this study and most concentratedly in Chapter 3. Some of it is ideological drapery, discussed mainly in Chapters 2 and 4; some inheres in the management of narrative voice, the concern of Chapter 5.

Other metaphors are always possible, and they lead in other directions. For the poet's method, and my own, I might use the Aristotelian image, adopted by Chaucer's eagle in the *House of Fame*, of a stone thrown into water, spreading larger and larger circles of ripples. Chaucer, like Aristotle, used the image to illustrate the movement of sound through air; I readapt it to represent the cen- trifugal motion of aesthetic minimalism such as found in the *Legend*.

Moreover, the "scientific" image might apply to the *Legend*'s fortunes as well as to its method, for the poem has had circles of influence that would surely have surprised its author.

In 1609, Chaucer's *Legend of Good Women* was enlisted in a worthy cause: to outlaw the abuse of married women. In that year, the Oxford clergyman William Heale published *An Apologie for Women, or an Opposition to Mr. Dr. [William] G[ager] in his assertion . . . That it was lawfull for husbands to beate their wives.* Heale wrote:

> All women (you saie) are altogether evil. . . . And are they evil all? Why then (ô grave Plutarch) how came it to passe thy wisdom so failed thee? ancient *Hesiode*, who corrupted thy mature judgment? . . . Chaucer, how miscarried thy golden pen? . . . Who deceived you al? for deceived you al are (if this position be received) who have severally written several tracts in honor of honorable women.[1]

Heale's booklet was commissioned by a woman: "Madam, your commaunde is effected," the dedication to Lady M. H. begins. On the title page there appears as epigraph the scriptural admonishment "Husbands love your wives, and be not bitter unto them" (Col. 3:19). Perhaps not surprisingly, given its polemical purpose, this epigram omits, in Wife of Bath–like fashion, the immediately preceding sentence: "Wives, be subject to your husbands; that is your Christian duty." I shall have more, much more, to say about textual management, for it is an important theme and process in the *Legend of Good Women*. Heale goes on to regret the time limit imposed by his patron, explaining that he could have done much better in so good a cause. Here he avails himself of an ancient trope and an equally ancient theme that are also relevant to the *Legend*: text as body, and the relations of nature and art: "For I know that this little body of my apologie is not so artificially featured, nor the limbs thereof so naturally jointed, that (as it should) it can seem a natural art, or an artificial nature." The "limbs" or chapters of the

---

1. Heale's pamphlet is in the British Library. The Chaucer passage is cited in Spurgeon, vol. 1: 183. Heale's opponent, William Gager (fl. 1580–1619), was an Oxford dramatist, Latin scholar, and assistant to clerics. His thesis "that it was lawful for husbands to beat their wives" was publicly defended at Oxford in 1608. The *Dictionary of National Biography* adds what might be interpreted as at least partial motivation if it is true: "In 1590 Gager seems to have been disappointed of a fortune which he expected from an uncle who died in that year. He attributed his disappointment to the action of his uncle's wife."

treatise take up the question of misogyny and wife-beating from the perspectives of natural law, the rules of "civill Pollicie," the traditions of civil and canon law, and the law of God. The book ends with exhortations to loving and peaceful marriage.

Despite his admirable intention Heale was not without his critics: the antiquarian and biographer Anthony Wood characterized Heale as "a zealous maintainer of the honour of the female sex . . . always esteemed an ingenious man, but weak as being too much devoted to the female sex."[2]

This was not the first time the *Legend* had been appropriated to make a feminist point—and I use the term "feminist" very loosely here to mean a point defending the rights or honor of women. Less than two years after the poet's death, Chaucer's disciple the hapless clerk Thomas Hoccleve used the *Legend* to make such a point. In his "Letter of Cupid," Hoccleve mentioned "my legende of Martires" (stanza 46), perhaps specifying his own personal copy of the poem; another version has the proud patriotic possessive "our" legend.[3] In both cases, though (despite other textual discrepancies), the reference is intended to demonstrate, against the supposed misogyny of Jean de Meun, that women do indeed suffer at men's hands: masculine betrayal is "to womman . . . nat unknowe."

Later on, a poet who perhaps was Chaucer's son's son-in-law[4] used the *Legend* to more immediate contemporary effect. MS. Fairfax 16 (Bodleian, Oxford) contains a series of twenty poems tentatively attributed to William de la Pole, first duke of Suffolk, who

2. Wood, vol. 2. Gager appears in the same place (cols. 87–89); of him, Wood asserts that he was "reputed the best comedian of his time," an assertion difficult to credit given not only the somewhat dour disposition suggested by the Oxford debate but also the competition, which included Shakespeare, Nash, Lyly, Heyworth, and Lodge.

3. The Fairfax MS (with "my") was used by Furnivall in his edition of Hoccleve's *Works*, while the Ashburnham MS (with "our") appeared in vol. 2, ed. Israel Gollancz, and is used by John Fleming in his interesting article on "Hoccleve's 'Letter of Cupid.'" Hoccleve's poem is an imitation and loose translation of Christine de Pizan's "Epistre au dieu d'amour," but the reference to the *Legend* is original with Hoccleve (although to be sure Christine is likely to have known Chaucer's work).

4. I leave aside the vexed question of whether Thomas Chaucer was the poet's biological son. A persuasive circumstantial case was made by Russell Krauss against Chaucer's paternity and for that of John of Gaunt. As for Suffolk's authorship, it was first proposed by H. N. MacCracken. Although other candidates have been suggested, the arguments for Sussex—though far from conclusive—remain at least as persuasive as those for anyone else. The most recent study is J. P. M. Janssen's. The series is printed in both Janssen and MacCracken.

married Thomas Chaucer's daughter Alice in 1431. The manuscript is an anthology of Chaucer's and others' poetry, including the *Legend*, and the influence of the *Legend* is particularly prominent in the poems attributed to Suffolk. Balade 3 is obviously derivative of Chaucer's balade "Hyde Absolon" from the *Legend*:

> O ye Lucresse, and also fair Eleyn,
> Thys I require yow of your gentylesse
> That in no wyse ye take yt in dysdeyn
> Though she which is my lady and maistresse
> Stand in your noumber, for in sothfastnesse
> I know her not alyve that in thys case
> Is bettir worthy ther to have a place.
> (Stanza 3)

More polemically relevant, though, is number 19 in the series, virtually a miniature replica of the scenario in the *Legend of Good Women*. The piece is entitled "How the lover ys sett to serve the floure," and the flower is the daisy "Wyth colours fressh ennewyd white and rede." The first-person Narrator, like Chaucer's Narrator professing "fayth" and performing "observaunce" to the flower, duplicates the Chaucerian use of the vocabulary of the religion of love. Like Chaucer, the fifteenth-century poet wishes for talent sufficient to praise the flower duly. Indeed, in apostrophizing the dead poet as it does, the piece not only pays pious tribute to a great literary predecessor but, if the poet is Suffolk, also offers filial tribute to someone about to become an ancestor-by-marriage in the Pole line.

Not only formally, but ideologically, the balade locates itself on what it sees as the terrain of Chaucer's *Legend*, for it vindicates the courtly versus the clerical-misogynist attitude toward women. This is expressed in an attack on John Lydgate, the "monke of bury," who—now that Chaucer is dead and buried—the poet considers the obvious candidate "After Chaucer to occupye his place." Yet the successor's worthiness is in doubt, for Lydgate composed a number of misogynist poems in the traditions of moral satire or moral exhortation: "Bycorne and Chichevache," "Examples against Women," "Beware of Doubleness," and others. He had also made, in *Fall of Princes*, the snide antifeminist guess that Chaucer's *Legend* remains incomplete of its full complement of nineteen good women because the great predecessor was unable "In al this world to fynde so greet a noumbre" (1.336). In *Troy Book*, Lydgate repeats at length the misogynist sentiments of Guido Colonna, his main source for that work. Though he adds that for every bad woman there are many good (such as the 11,000 virgins martyred at Cologne), Lydgate concludes that woman are "double naturelly" (3.4408) but that men should not blame them for it. There is plenty to choose from in Lydgate's oeuvre.[5] The Fairfax poet specifies no titles, but accuses Lydgate of writing "that love ys but dotage" and that women are untrustworthy and "unstedfast of nature."

Since no single one of Lydgate's poems is explicitly targeted, we may take the Fairfax verses as a composite remonstrance. The poet admonishes the monkish author that, since

> love ys of so grete autoryte, . . .
> It is your part in every maner wyse
> Of trew lovers to forther the servyse.

His analysis is ad hominem:

> What causeth this? for every creature
> That ys gylty, and knowyth thaym-self coulpable
> Demyth alle other [to] thair case semblable.

Echoing the opening section of the *Legend* the poet comments,

> Yit god defende, that everything were trew
> That clerkes wryte, for then myght thys be prevyd,
> That ye have sayd which wyll not be bylevyd,
> I late yow wyt, for trysteth verely,
> In your conseyt yt is an eresy.

He calls shame upon Lydgate the "envyous man," urges him to "Thynk whens thou came," and demands a retraction in much the same invective tone as Eros denounces the Chaucerian Narrator in the *Legend*'s Prologue:

> Thy corupt speche enfectyth alle the air;
> Knoke on thy brest, repent [the] now and ever
> Ayen ther-wyth, and say, thou saydyst yt never.

5. Another possibility is "Beware the Blind," printed in *Secular Lyrics of the XIV and XV Centuries*, ed. Rossell Hope Robbins, as item 211 ("Scorn of Women"). This suggestion was made by A. G. Rigg, but the attribution to Lydgate was not accepted by Robbins or MacCracken; indeed the attribution depends largely on certain verbal parallels between "Beware" and the Fairfax poem.

Thynk fully this, and hold it for no fable,
That fayth in women hath his dwelling-place;
For out of her cam nought that was unable,
Saf man, that can not well say in no place.
O thou unhappy man, go hyde thy face;
The court ys set, thy falshed is [out] tryed;
Wyth-draw, I rede, for now thou art aspyed.

Chaucer's *Legend*, then, had an early reputation as a serious and accomplished poem in defense of women, an instructive model of female fidelity, an enlightening beacon in the surrounding clerical-misogynist gloom. Or so it was for the readers cited. But even in the fifteenth century, not everyone saw it that way, not even admirers of Chaucer's art. I borrow the title of this introductory chapter from Osbern Bokenham, a fifteenth-century Augustinian friar living at Clare Priory in East Anglia. Bokenham was a Cambridge graduate, himself a poet, and an attentive reader of the *Legend of Good Women*. For his own all-female hagiography, the so-called *Legendys of Hooly Wummen* (1443–47), Bokenham loosely imitated the structure of Chaucer's mock hagiography.[6] It was an act of homage that also became a profound critique. The central legend in Bokenham's collection, that of Mary Magdalene, is preceded by a prologue and by a prologue to the prologue: a "prolocutory" as Bokenham calls it in one of his many neologisms. In this prolocutory he offers a poetic credo, specifying the ideological, polemical, and aesthetic angles of his work. Bokenham does not consider the religion of love to be much of a defense of women. On the contrary, he deplores the eloquence of "curyals" (courtiers)

In uttryng of here subtyl conceytys,
In whych oft tyme ful greth dysceyt is,
And specially for there ladyis sake
They baladys or amalettys lyst to make,
In wych to sorwyn & wepyn thei feyn
As thow the prongys of deth dede streyn
Here hert-root, al-be thei fer thens . . .
(5227–33)

6. The issues touched on here are developed at greater length in the Introduction to my prose translation of Bokenham's *Legends of Holy Women* (Notre Dame, Ind.: University of Notre Dame, 1992) and in my study of the poem, *Impolitic Bodies* (forthcoming).

Nor does Bokenham consider the imitation of classical rhetoric a suitable strategy for the Christian author. Particularly offensive is the invocation of classical deities—a fashion initiated by Chaucer and, in the *Legend*, carried to the absurd and possibly blasphemous extreme of invoking a daisy as muse, mistress, and "erthly god" (F, 95). Bokenham therefore refuses such tactics "As evere crystene man owyth to do" (5223). Instead of heroines of *cupiditas*, Bokenham portrays heroines of *caritas*; not woman as victim but woman teaching, healing, converting, and triumphant. Although Bokenham's indictment of courtly classicizers does not name names, Chaucer's *Legend* is one obvious target. If (as I shall argue further on) Chaucer parodies hagiography in order ultimately to validate its ideology, Bokenham misses or perhaps chooses to ignore the procedure: he parodies Chaucer in order to re-validate hagiography. It may strike us as odd that an Austin friar should present himself as a better champion of women than a worldly-wise urban courtier. I believe that Bokenham and his great predecessor are finally on the same side, even though one has to dig deeper for the *moralitas* in Chaucer. It seems, then, that even among its earliest audiences there would have been controversy about the poem, not least around the kind of question that continues to occupy us in connection with other authors, and not necessarily poets: Does the work offer a new dignity to women, or is it more of the same old thing?

In its modern history, the *Legend* appears less as an ethical exemplum or polemical tool than as an interesting variant in the annals of canonicity. Its authenticity has never been doubted, but its relative neglect during the present century has at times amounted to de facto exclusion from the Chaucer canon. Since the early years of the century, when John Livingston Lowes quashed the hypothesis of H. C. Goddard about the *Legend*'s ironic treatment of love, and until the past few years, studies of the poem were few and usually limited to source study or speculation about the occasion that might have called it forth. John Fisher noted, in the revised (1979) edition of Beryl Rowland's *Companion to Chaucer Studies*, that "up to 1940 . . . there were 115 articles and sections of books dealing mostly with the two forms of the prologue in their historical context. Since 1940 . . . there have been only 48 articles and books devoted to the Legend. . . . Since 1970 [there] have appeared . . . a book and three dissertations" (473). Tellingly, the original (1968) edition of the *Companion* had no essay on the *Legend*. The poem was and still is infrequently taught in Chaucer courses. Many critical studies of Chaucer's poetry do not discuss the *Legend*, and it is often excluded from or only partially printed in teaching editions. Robert O. Payne and Robert W. Frank have been important exceptions to the negative consensus, although Payne's study of the poem confined itself to the Prologue, and Frank's concentration on narrative technique left aside critical and intellectual issues that many readers will now want to address. Two recent books on the *Legend*, by Lisa Kiser and Donald Rowe, signal a renewed scholarly interest in the poem, as does the (still small but growing) number of papers on it at scholarly meetings.

The revival of interest lately in the poem is not, I believe, due only to a search for new ground in the burgeoning Chaucer industry. Rather it reflects two developments of the 1970s and 1980s. One is the revival of feminism and, with it, the development of feminist scholarship. The poem is not only a collection of stories, as Frank effectively reminded us; it is a collection of stories about women. It is a series of narratives about sexual relationships, about desire fulfilled and desire thwarted. I think it no accident that the three Ph.D. theses mentioned by Fisher were all by women, as were a disproportionate number of the (few) articles about the poem published during this same period.

The other influence I have in mind is the penetration into North American literary scholarship of European critical theory and speculation about language. In these Chaucerian short narratives, speech acts play a crucial role: promise, lament, prevarication, threat, revelation. Moreover, the *Legend* is a poem whose verbal texture calls attention to itself, foregrounding the act of its own production and that of its interpretation. This, at least, is how we are able to see it, if we wish to, because of paradigm shifts that have occurred in our profession. Books have their fates, and so do critical approaches. Both of them take us into history—but into what history?

Virginia Woolf made an interesting observation in "The Leaning Tower," a paper she read to the Workers' Educational Association of Brighton in 1940. She said that most English writers in the nineteenth century remained unaffected by the wars England engaged in during their lifetimes. The Napoleonic Wars were not mentioned by Jane Austen or Walter Scott. The Crimean War, the Indian mutiny, "all the little Indian frontier wars, and at the end of the century the Boer War" (164) do not find their reflection in English literature. They were, she said, very distant and remote without radio and telegraph and telephone.

In this light, Chaucer's notorious silence about the 1381 revolt and other important national and international events of his time appears not especially unusual: indeed, it appears prototypical. Of course, we can scarcely say the reasons were the same, when the poet was not insulated from these events but was himself a civil servant who traveled abroad on the king's business, who may have witnessed the entry of rebels into the city of London from his house atop Aldergate, and whose wife's patron's palace was sacked by the rebels. Yet it is not really—or only—technology that Virginia Woolf was after, nor explicit reference to events. She went on to discuss the privileged social position of the vast majority of English writers, their position in life, which she metaphorizes as the writer's chair:

> A chair is a very important part of a writer's outfit. It is the chair that gives him his attitude towards his model; that decides what he sees of human life; that profoundly affects his power of telling us what he sees. By his chair we mean his upbringing, his education. It is a fact, not a theory, that all writers from Chaucer to the present day, with so few exceptions that one hand can count them, have sat upon the same kind of chair—a raised chair. (168)

War may not have affected these writers directly, but peace certainly did, and all the so-called benefits of war: "the settled, the peaceful and prosperous state of England." Is there, Woolf asks, "any connexion between that material prosperity and that intellectual creativeness?" That is the theme she goes on to develop in the paper.

The kind of historicism represented in this study requires some comment. It is not the history of 1381 or of individual Ricardian political episodes that I have found most relevant to the *Legend of Good Women*, and neither have I sought the occasion—be it betrothal or feud—that the poem might allegorize or intervene in. This is not simply because the case for this or that occasion remains so unconvincing, but rather for a poetic and a historical reason. The poetic reason is that a writer can always invent, whatever and even despite the occasions. It is a terrible affront to the poetic imagination to reduce as densely layered a poem as Chaucer produces to a supposedly transparent reference to someone's birth, death, or marriage. There is an enormous expenditure of creative labor in such a work of the imagination, and to boil it down to a "real meaning" that is no more than a specific occasion may amount to an erudite philistinism.

The historical reason is that, as Fernand Braudel warns about events—whether major historical events or the "médiocres accidents de la vie ordinaire"—it is not the loudest actors who are the most authentic. Braudel means by this that the mass of events big and small does not constitute all of reality, "toute l'épaisseur de l'histoire sur quoi peut travailler à l'aise la réflexion scientifique" (46). It is a kind of thickness I hope to evoke in these chapters, a cultural environment—meaning social, intellectual, moral, aesthetic—in which the *Legend of Good Women* takes place, and takes its place.

At the same time I do proceed on the assumption that every human artifact is a historical document one way or another, regardless of the fabricator's intent and, as Edward Said remarks, "even when they [texts] appear to deny it" (4). The textual artifact cannot help telling us about its time and the maker's position in it, any more than any of us can help having a style when we speak or write. In both cases the alternative is silence. My interest, then—to borrow Woolf's metaphor—is Chaucer's chair.

So I have historicized the poem as ideology in a broad sense: a poem about nature, tradition, desire, language, women, and sexuality, and about the making of art as the site where these intersect. If, as Joe McCarney writes, "ideology is thought which serves class interests"; if it becomes, whatever its place of origin, "the medium in which class interests are articulated" (32–33), then how can the concept "ideology" be brought into any convincing relation with the text at hand? Not, I think, in any way transparently applicable to 1381. On the other hand, the *Legend* is not without its politics or its ideology. Its author was the product of urban commercial life in the capital, and of life at court as well; his audience was drawn from those layers of the population primarily but also from provincial gentry and nobility. The author worked for the government, and was intensely aware of the English national interest, as well as of the distinctively English culture he drew on and added to. The personae of the poem are aristocrats. The work depicts relations of power: political, marital, sexual, and parental. Its literary sources and its intellectual issues and procedures were those of an educated elite. Its deepest attitudes toward nature, women, sexuality, and authority are (I shall argue) entirely compatible with the orthodox Augustinian morality that suffuses both *Troilus and Criseyde* before it and the *Canterbury Tales* afterward. This is to clarify my use of the word "ideology," and to worry the anti-historicists and the occasionalists a little more; but in fact, with the exception of my excursus on Orientalism in Chapter 4, my main interest in writing about the *Legend* has not been to specify the immediate social referent and praxis of its ideas so much as to contextualize those ideas and elucidate the fact of their densely rich existence in a poem that has been trivialized for too long.

What about William Heale then, and before him the poet-polemicist anthologized in Fairfax 16? Were they wrong to use the *Legend* as feminist propaganda? Were they mistaken in their assessment of the poem as an authoritative text that could legitimately be co-opted to the defense of women? Or was Bokenham right to set his own moral vision against that of the classicizing courtier? As is so often the case with Chaucer, the answer has to be "yes and no." I hope that the following pages will make that ambivalence perfectly clear.

1

Reading and Writing

The *House of Fame* is a book about reading, the *Canterbury Tales* a book about writing. Between them comes the *Legend of Good Women*, a work "transitional" in several ways. Its meter, the innovative heroic couplet, would become the verse form for most of the *Tales*. Philosophically, the poet demonstrates his ability to integrate into his material the lesson of skeptical fideism so dramatically and painfully learned in the *House of Fame*. The Chaucerian Narrator is now an established poet concerned, not simply with how to use authoritative traditions, but additionally with his own place within those traditions. Therefore the *Legend* stakes out a territory, offering the theory and practice of a specific and developed aesthetic. That theory and practice will be explored in Chapters 2, 3, and 4, while the present chapter takes up, at some length, the *Legend*'s place in the making of a poet. The equivocal sense of this last phrase—how a poet evolves (is made), how a poet composes (makes)—captures quite accurately the double aspect of my interest here.

FROM READER TO WRITER

In moving through Chaucer's work, we observe a development in the figure of the Narrator. The Chaucerian Narrator is always both reader and writer, yet the balance of these functions is not constant. In the earlier dream-visions, the readerly function dominates as the Narrator confronts and absorbs various discourses, texts, and experiences. In some cases a specific text is named and summarized: Ovid's *Metamorphoses* and *Heroides*, Virgil's *Aeneid*, and Macrobius's commentary on the *Somnium Scipionis* are among them. This text provokes the Narrator's dream, which, when recorded, becomes the poem at hand. The narrative stance, then, is a passive or receptive one at the start of the poet's career. Over a period of about eighteen years, however, it shifts very perceptibly toward an active and self-conscious authorial position. The balance inclines progressively toward the writerly function, until in the *Canterbury Tales* we are very little aware of the Narrator as reader or scholar. Instead, we are invited to see him primarily as writer and artist, his ostensible sources no longer books but people and experience: "the book of the world," as a medieval cleric might say. In reality the *Tales* are of course every bit as bookish or intertextual as the earlier compositions. What I investigate here is not, however, actual literary sources, but rather the diegetic claim of the work, what the work asks us to believe about its Narrator and the processes of its own poetic production: a more speculative area of investigation than source study perhaps, but, for any writer, equally important.

It is probably well to address at the start the notion of chronology implied in these remarks. Robert O. Payne—to whose book *The Key of Remembrance* every Chaucerian interested in poetics must acknowledge a debt—thought the chronology of the Chaucer canon so precarious that "it would be foolhardy and pointless . . . to suggest any particular direction of development in [Chaucer's] poetics" (115). It is no depreciation of Payne's contribution to point out that this radical skepticism about order is exactly what his project requires, for his focus is "structural stereotypes" that cut across chronology. My hypothesis, on the other hand, while not originating in the traditional chronology, does tend to confirm it, although not rigidly (as will emerge later on). Hence the traditional chronology will be a useful, not a decisive, support for my hypothesis. There are limits to doubt, as my discussion of philosophical skepticism will note (see the second part of this chapter), and while we lack certainty about chronology, there is some probability.

In the *Book of the Duchess* (1368), the Narrator appears almost exclusively as reader. The setting of the dream-vision is the Narrator's chamber, where he is reading a romance in bed late at night. It is the story of Ceix and Alcyone (Halcyon) from Ovid's *Metamorphoses* 11, a tale whose theme of death and transfiguration anticipates the elegiac narrative to follow in the dream. After a lengthy retelling of this story, the Narrator falls asleep while reading. References by the Narrator to his authorial function are sparse and perfunctory. Lines 216–19, 226, 271, and 711 refer to the Narrator relating a story or a dream, not writing a poem, so that it could be maintained that these places do not constitute true authorial self-reference. For actual statements of writerly function in the Narrator's voice, only two appear, and these are extremely timid, particularly in comparison with what will come in later works. There is the "I, which make this book" of line 96, and at the very end of the poem:

> Thoghte I, "Thys ys so queynt a sweven
> That I wol, be processe of tyme,
> Fonde to put this swven in ryme
> As I kan best, and that anoon."
> This was my sweven; now hit ys doon.
> (1330–34)

Now there is a living poet in the *Book of the Duchess*, but it is not the Narrator. It is the Black Knight, whom the Narrator meets in the forest of his dream, and who is surprised in the very act of composing "a compleynte to hymselve . . . a lay, a maner song / Withoute noote, withoute song" (464–72). This plaint is reproduced in the Chaucerian text (475–86), and the Black Knight's subsequent elaboration of his loss—his gloss upon his own poetic composition—constitutes the body of Chaucer's poem.

What kind of poet is the Black Knight? He seems to be not only an active maker but an experienced and remarkably confident one, with, apparently, the faculty of virtually total recall of all he has ever composed. He claims to have made many songs and performed them often (1155–59); he associates himself through the modesty-topos with the archetypal scriptural and classical progenitors of the art, Tubal and Pythagoras (1160–70); he remembers and repeats his very first ("altherferste") youthful composition (1175–80). The Knight is equally self-conscious in other speech acts as well. He is able to recreate in detail his first confession of love to his lady (1181–1257) with all the psychological circumstances attendant upon this performance. These include his ambivalence about speaking, his worries about how to begin, and his nervousness at the possibility of a bad recital. The fear that causes him to omit part of his script ("many a word I over-skipte" [1208]) seems less a fear of the lady herself than of performing badly: "for pure fere / lest my wordes mysset were" (1209–10). He recalls, too, indeed he quotes from memory, the begging for mercy and swearing fidelity (1221–35), and notes his inability accurately to reproduce the lady's response except for its general tenor refusing his love (1236–44). Finally, he recounts the depression he suffered because of the lady's refusal.

The Black Knight, then, and not the Narrator, is portrayed as productive rhetor-poet in the *Book of the Duchess*. It is he who describes a poetic career, dwelling particularly on the launching of that career. He does so in the poem that is generally considered to have launched Chaucer's career as a courtly poet, not only because of its apparent priority in the canon, but also because of its engagement with a significant event of courtly social life, the death of John of Gaunt's Duchess Blanche. Onto the Black Knight, then, onto the fictional character, the poet has displaced active authorial function.

It is in this sense that I see the Black Knight as a kind of "alter ego" to the Narrator, rather than with respect to the issue of mourning, which has generally been the focus of criticism of the poem. Some remarks are in order here on the "alter ego" notion and on mourning. First, it seems obvious that in any literary work, every fictional character with any depth at all is to some extent a projection of its creator's inner life. In proclaiming, "Madame Bovary, c'est moi," Flaubert may have stated the principle with blunt unequivocality, but he can scarcely be considered unique in this matter in the history of Western literature. It would be ludicrous, I believe, to confine a discussion of "alter ego" to relations among characters and omit from it the author. My discussion is plainly one that in principle accepts the concept of character as at some level authorial "alter ego," although as I shall note further on, the extent of the relationship between author and narrator or author and character is neither constant nor predetermined in any Chaucerian text.

What I find odd in some recent uses of the "alter ego" notion is its application. In 1963, Bernard Huppé and D. W. Robertson, Jr., wrote of the Black Knight that he was not intended as the dream representative of John of Gaunt, but rather as a sorrowing alter ego of the speaker in the poem, like the poet himself representative of all those who have honored and loved Blanche and lost her in death (52). There is a peculiar circularity to this, which winds up negating its own initial assertion. John of Gaunt is excised; the Knight is alter ego to the Narrator, who in turn is "like" the poet, who in turn "represents" all who have lost Blanche—and would this not, after all, include her husband? In general structure this follows the pattern established by Bertrand Bronson in 1952. While reminding us that John of Gaunt was out of England during most of the nine years of his marriage to Blanche, including the time of her death, Bronson stressed the therapeutic function of the Narrator's dream. The Black Knight is the Narrator's "surrogate," his sorrow a projection or externalization of the Narrator's own "private grief" described at the beginning of the poem. A few pages later, however, the Man in Black also appears "as John of Gaunt," and the article ends with an orgiastic fusion of all personae including ourselves: "in the presence of death, Ceyx and Blanche, Gaunt and Alcyone, the Dreamer and Chaucer and his audience too, of which we now form a part, are become essentially one" (Wagenknecht, 294). A more sophisticated version of the position is offered in Judith Ferster's hermeneutically based discussion of "characters who are shadows of each other" (74), a narrator "who becomes a version of the knight" (92), and the evolution of each by his absorption of the other.

Such interpretations take a great deal for granted. In the most general, even banal, sense that we will all suffer the death of a loved one and require consolation, all the personae, including ourselves, do share something. But to focus on the issue of sorrow maintains the poem in a narrowly autobiographical mode, whether the sorrow is seen as that of John the Gaunt, the poet Chaucer, or the Chaucerian Narrator. This focus on sorrow can be called historicism, for it links the poem to a known historical event, Blanche's death in September 1368. It is a narrow historicism, though, and one that satisfies our own sentiment—indeed, our own sentimentality—by imposing on the past what we consider the "right" response to a noblewoman's death. We do this partly because we know that the real noblewoman was a "wife," and to this term there adheres a very considerable body of evaluation and response, conditioned partly by the development of family mores during the centuries after Chaucer's death. The realities of marriage and family were, however, rather different among late-medieval gentry and aristocracy, where matches often had little to do with the couple's taste, desire, or choice; where servants, tutors, and ladies- or gentlemen-in-waiting often performed the nurturing and disciplinary functions now associated with parents; where travel abroad or among a family's domestic territories kept a noble family dispersed. Then, just as now, practice often deviated from the recommended ideal—

surely this is why the ideal had (and has) to be recommended so often; but one ought not to take one for the other. There is anecdotal evidence for less than ideal practice; one thinks, for instance, of the Pastons' occasionally harsh treatment of their daughters.[1] As well, the "ideal" itself might be disputed or redefined from the perspective of intense religious commitment. St. Elizabeth of Hungary and St. Bridget of Sweden—both of them mothers of several children and well-known devotional models in Chaucer's England—pointedly renounced their family ties as hindrances to perfect spirituality.

A century or so after Chaucer, the anonymous secretary to Francesco Capello, Venetian ambassador to England, recorded the earliest extant Venetian account of the country. Besides English smugness, insularity, and superficiality, the young Italian deplored "the want of affection in the English . . . manifested towards their children; for . . . at the age of 7 or 9 years at the utmost, they put them out, both males and females, to hard service in the houses of other people."[2] Although this and my other examples of contemporary family relations are (somewhat) later than Chaucer, and do not constitute a "scientific" survey, they suggest a climate of opinion and practice. Nobles and gentry did send their children out to noble homes to learn manners and a career—Chaucer was a page in the household of Lionel, duke of Clarence—while bourgeois and artisan families often sent theirs out to apprentice in a trade; generally the children did not return home after their training but went on to work and marry. The fact of intra-familial murder among French and English noblemen of the period, for dynastic reasons, also makes my point about a different conception of familial obligation. So does the not inconsiderable evidence of infanticide and abandonment,[3] and so do the intra-familial lawsuits about money and property that went on at every level of society. All this is not to deny the existence of affectionate family ties—indeed the Paston letters are full of such affection as well as of friction and even abuse. It is

1. The Pastons were a Norfolk (East Anglian) family of prosperous business people and civil servants; their letters and documents cover the period 1418–1506.
2. In Sneyd, 24–25. For other information in this paragraph, see Gies and Gies.
3. Although the nature of medieval family life and attitudes is sharply disputed among social historians, nonetheless the sombre realities of infanticide and abandonment have been documented by Kellum, Trexler, Helmholz, and Boswell.

intended, however, to caution against automatic assumptions about the quality of a given marital or familial relation, and against the imposition upon medieval courtly life of the sentiments of our own domestic lives.

There is, therefore, a certain naïveté—it may alternatively be referred to as "the sincerity fallacy"—in assuming that the author of a courtly elegy is himself really in pain, or indeed that anyone is in pain, including the dead woman's husband. In the middle of the next century, the chronicler John Hardyng's dry comment on the marriage of John to Blanche of Lancaster was, "The duchy by hir had, men saied he had well sped" (330); and while Hardyng had a political-dynastic axe to grind, I doubt his estimate can have been unique. That John of Gaunt built an architectural monument for his deceased wife is no evidence to the contrary, notwithstanding that Donald Howard bids us remember, in support of his evocation of Gaunt's "towering" grief, the effigy erected on Blanche's grave. (The critic's perhaps unconscious wordplay with "towering" is very much in the Chaucerian spirit, as Chapter 3 will demonstrate).[4] The project proves nothing about John's feelings for his wife, although it certainly tells us something about his sense of social status and public display.

It is equally gratuitous to assume that the real death was perceived by the poet as anything other than an opportunity to write. Robert Burlin mentions the "ecstatic mutuality" that is Chaucer's "finest compliment to his lost Duchess" (63). Despite the homophonic allusion to Browning (there seems to be an irresistible pull to wordplay even among scholars concerned to establish sincerity of sorrow), I am not convinced that the intensity of the poem has anything to do with Blanche. I find Earle Birney's comment a refreshing antidote:

> The *Duchess* is not an ironical poem, yet is there any other elegy in the language with such playful passages and with such a general effect of lightheartedness? From what we know of Gaunt's character, and specifically of his readiness to remarry, it is likely of course that the husband's grief was more chivalric than intense; certainly Chaucer's lament seems delicately adapted to just such polite mourning.

4. Howard, *Chaucer*, 123. In "Chaucer the Man," Howard also writes of shedding "light on the Dark Lady."

I use the term "alter ego," then, in gingerly fashion, and in the context of the production of fiction rather than in that of loss and consolation. This might, I suppose, be considered equally auto-biographical, although in another register than the immediately and perhaps mechanically historical. I do not claim that the Narra-tor "is" Chaucer. The Narrator is a fictional character among others. Onto the Narrator, and sometimes onto other characters, the poet displaces certain of his own activities, particularly the reading and writing that are my concern here. From the proportionality of this displacement, we may be able to infer something about Chaucer's sense of himself as a developing poet.

That the Black Knight should be so strongly characterized as maker, and the Narrator play so depreciated a role with respect to writing, is no mere flattery of a recently bereaved patron. Surely we may also read in this displacement of function the real poet's ambiv-alence or uncertainty about his own social role and his burgeoning poetic powers. For Chaucer was still between twenty-five and thirty years of age; he had recently married the royal mourner's future sister-in-law, Philippa Payne de Roet, a woman far above her hus-band in social rank. He was a relative newcomer to the king's service, although he had been trained for it since early adolescence. With the *Book of the Duchess* he was making a bid to become some-thing more at court than a minor diplomat: both an acknowledged poet and a lucratively rewarded courtier. For the moment, however, the future was uncertain.

With the *House of Fame*, we enter the heart of uncertainty. This begins with the date of the poem, which has been estimated as between 1374 and 1385. It is generally agreed to be later than the *Book of the Duchess* and probably dates from about 1375. Although much else is at issue in the *House of Fame*, Chaucer has at least now incorporated the role of writer into his first-person narrative per-sona. The Narrator is both reader and writer from the start of the poem, but the readerly role continues to dominate and the writerly role is marked by uncertainty.

The 65-line Prologue reflects the Narrator's experience as reader. His puzzlement about conflicting theories of dream produces an agnostic stance ultimately eased by the fideistic transfer of respon-sibility to divine power:

For I of noon opinion
Nyl as now make mensyon,
But oonly that the holy roode
Turne us every drem to goode!
(55–58)

No such easy route will be available in the writerly role, where responsibility for error is untransferable (although, as the Retraction to the *Canterbury Tales* acknowledges, good effects may be attributed to divine influence). Self-referential comments about authorial function in the Proems and Invocations to each of the three divisions of the poem are timid, self-doubting, and modest. They reveal anxiety about accurate narration of the dream (79 and 527), about the technical ability "to endite and ryme" (520), about the difficulty of reproducing one's idea (1101–3). These are, of course, among the important questions for any artist, but they usually loom largest at a relatively early stage of a writer's career. They must be resolved before another set of important questions can be dealt with, such as the artist's social and moral responsibilities, attitudes toward love and nature, place in a tradition, and so on. The curiously vehement blessing and curse on the good and bad audience (81–108) suggest the defensive maker, unsure of his reception and despising in advance any potential malicious or philistine misinterpretation of his work.

The content of the dream-vision is highly literary and traditional: again it is a scholar's dream, this time centering on the story of Dido and Aeneas. Yet if the sources of the main story are undeniably literary—derived from those two authoritative (and conflicting) texts, Virgil's *Aeneid* and Ovid's *Heroides*—nonetheless the diegetic representation of this story is far from being straightforwardly literary. There is in fact a very odd mixture and confusion of media in this section of the poem: surely one of its most disorienting features. *Ekphrasis*, the representation of one medium in another, is an important technique in Ovid's *Metamorphoses*, as Eleanor Leach has shown. But it is most probably from Virgil that Chaucer borrowed it, for when Aeneas first arrives at Carthage, he sees, upon the walls of the Temple of Juno, the visual representation of his own history and the fall of Troy (*Aeneid* 1.453–93). Whether the medium is tapestry, painting, or relief is not specified, but the verbal representation of the visual representation is at least clear and consistent, and if supplementary explanation of a scene appears, this can be attributed to the viewer's—Aeneas's—intimate knowledge of the persons and events portrayed (e.g., the interjection about Troilus, "infelix puer atque inpar congressus Achilli": "unfortunate boy, and unequal to the meeting with Achilles" [1.475]). Nonetheless, both Virgil and Chaucer offer, in a sense, a double *ekphrasis*. Neither of them verbally represents a simple three-dimensional art object; rather they represent something ornately decorated that—like Achilles's shield in *Iliad* 18 and Keats's urn—in turn represents narrative. If *ekphrasis* is, to borrow Murray Krieger's phrase, language attempting to "freeze itself into a spatial form" (10), then the *ekphrases* discussed here re-freeze a spatial form that has already frozen into spatial form the language-exchanges and the actions it represents.

Not all classical or later *ekphrasis* is as clear as Virgil's. Discussing the representation of maps in painting, Svetlana Alpers notes that the only Greek word the Alexandrian astronomer Ptolemy (2d century c.e.) had available for referring to a maker of pictures was *graphikos*, a suffix denoting one who writes, draws, or records. Later,

> where the word description is used by Renaissance geographers, it calls attention not to the power of words, but to the sense in which images are drawn or inscribed like something written. It calls attention, in short, not to the persuasive power of words but to a mode of pictorial representation. . . . When we look back at Ptolemy now we have to say that his term *grapho* was opened up to suggest both picture and writing. (Alpers, 136)

Closer to home, the medieval commentaries on classical myth often employed *ekphrasis* in their verbal representation of visual representation. The operative word is *pingitur*, from Latin *pingo*, to represent pictorially whether in drawing, painting, embroidery, or tapestry. Beryl Smalley notes that Fulgentius, writing in the late fifth century, occasionally uses the word; Alberic of London about 1200 uses it more often, and the fourteenth-century commentator John Ridevall "never omits it." Smalley goes on to observe that "Ridevall's 'pictures' did not lend themselves to visual representation and the results were as clumsy as might have been expected. Ridevall described Juno as 'redolent of unguents'. The poor artist could only set an open flask beside her head" (*English Friars*, 112–13). What we encounter in these cases seems to be an aspect of manuscript culture and early print culture, where modes of apprehension interpenetrate. Part of this is doubtless due to the relative novelty and marginality of writing itself, an art whose boundaries had not yet become rigidly fixed.

The Chaucerian Narrator, like Aeneas, also finds a visual representation on the walls of Venus's temple; it is not only the history of Troy but of the entire *Aeneid*. The treatment of this motif, however, is very different from that in the classical source. To begin with, Virgil's succinct comment that the Temple of Juno is *donis opulentum* ("opulent with gifts" [447]) is amplified into an architectural nightmare. The Chaucerian Temple of Venus is an unusually bizarre and grotesque example of high Gothic architecture (121–27): it is made of glass and profusely filled with images, niches, altars, towers, statuettes, and paintings. The setting is thus as chaotic as the representation of the ancient story will shortly prove to be. About this puzzling edifice the Narrator knows only that it is the Temple of Venus, for he sees a painted portrait of Venus surrounded by her usual iconography (129–39). Next he finds a brass tablet on which is written a translation of the opening lines of the *Aeneid* (140–48): "And tho began the story anoon, / As I shal telle yow echon" (149–50). This transitional couplet leads us to expect a smooth passage into the rest of the story, and to expect that it will appear to the Narrator in the same medium as what he has already seen—that is, as words written on a brass tablet. Yet such is not evidently the case. At no time, for instance, does the Narrator use the word "read" as we might expect with a written account; it is always "see," more appropriate to visual than to verbal representation. On the other hand, what the Narrator "sees" includes motivation, lament, and emotion—in short, narrative with all its rhetorical features. The frequent recurrence of the phrase "sawgh I graven" and other forms of the verb "graven" only intensifies our uncertainty, for the word may mean to carve, as in statuary (a "graven image" is an idol), or it may mean to incise either words or images on metal or stone.

In line 211 appears the phrase "peynted on the wal." This seems unequivocal enough, except that the appearance of the word "peynte" a few lines later (246) to mean verbal rhetoric once again confuses the picture. Perhaps it is well that we are forced to problematize appearance, since the question of deceptive appearance is highlighted as the core of the love story (263–92). Next, the Narrator appears to abandon the fiction of visual art in referring us to books if we want to know the details and the analogues of the love story (375–432). Then the ambiguous "sawgh I grave" formula reappears several times. Finally, the Narrator reflects on the "noblesse / Of ymages" (471–72) he has seen and his ignorance of "whoo did hem wirche" (474), reverting to the imagery of the visual arts. The episode ends with the Narrator as confused as his reader. Indeed, it is the Narrator-as-reader who is confused, with no one to advise or inform him ("rede or wisse" [491]) about the unfamiliar desert landscape he now confronts and is unable to interpret.

And, after all, interpretation has been the problem all along. What we find in the Dido and Aeneas story is something analogous in literature to the portrayal in painting of a written inscription. Mieczyslaw Wallis has called this, rather than *ekphrasis,* a "semantic enclave": part of a work of art that consists of signs of a different kind or from a different system than the signs of which the main body of the work consists. This might be, in a text, the insertion of a different language for part of the text, as in macaronic verse; or it might be the use of illustration, as in an illuminated manuscript. In a painting, the autonomous semantic enclave might be the representation within the painting of a map, a musical score, a heraldic device, or an inscription, whether free-floating or placed on an object (e.g., a book, banner, robe, etc.). Cubist, dadaist, or surrealist collage would be modern examples.

While the text at hand remains integrated in the sense that it is all in the same language, nonetheless it seems to me that the constant shifting of ground between visual and verbal registers in this portion of the *House of Fame* operates as an oscillation between semantic enclaves, reminding us, as it must remind the Narrator, of the proliferation of languages, texts, and meanings: the unreliability of communication generally that is the lesson to be learnt at the houses of Fame and Rumor.

For, of course, it is not only the desert landscape the Narrator-as-reader is unable to gloss, but his experience in the Temple of Venus. The dual Virgilian-Ovidian tradition of the Dido and Aeneas story is quite as problematic for a reader as the multimedia representation of it the Narrator has just given. In that sense, the Dido-Aeneas story is paradigmatic of other written traditions to be encountered by the Narrator, traditions in science, myth, and history whose internal contradiction will pose a similar problem to that of the classical love story and be resolved, as I have argued in *Poetics of Skeptical Fideism*, in a similar way.

The inner structure of the *House of Fame* thus centers on the Narrator as reader: more generally, as observer-interpreter. Its plot, however, focuses on his role as writer, and one notes that it is in this text that, for the first time, the author names his Narrator with his own—the author's—proper name: "Geffrey, thou wost ryght wel this" (729) are the words with which the kindly Eagle begins his lecture on sound. Geffrey's journey to the houses of Fame and Rumor is his reward for perseverance in poetic making. But when the great eagle, Geffrey's psychopomp, says to his passenger,

> when thy labour doon al ys, . . .
> Thou goost hom to thy hous anoon,
> And, also domb as any stoon,
> Thou sittest at another book
> Tyl fully daswed ys thy look . . .
>   (652–58)

we do not know whether it is as reader or as writer that Geffrey dazes himself in front of another book. The ambiguity encapsulates my point about the poem's dual representation of narratorial roles.

The aim of the aerial trip is to reward Geffrey as poet by providing him with "tydynges" (information) about "Loves folk" that will amuse and instruct: it will be a diversion, and the implication is that the tidings may furnish some vicarious experience of love or even material for further making, although these latter purposes are not specified. The emphasis is firmly on hearing, not on utterance. Accordingly, the Eagle's farewell benediction to Geffrey is not that he write well about his journey, but that he have the grace "Some good to lernen in this place" (1088). The true center of the poem is not yet the production of discourse but its reception.

In the Proem to book 3, the Narrator at first appears as writer, placing himself under Apollo's aegis. Nonetheless he quickly reverts to the receptive-scholarly position as he confronts, in the narrative, a central readerly problem: the unreliability of *fama* (fame, reputation, tradition) and especially the coexistence of mutually contradictory versions of the same events. Given the evanescence and ambiguity of tidings, it is scarcely surprising that none can be produced as a climax to the poem despite the scene of frenetic anticipation with which it ends. Even with its intermittent glimmers of authorial self-assertion, the *House of Fame* remains essentially a book about reading, with writing submerged as a kind of by-product of reading.

The equilibrium of roles in the *Parliament of Fowls* (dated between 1374 and 1380) is fairly similar to that in the *House of Fame*. John Fisher has remarked that although the conventional placement of the *House of Fame* before the *Parliament* is "satisfactory, . . . the reverse order would do just as well" (208), and so it would for my present purpose. Again the Narrator enters the poem as a reader; again the dream-vision is stimulated by his reading of a classical literary source; again he requests the ability to rhyme and "endite" (119); again the dream-journey is a reward for labor, although here it is the scholarly labor of reading Macrobius's commentary on Cicero's *Somnium Scipionis* (109–12) rather than of writing love songs. The purpose of this journey is not simply to acquire information but now explicitly to acquire poetic material, for the psycho-pomp Africanus says, "I shal the shewe mater of to write" (168). Yet this offer of poetic material is undercut by the snide comment of Africanus: "And if thow haddest connyng for t'endite . . . " (167). So an ambivalence prevails with respect to the writerly role.

The dream-content is at first extremely static, emblematic, and mythological. It demands interpretation or at least a syntax: its self-evident metonymies (Bacchus/Ceres/Venus, Cupid/Will, Behest/Art et al.) require to be ordered by the observer into some sort of structured, intelligible statement about love. But this scenario shortly gives way to the dynamic, colloquial, and rapid-paced bird-parliament in Nature's Park, where utterance, albeit not the Narrator's utterance, is the center of interest.

As in the *Book of the Duchess*, the *Parliament* offers another poem within a poem, the concluding rondel. As in the *Duchess*, performance is ascribed to fictional characters (here, the birds) rather than to the Narrator. Composition is left anonymous, both for words and music: "The note, I trowe, imaked was in Fraunce, / The wordes were swiche as ye may heer fynde" (677–78). While the *Duchess* ends with the promise of writing, the *Parliament* promises further reading and hopes for more dreams that will in turn effectuate improved experience:

> I hope, ywis, to rede so som day
> That I shal mete som thyng for to fare
> The bet, and thus to rede I nyl nat spare.
>   (697–99)

We know that dream operates as a metaphor for composition, but composition itself is effaced in this ending.

Anelida and Arcite (of uncertain date) seems, despite its brevity and lack of poetic distinction, to suggest a more even distribution of functions than appears in the *House of Fame*, with the writerly coming more into prominence. (My reading thus tends to confirm that of J. Norton-Smith, who links the work with the *Legend* both chronologically and thematically.) To begin with, Chaucer plays fast and loose with sources. He claims to be translating an old Latin story (8–10) but no such text has been identified. He claims to follow "Stace, and after him Corynne" (21) and even if scholars were agreed on the identity of Corynne, he or she has left no literary remains. The *Thebaid* of Statius may have provided some details at the beginning of the poem, but not its body; and Boccaccio's *Teseida*, also used, is not mentioned at all. "Scholars are loath to credit anything to pure invention," observed F. N. Robinson in his introductory remarks to the poem. To credit invention here is to acknowledge an important step beyond the *House of Fame*, for it means we are now dealing with an author who accepts the autonomy of fiction. A more stable equilibrium of readerly and writerly functions has been achieved than in the earlier work. Thus, according to the Invocation, the Narrator-reader has found material that the Narrator-writer will now present.

Besides a source, the poet devises a purpose, indeed, a mission both patriotic and socially responsible: to translate into English an old story that age has already nearly effaced from memory:

> For hit ful depe is sonken in my mynde,
> With pitous hert in Englyssh to endyte
> This olde storie, in Latyn which I fynde,
> Of quene Anelida and fals Arcite,
> That elde, which that al can frete and bite,

As hit hath freten mony a noble storie,
Hath nygh devoured out of oure memorie.
(8–14)

The preservation of old stories is a theme that will reappear in the Prologue to the *Legend of Good Women*. Here, the (evidently nonexistent) "nygh"-forgotten ancient material is assumed to be without complications: unambiguous and therefore writable. The skeptical abyss is temporarily healed over, disbelief is for the moment suspended. What is read can be assimilated and in turn produced.

It is with *Troilus and Criseyde* (1385 or after) that a decisive shift occurs in the earlier proportioning of readerly and writerly functions. The Narrator cannot be entirely divested of his readerly stance, because he is working with an older story, which he claims to have translated. This source is Boccaccio's *Filostrato*, but Chaucer effaces Boccaccio from his text, substituting the nonexistent "Lollius." Evidently he believed in good faith that there was a Lollius, but the substitution itself was no error: it was a conscious fiction. This takes us a step beyond "Anelida," where a real author (Statius) was used to cover invented material. Here an invented author is used to cover real material and to displace its known author. Hence the treatment of source evinces authorial initiative rather than scholarly receptivity. Why does Chaucer need Lollius at all? I think it is somewhat more complicated than the medieval "respect for authority" such as is generally said to have led Chrétien de Troyes and Wolfram von Eschenbach to invent ancient books as sources for their chivalric romances. (Perhaps it was more complicated for them also.) Chaucer has not at this point arrived at a definitive author-narrator distinction; in my view, he never fully achieves this, despite valiant efforts to do so. The closest he can come at this point, I suggest, is an author-translator distinction: a more limited version of the impulse to the autonomy of fiction. To this end he requires a text to translate, an old text in an authoritative language. Boccaccio is simply too close to provide the necessary distancing. As a recent contemporary writing in the vernacular (for *Filostrato* in any case), Boccaccio was simply neither distant nor, therefore, different enough to justify a credible disjunction between author and translator.[5]

5. David Wallace offers another and intriguing possibility: that Chaucer wanted to avoid being compared with Boccaccio, an author whose "poetic evocations of

Despite various references to "myn auctor" and such phrases as "I fynde ek in stories" or "as I rede," the dominant image of the Narrator in *Troilus* is that of writer. This image is built up in numerous ways. To begin with, there are the long, important, and poetically intense invocations to each of the five books of the poem. In these the Narrator represents himself as the transparent "instrument" (1.10) of his material and single-minded servant of the servants of love (1.15–51); as disinterested translator of his Latin source (2.12–21) and cultural relativist (2.22–42); as bard of universal principles of love (3.1–49); as sympathetic moralist (4.1–14). Beside the invocations, with their acute awareness of the production of literature, there are other lengthy reflections on changing language as a problem for the modern writer (2.22–49 and 5.1793–98). At another level, there is the evolving view of Criseyde, whom we see early on as auditor of the romance of Thebes (2.80–108), but who by the end (5.806–26) has become the iconic figure in a new romance, a new tradition that bears her name and that of Troilus. This placing or distancing can have been accomplished only through the active intervention of a new author.

Finally, and especially, there is the profoundly self-conscious coda to the poem (5.1765–1869), which pulls the text definitively into range of mature authorial concern. Here Chaucer or his Narrator (the distinction is not significant for my purpose at this point) addresses himself to narrative proportion (1765–71), audience response (1772–78), authorial motive and intent (1779–85), future authorial production (1786–88), relation to tradition (1789–92), changing language and the transcription of manuscripts (1793–96), the moral implications of his own work (1828–55), and commendation of the text to friends (1856–62).

The story itself continually emphasizes the importance of discourse, both verbal and written: not simply the reception of discourse, as in the *House of Fame*, but its production as a psychological and ethical phenomenon. We are required to come to terms with the

---

cortesia actually furthered the debasement of courtly language. . . . Perhaps this is why Chaucer was anxious to publicise his admiration for Petrarch and Dante whilst passing over Boccaccio in silence" (152). This does not contradict my hypothesis, for careerist and poetic motives might well overlap and reinforce one another. In his psychoanalytically oriented article on the same topic ("Chaucerian Authority"), A. C. Spearing also suggests that Boccaccio is "dangerously close, a father rather than a distant ancestor," but he does not fully account for *why* Chaucer tends to suppress his father-figures.

frightening power of the word as it emanates from various characters in monologue, dialogue, songs, and letters; in persuasion, promise, threat, praise, self-justification, lament, blasphemy, pun—an immense variety of speech-acts. We are required to consider the relation of discourse to external circumstance and to the utterer's will. Alfred David asserts, in another but related connection, that "in *Troilus and Criseyde* the narrator at last steps into the pulpit that is the poet's rightful vantage point" (27).[6] To extend this point, I propose that in *Troilus* Chaucer is able for the first time definitively to appropriate to his first-person Narrator the active authorial role, grasping the nettle to achieve the mature (although not necessarily unambiguous) voice that we recognize as the voice of the *Canterbury Tales*.

Although the tales were composed at various times during Chaucer's career, the General Prologue was evidently done in 1387. As a group, the pilgrims are fairly active readers (or, in some cases, hearers) of assorted texts. The up-to-date Man of Law has read the poetry of Chaucer; others read Aristotle, medical texts, romances, misogynistic anecdotes, Breton *lais*, Petrarch and Ovid, Marie de France's fables, saints' lives and miracles of the Virgin, Roman history, the Bible, treatises of moral edification, and tragedies of the fall of great men. They are also narrators and performers, many of them quite self-conscious about the sources, style, content, and interpretation of their own and each other's recitals. But with the exception of Pardoner and Parson, they are not professional rhetors: the fiction we are asked to accept is that these ordinary folk, amateurs, speak spontaneously out of their experience and their reading.

The Narrator, too, has done his reading, as his tales show: he has read in "bourgeois romance" and in compendia of ethical advice. Nonetheless he is presented primarily as speaker, reporter, and maker. Lest in our fascination with other characters we forget his shaping role, it is emphasized often, in the Narrator's own voice, as organizational interjection (GP 35–42, 715–24), opinion (GP 183, 385, 691, *Canon's Yeoman's Prologue* VIII.568–73), disclaimer (GP 284,

---

6. David's emphasis here, and mine, is in contrast to Howard's in "Chaucer the Man," which stresses that the Narrator of *Troilus* "is a *reader*" (39; italics in original).

330), and apologia (GP 725–46, *Miller's Tale* I.316–86). In this poem foregrounding the production of discourse, the Narrator is constantly kept before us as the primary producer, the filter through whom all the others are apprehended. What we find, then, is a reversal of the proportions I have noticed in the *Book of the Duchess*: not a complete or exclusive reversal, but a general shift. There the first-person Narrator functions within the fiction primarily as reader, with discursive activity displaced onto another fictional character, the Black Knight. Here the first-person Narrator functions within the fiction primarily as producer of discourse, with readerly activity displaced onto the fictional characters, the pilgrims.

This development in the assertion of authorial function might interestingly be approached from the standpoint of naming, for a parallel evolution can be traced through the poet's career. In the *Book of the Duchess*, the Narrator is nameless, and likewise in the *Parliament*, even though there exists in the latter text an interlocutor—Africanus—whose dominant role and condescending tone might have allowed him to name the Narrator. In the *House of Fame*, the Narrator is for the first time named—by his interlocutor, the chatty Eagle—and with the poet's real proper name (729). He also expresses a nervous concern that "no wight have my name in honde" (1877). In *Troilus*, the Narrator is again unnamed: there is no interlocutor who might address him, but then an occasion for naming could have been invented, or a narratorial name included with those of Gower and Strode at the end. In any case, the pronounced authorial self-consciousness in *Troilus* is not expressed in naming. Nor is it in the *Legend*—not, at least, directly. There is a fair amount of naming in the *Legend*: various sources and authors are named throughout, and the naming of Alceste is an important feature of the Prologue: she names herself (F 432, G 422), she is named by Cupid (F 511, G 499), and the Narrator acknowledges her by name (F 518, G 506). Moreover, though the Narrator is not named, his previous works—which also happen to be the works we recognize as Chaucer's—explicitly and profusely are both named and evaluated. What seems to happen is that personal self-referentiality is displaced onto Alceste, while the poet himself exists as maker of his works and as object of a critical discourse. Whatever his personal fate, the poet seems to realize that he will live as the author of works that, unlike so much medieval literature before (and even after) him, will not be untitled or anonymous; in short, his name (albeit here suppressed) is going to have a function—the one, I suggest, that Michel Foucault has called an "author-function."

I do not want to claim for Chaucer the fullest sense of this Foucauldian term, for it is unlikely that any poet or belletrist can found a discursive practice that will be "embodied in technical processes, in institutions, in patterns for general behavior, in forms for transmission and diffusion, and in pedagogical forms which, at once, impose and maintain them" (*Language,* 200). What I do want to get at, though, is the process we know Chaucer witnessed already in his life, a process that the Prologue to the *Legend* fictionally represents, namely, the hardening of himself and his work into a figure, something beyond the merely personal or autobiographical. As Howard observes, "Chaucer was recognized as a major poet in his own lifetime. He was praised over and over as a 'philosophical' poet, a great rhetorician and translator; he was imitated by lesser poets like Usk and Hoccleve" (*Chaucer,* 524). In this light, it is legitimate to infer a developing attitude toward his own work. "The comparisons we make, the traits we extract as pertinent, the continuities we assign, or the exclusions we practise" (Foucault, *Language,* 127): these aspects of the author-function are surely recognizable as what Alceste and Eros do to Geffrey and his writing, and it is an experience at once exhilarating and frightening.

The effect, I believe, is that the poet is becoming aware of producing not only works but texts, a discourse in a receptive field (that is, a field of divergent receptions). It is a discourse because it is a body of work with a recognizable style and subject matter and an ideological position. It can generate both imitators and opponents—sometimes both in the same person, as in the case of Osbern Bokenham. The maker, I suggest, is concerned about the status of his discourse in much the same way that Criseyde sees herself becoming frozen into a tradition "rolled . . . on many a tongue," hated especially by women for dishonoring them (5.1054–68). It is precisely the charge laid against the poet-Narrator of the *Legend.* To his readers—the two of them represented in the *Legend*—he protests, as it were, that it is more complicated than they think. He proceeds to show them how complicated it is by writing yet another book, this one about writing books.

It is as if that act frees the poet (relatively) from this obsessive concern with his role to produce a work that looks at the world rather than at its own feet: the *Canterbury Tales*. There, the bumbling, scholarly, versifying "Geffrey" no longer exists. Instead, we have "Chaucer" (*Man of Law's Prologue* II.47)—the formal, dignified patronymic that will survive through history and set the poet apart from any other Geoffrey. (It is not irrelevant to recall in this connection that when Mary Serjeantson edited Bokenham's legendary for EETS, she mistakenly identified "Galfryd of ynglond" as Geoffrey Chaucer rather than as Geoffroi de Vinsauf. So far from being subsumed by any other Geoffrey, Chaucer has come to subsume all the others!) In the Man of Law's recital, Chaucer's works are named and discussed, and by a far more sympathetic reader than Alceste. This naming, in context of a multi-class pilgrimage, suggests a self-confident awareness on the real author's part that such reference would not be completely inappropriate on such an occasion: that his name might be dropped by a lawyer, and that it might be recognized by at least some of his companions.

We may like to assume that this named Chaucer is identical with the "I" who narrates the entire set of stories and who, within it, tells the tales of Melibee and Thopas. This was the scribal assumption (and it is worth remembering that all extant manuscripts of the tales postdate the poet's death). It is duplicated in incipits and explicits that make their way into editions, it is taken for granted by every scholar, and it makes for delicious ironies; but there is no actual evidence within the poetic text for such an identification. The Narrator evinces no response either to the Man of Law's praise or to the Host's denunciation of his tale that might suggest real authorial status at stake. As far as textual evidence goes, the Chaucerian-narratorial " 'je' est un autre" (as Rimbaud put it), and the absence of indication of originary authorial intent permits the speculation that we may see the Narrator as not-Chaucer. Strictly speaking, there is no "Chaucer the pilgrim" on the pilgrimage. Once again we have an unnamed Narrator. He is distanced, as far as present evidence lets us judge, in a number of ways from the poet designated "Chaucer," among them his (the Narrator's) apparent poetic ineptitude. If the first-person Narrators of the earliest works were nameless because a lack of poetic security prevented the maker from naming himself, the first-person Narrator of the *Tales* is nameless because the maker's name is borne by someone else, someone outside the fiction who is already famous. David Lawton rightly emphasizes the rhetorical, not characterological, function of Chaucer's narrators, writing of "not one device but a scale, a register, of different ones" (7). My own image for the relation of author to narrator is that of the U.S. and Canadian dollars: sometimes so close in value as to be exchangeable at par, at other times very far out of phase. It is because of this flexibility, this shifting signifier that is the narratorial persona, that virtually everyone who writes about Chaucer's narrative voice is right—at least in places.

THE TWO PROLOGUES

What position does the *Legend of Good Women* occupy in this progression from readerly to writerly concerns? The period of composition is generally agreed to be between *Troilus* (to which F and G Prologues both refer) and the General Prologue to the *Tales*, hence about 1386. It is a book about the reception of texts and the production of texts, but the balance has definitively shifted, as we should expect from *Troilus*, in the direction of writing. So much is this the case that the texts whose reception is at issue are those of the Narrator himself: certainly in the Prologue, and, as I shall propose in Chapter 5, in the legends as well. The placement of the *Legend* in this discussion becomes somewhat more complicated than for other of Chaucer's works because of the existence of two versions of the long Prologue to the *Legend*, one of them a revision of the other.

One version, usually designated "G," exists in a unique copy, MS. Gg 4.27, in Cambridge University Library.[7] The other, designated "F," exists in several manuscripts. None of the extant manuscripts is complete (although some are fuller than others) and none is earlier than about 1425. Which version precedes the other, and which is the revision, has not been proven, despite the assurance of A. S. G. Edwards and M. C. E. Shaner, in the *Riverside Chaucer*, that this "formerly vexed question . . . was resolved by John Livingston

---

7. MS. Gg 4.27—the earliest collection of Chaucer's major works (it also includes *Troilus*, the *Canterbury Tales* and the *Parliament of Fowls*, as well as various shorter pieces by him and by other authors), and the only one extant from the fifteenth century—has been published in facsimile by M. B. Parkes and Richard Beagle.

Lowes" (1178) in 1904 and 1905.[8] About the turn of the century, G was considered the original: F. J. Furnivall thought so, as did Walter Skeat and numerous others. The consensus among modern scholars has reversed this judgment, largely, it seems, as a consequence of Lowes's arguments. But in fact an agnostic position is the only realistic one. The many and mutually cancelling historical/occasional arguments for dating that have been produced over the decades are hypothetical in the extreme, and as Robert Frank drily notes, "We know nothing about specific censorship or a royal directive or a queen's request" (27). From an editorial viewpoint, the most that can be said about G is what George Kane says: that G has no special authority but "uniquely preserves an authorial version of the Prologue copied by an immediate scribe notably subject to error" ("Text," 58).[9] For my purpose in the present discussion about reading and writing, the question of priority is not crucial, for the versions are sufficiently similar—even given their frequent differences in wording and tone—that I might, with one or two exceptions, use either one. My procedure in this book as a whole is to use both, moving between the two versions in order to construct an inclusive picture of Chaucerian concerns. I shall generally quote from F as the fuller and (by my standards) more aesthetically interesting version, noting any significant difference from G. More important to me is the relative position of the *Legend* as a whole—one Prologue plus lives—within the canon, and in this I have accepted the traditional placement as noted above.

Nonetheless, since debate over the priority of F or G has raised significant but unexamined critical questions, I should like briefly to note some of the premises that have come into play. There is very little in the Chaucer canon that can be dated with any accuracy, and often the criteria for dating are peculiarly subjective or naïve. Nowhere, it seems to me, has this been more blatantly so than with the Prologue to the *Legend of Good Women*.

For example: A detailed comparison of differences between F and

8. The two relevant articles by Lowes are both short-titled "The Prologue to the *Legend of Good Women*."

9. It is to be noted, however, that the question of scribal carelessness is controversial in this case. Some scholars have thought the scribe was foreign; others see him or her as a conscientious editor. Parkes and Beagle diagnose lapses of attention combined with an effort to "translate" the text into East Anglian dialect forms.

G shows G to be drier and more austere in tone than F. It strikes one as a work on the whole less subjective than F, less insistent on art in general, and more modest in its presentation of the Narrator as poet. Some instances: F has but G lacks the important and powerful passage on the daisy as the Narrator's muse, inspiration, and "erthly god" (F 84–96). F has but G lacks a mini-portrait of erotic desire (F 103–14). In F, the birds defy the fowler "and al his craft" (139), while G has no reference to craft. F has but G lacks a coy, semi-sexual invitation to construe the previous line (F 152). In F, it is the Narrator who proudly sings the beautiful balade in praise of Alceste; in G, it is Alceste's retinue of ladies who perform the song. In F, the refrain to the balade begins "My lady cometh," while in G it begins "Alceste is here," a phrase that makes the balade less public, less generally applicable, hence less susceptible to being taken out of context and used on its own as a love song. The broadly applicable "ymagynacioun" of F 355 is the narrower, moralistic "jelos ymagynyng" of G 331. F ends with reading, dream, and experience fused in the creative act:

> And with that word my bokes gan I take,
> And ryght thus on my Legende gan I make.

In G, the penultimate line reads, "And with that word, of slep I gan awake," omitting the books and the possessive pronoun.

What can be made of such differences? It has been maintained that the "juicier" version, F, is clearly that of a younger man, while the more modest and moralistic G displays the wisdom and elevated consciousness of the aging poet contemplating death. Thus Lowes opined in 1905 that "a revision will be apt to possess . . . more intellectual, fewer sensuous or emotional qualities than its original"; it will show "calculation rather than abandon" (799). The aesthetic implied here would horrify or amuse many a poet. Certainly it has little in common with the principles of medieval rhetoric (one thinks especially of Geoffroi de Vinsauf's *Poetria nova*), which are strongly for sensuous qualities.

From another angle, here is D. D. Griffith's motivation of his preference for G as revision: "It seems tenable that Chaucer in his maturer life became more formally religious and regarded the analogies between the service of the Roman church and the service of Cupid as blasphemous." Such a position is predicated on stereotypes about youth and age. Moralism, modesty, and austerity are seen as by-products of aging; confidence and desire as aspects of youth. (Let us note parenthetically that we are speaking here of a poet whose approximate age in 1386 would have been forty-four, and, if the revision came ten years later, fifty-four at the time of revision. He is middle-aged in both cases, neither young nor old. We may add in this connection that the Middle English alliterative poem *The Parlement of the Thre Ages*, probably composed during Chaucer's lifetime, gives Youth the age of thirty, Middle Eld sixty, and Old Age a hundred: figures that are presumably to be taken as terminal for each category. It is important too not to misinterpret low life-expectancy figures to mean that no one lived long; they are statistical averages reflecting the high rate of infant and child mortality.) Stereotypes about age may well be inaccurate, for many people feel freer as they age to reject the rigid moral norms they once accepted. As for the medieval literary artist, the existence of an authorial holograph revision of the *Decameron* dating from the author's last years suggests that Boccaccio at least did not lose interest in his youthfully frivolous productions. I would argue as well that Chaucer always saw the religion of love as blasphemous, particularly in the *Troilus*.[10] Finally, the fuller and more art-conscious version of Chaucer's Prologue may well represent the sensibility of the maturer, more buoyantly confident poet. Alfred David writes of "loss of faith in the defense of poetry" (49), but equally likely— particularly in view of the pattern of increasing writerly self-assertion traced in the previous section of this chapter—is the reverse: that in G, faith in the defense of poetry has not yet been attained.

It is true that G has three references to age that do not appear in F. They are:

> "Wel wot I therby thow begynnest dote,
> As olde foles whan here spiryt fayleth"
> (261–62),

> "Although thou reneyed hast my lay,
> As other olde foles many a day,
> Thow shalt repente it"
> (314–16),

10. See Delany, "Techniques of Alienation."

and

"Whil he was yong, he kepte youre estat"
(400).

It has often been assumed that these carry a straightforward autobiographical message: "thou" refers to the historically real Chaucer,
Chaucer is now old, therefore the G text is the revision.[11] I have
already noted that Chaucer was not old either at the time of original
composition or at the time of revision. Moreover, the first two
passages are spoken by the God of Love, attacking the Narrator; the
last by Alceste, defending him. Neither one is an entirely trustwor-
thy reporter. The God's aim is to insult the Narrator—earlier he has
called him less worthy than a worm (F 318; G 244)—so that the
charge of foolish old age suits his overall invective. The God of Love
would certainly be the right character to use age as an insult, since
courtly love was codified as unsuitable for any but the young. In
short, the God of Love's remarks do not tell us either that Chaucer is
old or that the Narrator is old. Furthermore, it is important here to
take account of the rhetorical status of the comments, for they are
similes, telling us that the God considers the Narrator to be acting as
if he were old. Alceste's remark also does not tell us that the Narrator (much less the poet) is old, only that he is no longer young, a
comment quite applicable to middle age. If G came first, the age-as-
insult motif could have been excised in revision as irrelevant to the
newly foregrounded theme of artistic self-awareness.

From the perspective of metrics and simple poetic effectiveness,
a strong argument can be made for G as original, for the meter and
language of G are consistently rougher than those of F. One would
scarcely expect a matter so apparently straightforward as meter to
be contentious, but so it has proved in the checkered history of
Legend scholarship. In 1890, John Koch took G as original, partly
(although not only) on metrical grounds, for "it often enough spoils
the sense and the metre entirely"; J. B. Bilderbeck agreed in 1902,
also on metrical and aesthetic grounds. Ernest Amy's 1916 study—

---

11. Shea, ch. 5. Howard, too, cites these references to old age as among the
reasons to consider G a revision (*Chaucer*, 468). Howard's treatment of the question is
curious: he asserts that "in recent years it has been established" that G is later, but
gives no note to support this contentious claim. For a concise discussion of the
tendency to autobiographical inferences, see Kane, *Autobiographical Fallacy*.

still frequently cited as authoritative—offers an interesting example of how the metrical argument has been fudged. Amy several times characterizes G as "metrically and grammatically accurate," even while admitting that "large numbers" of its lines "are headless or somewhat rugged" and that in a twelve-line sample (G 127–38), "half . . . are strangely imperfect in the MS" (51, 94). As if this inconsistency were not enough, Amy eventually insists that G is later despite its "metrical imperfections"—because of Lowes's study of the poem's relation to its French sources! In short, he retreats completely on the question of meter, shifting ground to sources instead (but failing to offer any assessment of Lowes's far-from-conclusive hypothesis). Later, Kemp Malone compared two parallel passages, lines 27–39, in F and G. Much of his argument is circular, depending as it does on a prior acceptance of F as original; as, for instance, his observation that three run-on lines in F (27, 32, 36) are end-stopped in G: "It would seem that Chaucer looked upon a run-on line as metrically inferior." This is a gratuitous inference, for it could more convincingly be argued that F's enjambment is a mode of variation introduced in revision. Similarly, the presence of "I" once in G 30 but thrice in corresponding F (29–31) "is to be reckoned a stylistic improvement, an avoidance of repetition"; but I think the repetition improves the text, making it more direct and intense. Assuming that F 39 is original, Malone wishes that Chaucer had let the line alone, and he acknowledges that the "changes" "take away something of the freshness and spontaneity so marked in" F: Chaucer "loses more than he gains." Chaucer's genius, he concludes, "found better focus in the heat of original composition than in the cold of critical revision." Again, therefore, the critic's conclusion is not only based on prior acceptance of a debatable order, but on a romantic ethos that privileges the fiery and spontaneous creative-imaginative moment over painstaking analytic-revisionary labor, making "original" stronger than "revision"!

Of course, the problem with a metrical approach is whether such variants are typical transcriptional (scribal) errors and anyhow too minor to be taken seriously, or whether they represent authentic readings (a quarter-century after the author's death). I suppose the question is where we draw the line. We do not think a scribe could have been responsible for inserting whole sections of verse. We do think a scribe could have regularized meter, at least sometimes:

these views are supported by Kane's conclusion. But there is a gray area between these kinds of maximal and minimal revision into which the *Legend* falls: not only occasional but persistent and detailed metrical regularization; not only regularization of meter but improvement of the poetry in other ways as well. Here Kane's comment leaves an opening for further speculation: "As to the smaller differences, the indication is that any which relate intelligently to the meaning or feeling of their context, or show any command of expression, or answer to the better hypotheses of revision, are not to be attributed to [the G scribe]" ("Text," 52). The case warrants a closer look.

Taking the first thirty-nine lines as a sample, I note the following: In line 4, "this" (G) is "yet" in F, which eliminates the somewhat tongue-tying alliteration of *th* from the preceding "natheless." The same alteration is produced by the presence in line 5 of "dwellyng" (F) rather than "that dwelleth" (G) in a line that without the alteration has no fewer than five alliterations on *th*. (I note that *th*-alliterations may have posed a problem for the G scribe: G 93, for example, has four—"And that the sonne out of the south gan weste"—and this is likely to have caused the scribe to build a lisp into the following line, writing "clothed" for "closed." It is necessary to consult the facsimile published by M. B. Parkes and Richard Beagle here, for the reading does not appear in F. N. Robinson's version or the *Riverside Chaucer*, but is listed in *Riverside* under "Readings of Gg rejected by all editors" [1180].) Moreover, the shift to present participle in F cuts off two extra syllables, thus regularizing the line. In 20–21, the shift from "Yeven" (G) to "Yeve" (F) gives a smoother meter by eliminating two adjacent unstressed syllables, while the elimination of G's "trowen" removes the redundancy produced because of "credence." In lines 24–25, the reversal of infinitive forms from G to F (make/maken, weren/were) produces a more regular meter. G 28 has three alliterations on *th*, a repetition of "there," and eleven syllables (or even twelve, if we sound the final -*e*); the corresponding F line, 28, eliminates all these minor infelicities. The phrase "feyth and ful credence" in F 31 is far more effective than "swich lust and swich credence" in G 32 in eliminating both the repetition of "swich" and the possibly ambiguous "lust," while intensifying the devotional theme also introduced in "devocioun" (F 39). The eleven-syllable G 35 is matched by the perfectly regular F 35. G 36, "the joly tyme of May," is trite; F's "the month of May" less so.

Another argument that has been made for the priority of F is that it has, while G lacks, what is evidently a compliment to Queen Anne: "And whan this book ys maad, yive it the quene, / On my byhalf, at Eltham or at Shene" (F 496–97). Since Queen Anne died in 1394, it is assumed that the reference was removed at or soon after that time in deference to the king's grief. It is also this locus, there-fore, that accounts for the supposition of an eight- or ten-year gap between original and revision. On the other hand, one might equally well hypothesize that G was composed first, about 1386, without the reference to the queen's favorite palaces, and that F, the revision, added the compliment at some time before 1394. There would be no need to remove it when she died: it could stand as a compliment to a dead noblewoman, much as the *Book of the Duchess* does to Blanche. A more recent "occasional explanation" of G as revision, by John Fisher, hinges on the presence of "lylye flourys" in Love's garland (G 161), which do not appear in F. This is construed as an allusion to Richard's betrothal to Isabel of France in 1396. Given the very frequent exchange of personnel with the French court, though, this could be a compliment to any French visitor after 1385, not necessarily female and not necessarily royalty. Or it could allude, as Skeat long ago suggested, to the English claim to the French crown.[12]

Another striking difference between F and G might be taken as support for the precedence of G. It is the memorable phrase I have borrowed for the title of this book, "the naked text" (G 86), lacking in F. As I shall show in Chapter 3, the phrase was intimately linked with the Wycliffite project of Bible translation. This was always a controversial project; yet if there is a historical reason for the omis-sion from F of this phrase, I believe it is less an ideological gesture related to Wyclif's condemnation for heresy by English clerics in 1382 (an event in any case preceding the composition of either

---

12. Judson B. Allen offered another occasional explanation: that the poem repre-sents Queen Anne's failed intercession before the count of Arundel for the life of her and Richard's favorite Simon Burley in May 1388 (264). Paul Strohm's discomfort with occasional interpretation of the *Legend* (which he nonetheless accepts) emerges in the numerous qualifiers in a paragraph devoted to it: "apparent . . . presumably . . . almost certainly . . . probably . . . evidently . . . undoubtedly . . . must have" (171 n. 53).

Prologue, and not taken very seriously by the English at that time) than a tacit and prudential acknowledgment that any association with Lollardy was impolitic in the increasingly censorious climate of the later 1380s and 1390s. For a variety of reasons, Wyclif himself fell out of court favor after 1378, but he continued to enjoy the support of John of Gaunt until his, Wyclif's, death in 1384. He never broke with the pope, withdrew from the Church, or was excommunicated; he was buried in hallowed ground. However, the Church's success against Wycliffism at Oxford, the spread of Lollardy among the working and artisan classes, and the potential danger of Wyclif's ideas on dominion to ecclesiastical and secular realms alike generated a long campaign against Lollardy. Lollards were prohibited from preaching (1387), royal commissions were appointed to confiscate Wycliffite literature and arrest its owners (1388–89), several prominent Wycliffites recanted (1390–91), and Wyclif's *Trialogus* was examined and condemned by the chancellor of Oxford under royal mandate (1395–96). Throughout the period there was a growing frequency of arrests, trials, seizures of material, inquiries, excommunications, and abjurations. In 1397 the prelates asked Parliament for the death penalty for heresy, and this was at last granted in the 1401 decree *De haeretico comburendo*. Only in 1428 were the scholar's remains exhumed and burnt, the ashes scattered and, as Kenneth McFarlane poignantly puts it, "cast into a nearby stream" (*Wyclif*, 106). What becomes clear from this history is the slide of Wyclif and his doctrines from court approval in the 1370s into ambiguity during the mid 1380s, and eventually into the general opprobrium of civil and ecclesiastical authority. Given this changing climate, it is far easier to imagine the ever-diplomatic Chaucer removing the distinctively Wycliffite phrase "naked text" from his G Prologue than adding it to F.

My last instance of critical illogic in relative dating of the two prologues has to do with the refrain to the balade "Hyd, Absolon, thy gilte tresses clere" (F 249–69, G 203–23). In F, Alceste's name appears nowhere in the balade, and the Narrator is blamed for having omitted it (F 537–43). Lo and behold, in G, Alceste's name appears in the refrain of the balade. QED, Chaucer the poet has followed the advice of the God of Love, and G is later. The naïveté of this is patent in the many ways in which it relies upon an autobiographical literality of the text. In fact, to omit Alceste's name as F does is to create a more interesting poetic structure: it defers the revelation of her identity, thus creating suspense and a climax lacking in G. It also adds another fault that the God of Love can blame the Narrator for, intensifying the guilt-and-expiation theme that fictionally motivates the composition of the legends. In terms of aesthetic logic, then, it is far easier to believe that Chaucer took out Alceste's name in his revision than that he put it in. This is so despite apparent chronology, because the appearance of chronology is imposed by the scholar in accordance with a wish to prove the priority of F. There is no chronology, no compositional sequence to these fictional events, not even an implied one.

If I seem to have dwelt overlong on matters of relative dating, it is because they tell us something about critical assumptions. These are not limited to dating, of course; they recur throughout the present century as interpretations and as obstacles to interpretation. Nor are they limited to determining the priority of medieval manuscripts. The interesting history of two unique printed versions of Marlowe's *Doctor Faustus* (1604 and 1616 texts, called A and B), reversing earlier critical assumptions about priority, also opened windows onto conditions of cultural production and cultural criticism. My excursus on dating is thus a metacritical exercise, and with this in mind I should now like to return to my earlier question about the relation of reading to writing in the Prologue to the *Legend of Good Women*.

READING, KNOWING, AND MAKING

There is in the *Legend* no single named generative text, as there were in the *Book of the Duchess* and the *Parliament of Fowls*, to provoke a dream or to provide thematic material. Instead, there is tradition at large, literary tradition as a source of information, or at least of stories about all sorts of things:

> Of holynesse, of regnes, of victories,
> Of love, of hate, of other sondry thynges,
> Of whiche I may not maken rehersynges.
> (22–24)

The poem starts neither with tradition nor with the search for information, however, but with something more basic. Chaucer backs up to take a long running leap at literary tradition, and so must I in approaching the question I have posed about reading and writing.

The poem opens with an epistemological inquiry: how do we know, and what are the sources of knowledge? This is a reader's problem, for it seeks out the rules governing the reception, interpretation, and evaluation of propositions:

> A thousand tymes have I herd men telle
> That ther ys joy in hevene and peyne in helle,
> And I acorde wel that it ys so:
> But, natheless, yet wot I wel also
> That ther nis noon dwellyng in this contree
> That eyther hath in hevene or helle ybe,
> Ne may of hit noon other weyes witen
> But as he hath herd seyd, or founde it writen;
> For by assay ther may no man it preve.
>
> (F 1–9)

The nature of evidence had preoccupied the medieval intelligentsia since the mid twelfth century, when Latin translations of Aristotle and of Aristotle's Arabic commentators brought to the attention of Christian Europe a worldview considerably more rationalist and materialist than that of Christianity. In the *Sophist,* Plato describes the conflict of idealism and materialism as a perennial gigantomachy, a battle that "rages, as it has always raged, with unabated fury" (246C). In the high and late Middle Ages, this unabated fury took the form of book-burnings, excommunications, heresy trials, and lists of books banned by the Church from university curricula. Yet these tactics were far from effective, and others were devised than open warfare. Some scholars accepted from classical and Arabic philosophy what harmonized with Christianity, rejecting the rest; others attempted to produce a synthesis by christianizing Aristotle; still others took Aristotle as he was but severed philosophy from faith. The work of Aristotle and, eventually, of those who went beyond Aristotle, flourished in the universities of France, England, Germany, and eastern Europe.

Without being a university-trained intellectual, Chaucer was nonetheless well placed to appreciate some of the important philosophical issues of his day in their empirical manifestations, particularly as these related to the nature of evidence. The problem of faith versus experience was posed in the most immediate way by several major disasters of the period. The defeat of the Crusade movement toward the end of the previous century showed (or might be construed to show) that Christian faith does not necessarily suffice in combat against pagan hordes. Later, one did not have to be an intellectual, or even literate, to observe that the Black Plague that swept Europe in several waves beginning in 1349 made no discrimination of good or evil, just or unjust, baptized or unbaptized. And anyone might feel the deleterious impact upon faith of two (indeed, at one point, three) competing popes with their bureaucracies in Rome and Avignon after 1378. What was the moral and historical meaning of these fiascoes? Was retributive justice a valid concept? What was the value of a virtuous life, the efficacy of one's priest or of confession, the nature of evidence, demonstration, authority, or truth? These questions were not limited to clerics or professional philosophers, but were of concern to the populations of Europe, "lerned and lewed."

Chaucer would have had a more intimate appreciation of these issues than many, for during the hair-raising events that precipitated the Great Schism of 1378, he was in Italy, part of an English team negotiating with Bernabò Visconti, lord of Milan and old enemy of popes and priests. Visconti's niece Violante had married Chaucer's former patron Prince Lionel in 1368, and it is possible Chaucer attended the wedding in Milan. Visconti's militarism had made him one of the most powerful men in Italy and a threat to the Papal States. He had been excommunicated as a heretic in 1363 by Urban V, who also—in what Barbara Tuchman calls "one of the century's more futile gestures" (249)—preached a crusade against him. Visconti was a not unsuitable ally for the English, who— although loyal to the Roman pope, Urban VI, during the schism— were generally resentful of papal interference in domestic ecclesiastical affairs. The schism was exclusively a political event, with no doctrinal content whatever, and although the English were not negotiating the schism, still ecclesiastical politics must have been very much on Chaucer's mind.

Not for the first time, either, for it is likely Chaucer was acquainted with the doctrines of John Wyclif—perhaps with Wyclif himself, at least in passing. During the 1370s, Wyclif was a zealous proselytizer for subversive anti-papalist doctrines such as had previously been expounded by Marsilius of Padua and William of Ockham. This was precisely what recommended him to the English ruling elite as a theoretician and propagandist of national independence from papal supremacy. Wyclif entered the royal service in the early 1370s. He was present as a spectator at the 1371 Parliament; subsequently he was the king's chaplain and a protégé of John of Gaunt's. In 1374 he was among the king's envoys in negotiations with a papal delegation in Bruges. Wyclif had followers, the so-called "Lollard Knights," among Chaucer's friends and colleagues at court, and Michael Wilks claims that Wycliffism was, during the 1370s, "a court-centered movement . . . the expression of an officially approved reform programme, which carried the seal of royal authentification" (65–67). Moreover, Wyclif's ideas were frequently preached in London churches during the 1370s and 1380s, both by himself and by other priests, so that Chaucer would have had ample opportunity to encounter them; indeed, he would have been unable to ignore them. In short, Wyclif was genuinely part of the Chaucerian milieu for close to a decade: the decade usually considered formative for Chaucer the poet. Wyclif's ideas, far from being abstruse academic or theological theories, were in favor by reason of their applicability to the relations between Church and state. Had the ruling elite taken Wyclif's advice to its conclusions, the English Reformation might have occurred a century and a half before it did, for Wyclif supported the disendowment of Church properties—a not-unpopular idea in France at the time either.[13] There is no hard evidence that Chaucer supported Wyclif's doctrines, even during the period of Wyclif's popularity at court, but there is every reason to believe that Wyclif and his London followers conveyed key contemporary issues of faith, experience, and tradition to Chaucer. As we shall see in Chapters 2 and 3, it is equally likely, too, that Wycliffite literary activity helped focus Chaucer's concern about matters of translation and interpretation.

Another fairly obvious channel for such issues was the "philosophical Strode" addressed, at the end of *Troilus* (5.1857), along

13. Anne Hudson's definitive new study, *The Premature Reformation*, confirms this view, as its title indicates. On other aspects of Wyclif's career, particularly the political, see McFarlane, *Wyclif*. It is to be noted that while McFarlane and Joseph Dahmus cover much of the same territory, their aims are different, Dahmus's being to deflate what he considers an exaggerated estimate of Wyclif's political importance.

with "moral Gower" as a special patron spirit of the poem. Ralph Strode was a friend and critic of Wyclif, fellow of Merton College before 1360, and, according to Robinson, "an eminent Thomist philosopher and authority on logic" whose works are now for the most part lost, although some responses to them exist in Wyclif's work. Robinson makes a case for identifying the scholarly Ralph Strode with the lawyer Ralph Strode who lived in London and who was associated with Chaucer during the 1370s and 1380s. The dedication is, I suggest, more than a gesture of goodwill toward a learned colleague, for it is possible to see *Troilus* as an exploration of key philosophical problems at Oxford of the previous generation (i.e., Strode's generation): a medieval "Philosophy in the Bedroom" if you will. Troilus's agonized question "If no love is, O God, what fele I so?" (1.400) has impeccable literary roots in a sonnet of Petrarch's, but it is nonetheless, for any scholar, a serious philosophical question, raising not only the problem of universals but also those of cognition and will. Elsewhere, the characters implicitly and explicitly pose several important questions about "entente" (will, intention). Has will a cognitive function? Does will preserve its independence despite its dependence on God? Is it possible to measure the intensity of will, especially in the context of love? As Konstanty Michalski shows, these were three prime problems explored by Oxford philosophers in the second and third quarters of the century, and if Chaucer was able to shape the courtly erotic romance to accommodate them, that is further affirmation of his consummate art.

That there is joy in heaven and pain in hell is what one hears and reads but can never prove by logic or experimentation. The impossibility of verification opens the way to strict empirical skepticism, for one might wish simply to dismiss the unverifiable. This possibility the Narrator rejects with horror:

> But God forbede but men shulde leve
> Wel more thing then men han seen with ye!
> Men shal not wenen every thing a lye
> But yf himself yt seeth, or elles dooth;
> For, God wot, thing is never the lasse sooth,
> Thogh every wight ne may it nat ysee.
> Bernard the monk ne saugh nat all, pardee!
> (F 10–16)

The passage echoes John 20:29: "Jesus said to him, 'Have you believed because you have seen me? Blessed are those who have not seen and yet believe.'"

But it also echoes real philosophical controversies of the period. The nature of visual perception was a major topic in European and English universities during the fourteenth century. In fact, the bold investigation of vision theory, with its skeptical and empirical tendencies (or its deviations and distortions, as the more conservative said), was distinctively and notoriously English. Richard de Bury—bibliophile, bishop of Durham, and lord chancellor of England—boasted of his countrymen's tendencies and influence when he wrote, in *Philobiblon* (1344), of English perspicacity ("Anglicana perspicacitas") and of the English subtleties ("Anglicanas subtilitates"), which, publicly condemned, were furtively pursued at night.[14] A far more hostile attitude was expressed by Petrarch, who met Bury at Avignon during the years of papal residency there (1309–78, the so-called "Babylonian captivity"). Petrarch showed little of the British cleric's enthusiasm for dialectic. His attitude toward it resembled that of George Bernard Shaw toward socialism: the man who does not follow it at twenty has no heart, the man who still follows it after forty has no brain. Writing (about 1350) to Tomasso Caloiro da Messina, a friend from his student days in Bologna, Petrarch conceded that dialectic is "not a useless armor for those stepping into the thorny way of the philosophers. It rouses the intellect, marks a way of truth, teaches the deceits to be shunned. In short, if nothing else, it makes men resolute and very keen. . . . But," warns Petrarch,

> a place we pass through once and enjoy is not a place where we can justifiably linger; just as indeed it is insane for a pilgrim to forget the goal of his journey because of the pleasantness of the road. And who among us is not a pilgrim? . . . Dialectic can be part of the journey; but it is certainly not its goal. . . . If as old people we are unable to abandon the school of dialectic because we had fun with it as youngsters, we should not be ashamed by that same token either to play the

14. The passages are cited, translated, and discussed in Neal Gilbert's essay "Richard de Bury and the 'Quires of Yesterday's Sophisms.'" He argues that the impact of British logic in Paris was not limited to the work of Ockham but included the writing of several other scholars, such as Bradwardine, Burley, and Kilvington. John E. Murdoch has studied the influence of the British group, and particularly "the English calculatory tradition" (67) on two Parisian Cistercian theologians.

game of odds and evens or ride on a trembling reed or be rocked in the cradle of children.

Petrarch considered British dialecticians responsible for this folly, which had now infected even Sicily:

> Where will we flee from the presence of these madmen if even the islands are not safe from them? Can it be that neither Scylla nor Charybdis kept the passage of this plague from Sicily? Indeed it has now become a pestilence peculiar to the islands that to the ranks of British dialecticians is now being added the swarms of new Cyclopes from Aetna.[15]

Whether or not Petrarch knew the dialecticians' work directly, nonetheless, as a courtier at Avignon, where various doctrines were examined, tried, and condemned, he was well placed to know something about the potentially subversive inclinations of the British.

English logic, natural philosophy, and the new theology they generated constituted, in the fourteenth century, an international tradition derived largely from the immensely influential work of the English Franciscan William of Ockham. Although the label "Ockhamist" did not exist at Oxford as it did at Paris, nonetheless William Courtenay reminds us that throughout the century, "Ockham's name and ideas did remain at the forefront of philosophical and theological discussion. He was in no sense forgotten or ignored. . . . The elements [of his epistemology] that best survived . . . continued to make Ockham controversial in the more conservative atmosphere of Oxford in the 1360's and 1370's" (107). Some of the more radical scholarly formulations of this tradition show that Chaucer was by no means operating in an intellectual void when he composed the Prologue to the *Legend of Good Women*. Given the internationalism and ease of diffusion in this intellectual milieu, almost any text will serve to illustrate the tendencies within it. I have chosen one that is fairly close in its concerns to those of the opening lines of the Prologue. It is by Gottschalk of Pomuk, a Cistercian of the 1360s, on the impossibility of proving either the

---

15. *Le familiari*, ep. 1.7, trans. Bernardo, 37–39. On the date, cf. Introduction, xxvi. Also note ep. 1.2 to the same recipient, with its reference to "those who spend every minute of their life in debates and dialectical scoffing and who are constantly stirred up by inane trifling questions" (18).

existence of God, or the original creative act, or eternal blessedness of heaven or pain in hell. The passage is excerpted by Michalski from Gottschalk's commentary on Lombard's *Sentences*:

> Nullus viator potest naturaliter demonstrare aliquem articulum fidei. . . . Tertio infero, quod beatitudinem nostram finalem non potest aliquis naturaliter probare . . . , quia est mere creata et probatur est ex alio, quia si posset naturaliter probari, quod justi praemiabuntur post hanc vitam, eodem modo posset probari naturaliter, quod mali punirentur post hanc vitam. Sed hoc non, quia hoc videtur repugnare rationi naturali . . . , quod aliquis cruciatur ardoribus in perpetuum. (247)

> No one [lit.: no pilgrim] can by natural means demonstrate any article of faith. . . . Third, I infer that our final blessedness cannot be naturally proved by anyone . . . , because man is merely a creature and it is proved on other premises, so that if it could be proved by natural means that the just are rewarded after this life, it could be shown by the same natural means that the bad are punished after this life. But this can't be done . . . , because it seems to oppose natural reason . . . , that anyone should be confined to flames forever.

The empirical attitude was confined neither to England nor to university-clerical intellectuals. It filtered down, partly through the example and pressure of events, as noted above, partly through the very interpenetrated relations of ecclesiastical and lay life, courtly and urban life, courtly and university life. One instance will have to suffice for many. Marie-Christine Pouchelle writes brilliantly of Philippe le Bel's surgeon Henri de Mondeville, who composed a treatise on surgery during the first quarter of the fourteenth century. Mondeville's polemical aim was to overcome the then-dominant contempt for surgery as a particularly dirty manual craft—that is, to overcome the theory-practice split in contemporary medicine that elevated physicians at the expense of surgeons, the diagnostic function over the operative. To do so, Mondeville had to rehabilitate the senses—hand and eye—as means of knowledge, and thus risk contradicting a long and authoritative medical tradition not founded in experiment or detailed observation. At one point he writes:

> Ce sujet étant donc litigieux et obscur, j'ai songé à procéder d'après l'observation *sensibiliter et grosso modo* . . . quoique ce ne soit pas en accord avec les auteurs et les practiciens, ni peut-être avec la vérité. (44)

> This subject [diseases of the skin] being disputed and obscure, I
> decided to proceed according to observation empirically and crudely
> . . . although this may not be in accord with [medical] authorities and
> practitioners, nor perhaps with truth.

Noteworthy in this short but poignant passage is that its author
continues to reserve the word "truth" for the theoretical formulations he knows are "wrong"—that is, in conflict with his own
observations. But his medical practice will be on the basis of personal observation nonetheless. It is, in its own way, the doctrine of
two truths on a small, intimate, and accessible scale.

If empirical skepticism questions all but the sensible, an even
more radical extension of the impulse is what one might call "ideal-
ist skepticism": to question the existence not only of the unseen but
of the seen, for how can there be any certain knowledge except of
one's own consciousness ("soul")? As Etienne Gilson summarizes
the position:

> If God can conserve in us the intuition of something that is not
> actually existing [e.g., in dream, hallucination, or miracle], how shall
> we ever be sure that what we are perceiving as real is an actually
> existing thing? In other words, if it is possible for God to make us
> perceive as real an object that does not really exist, have we any proof
> that this world of ours is not a vast phantasmagoria behind which
> there is no reality to be found? (80)

Such extremism was fashionable in Chaucer's day at Oxford, Paris,
and other European universities, where some enthusiasts of the so-
called "Ockham's razor" had taken a fairly sensible rationalist caveat to the point of absurdity. This was especially the case in connection with the nominalist notion of the perfect freedom of God's
will; for if God has both absolute freedom and absolute power, then
he can at any moment alter any physical phenomenon or moral law.
Therefore it is not a necessary and self-evident assertion that fire
will burn wood, that incest is bad or honesty good, that the sun will
rise tomorrow, and so on. Neither causal nor predictive assertions
can be accurately (i.e., certainly) made. No thing can be demonstrated to be absolutely and eternally better than any other thing.
The only possible first principle is "If something exists, something
exists" (Si aliquid est, aliquid est).

Similar positions were advanced in what has been called "the

most famous discussion of cognition at Paris in the 1330's,"[16] the
debate by correspondence between Nicholas of Autrecourt and a
respected Franciscan scholar and teacher, Bernard of Arezzo.[17] Bernard's side of the correspondence does not survive, and all we have
of it is two of the nine letters of Nicholas. From this scant evidence,
scholars deduce that Nicholas defended a somewhat moderated
skepticism against arguments by Bernard that he, Nicholas, believed were an inadequate defense against complete skepticism.
The debate centered on vision, as was common in epistemological
discussions derived from the Ockhamist tradition (cf. McGrade).
Apparently Bernard had stated propositions whose logical consequence would be the denial of any certitude about anything at all.
The implication of Bernard's position was, according to Nicholas,
that

> you must say that you are not certain of those things which are
> outside of you. And thus you do not know if you are in the heavens
> or on the earth, in fire or water; and consequently you do not know
> whether today's sky is the same one as yesterday's, because you do
> not know whether the sky exists. Just as you do not know whether
> the chancellor or the Pope exists, and whether, if they exist, they are
> different in each moment of time. Similarly, you do not know the
> things within you—as, whether or not you have a beard, a head,
> hair, and so forth. And *a fortiori* it follows from this that you are not
> certain of the things which occurred in the past—as, whether you
> have been reading, or seeing, or hearing. Further, your position
> seems to lead to the destruction of social and political affairs, because
> if witnesses testify of what they have seen, it does not follow, "We
> have seen it, therefore it happened." Again, I ask how, on this view,
> the Apostles were certain that Christ suffered on the cross, and that
> He rose from the dead, and so with all the rest.[18]

To avert these dreadful consequences, Nicholas affirmed the cognitive and evidential validity of the five senses and of formal experiment, while limiting the kinds of inference that can be made from

16. Tachau, 335. One notes that the epigraph to her book is from the *Canterbury
Tales: Squire's Tale* 225–35.

17. The birthplace of Petrarch in 1304, and of Aretino in 1492, Arezzo was a
literary and intellectual center in the thirteenth century. As a Ghibelline city it was
disrupted by warfare early in the fourteenth century, so that many of its students and
faculty went to Florence instead (see Wieruszowski).

18. The two letters are translated in Hyman and Walsh, 707–8. They also appear
in Shapiro, 509–27.

such evidence. In other words, although we may be sure that the sun rose today, we predict its rising tomorrow only as a probability based on experience, but not as an absolutely certain truth.

Whether the propositions on either side were made "in earnest or in game" is hard to judge, for when summoned to Avignon to be examined for heresy, Nicholas claimed that he had engaged in disputation only to show that very startling assertions could be made without logical contradiction, and that his logical speculations were possible but not probable. In 1347 he publicly recanted his positions in a sermon in Paris and burnt his own theses and tractate. "His moderation," Hastings Rashdall writes, "was not unrewarded. In 1348—two years after his condemnation—he is Dean of Metz, and the friends who shared his errors seem for the most part to have likewise achieved satisfactory ecclesiastical careers" (5). Obviously, many who flirted with philosophical radicalism were satisfactorily reintegrated into the establishment, though its initiator and best-known spokesman, William of Ockham, died unreconciled with the Catholic Church, while some of Ockham's serious followers, like Hus, died at the hands of the Church. Still, Autrecourt's story suggests the currency and the availability of the new ideas. I do not want to make overmuch of the attractive coincidence of name, topic, and philosophical orientation, but the traditional identification of Chaucer's "Bernard the monk" ("Bernard the monk ne saugh nat all, pardee!" [F 16]) with St. Bernard of Clairvaux has always struck me as rather tenuous. This is because the saint was so much more than a monk; because the acerbic tone of the line implies a criticism; and because the philosophical content of Chaucer's passage seems to require a rather more controversial figure than an orthodox and canonized eleventh-century theologian. However, since nothing can be proved, I rest content with nominating a candidate who, even though he was a friar rather than a monk, has as good credentials as many another Bernard.

When Nicholas of Autrecourt conceded, at his examination for heresy, that his propositions were logically possible but not probable, and when he was able therefore to conclude that "we should adhere to the Law of Christ, and believe that reward and punishment take place in the way in which it is expressed in the sacred law," he availed himself of the so-called "doctrine of two truths" or "leap of faith" that enabled many medieval (and later) intellectuals to pursue their logical investigations while maintaining their status as Christians. It is essentially the same solution that Chaucer came up with in the *House of Fame*: to evade evident contradiction or a difficult choice by asserting faith:

> "Y wot wel y am here;
> But wher in body or in gost
> I not ywys; but God, thou wost!"
>   (980–82)

These lines exemplify the fideistic paradigm, and so do the first twenty-eight lines of the Prologue to the *Legend of Good Women*. The Narrator has already rejected a thoroughgoing skepticism and asserted (10–16) that where we do not know, there we must believe. We are warned, therefore, against the inadequacy of mere personal experience, mere phenomenology, as a basis for judgment. To rely on personal experience alone is to risk vulgar empiricism and solipsism; the antidote is faith.

Let us inquire at this point what the epistemology set out in the first sixteen lines of the Prologue (both F and G versions) means for the portrayal of women that is to come. It implies, first, that in general there is more than meets the eye. I do not mean this in the narrowly cynical sense that "women are deceptive," particularly not in a text that shows quite amply the deceptiveness of men. The implication is larger: no one's personal experience of human nature can be definitive, for no one sees everything. Furthermore, conjecture about the past, its events and personalities, is an unverifiable hypothesis, "For by assay ther may no man it preve" (9). History, as Hayden White has it, is necessarily "metahistory." From these principles enunciated in the poem's opening lines, then, we might legitimately deduce a very nuanced, and possibly ironic, treatment of the individual stories to follow, a treatment making fairly free with its sources.

What can be done to supplement the inadequacy of experience just stated? The second movement of the Prologue offers what appears to be a solution. "Than mote we to bokes that we fynde," the Narrator continues,

> Thurgh whiche that olde thinges ben in mynde,
> And to the doctrine of these olde wyse,
> Yeve credence, in every skylful wise . . .

And yf that olde bokes were aweye,
Yloren were of remembraunce the keye.
Wel ought us thanne honouren and beleve
These bokes, there we han noon other preve.
(F 17–28)

This is a key (important) passage in its proposal of a key (solution) to the skeptical puzzle. In Middle English pronunciation, the word *key* and the letter *k* were exactly homophonic; moreover, the written letter as it appears in manuscripts closely resembles a late-medieval key with its handle and teeth. For whatever reason, the passage evidently struck a chord. John Lydgate, in a couplet echoing this Chaucerian locus, wrote,

For yiff pennys & writyng were a-way,
Off remembraunce we had lost the kay.[19]

This is the passage that commended itself also to a younger noble contemporary of Chaucer. Edward Langley, second duke of York, dedicated his *Master of the Game* (a translation of a French hunting manual) to King Henry IV, justifying his literary effort with these words:

And for I ne wold that his hunters ne yours that now be or shuld come here aftir weren unknowe in the profitenesse [should probably read "parfitnesse"] of this art for thi shall I leve this symple memorial ffor as Chaucer saith in this prologe of the *xxv* good wymmen. Be wryteng have men of ymages passed for writyng is the keye of alle good remembraunce. (Spurgeon, 1: 18)

In practical matters as well as metaphysical ones, textual authority must take over when experience falters.

In the *Legend*, the leap of faith is to books, secular books, and in noting this we note a subtle but significant tactical shift in the terms of discussion. The poem opened with heaven and hell—doctrinal matters to be adjudicated by Scripture and its ecclesiastically approved supplements and interpreters. Now the subject is history as it appears in secular books of various genres whether hagiography, encyclopedia, chronicle, epic, or romance—that is, books telling

19. "Horse, Goose and Sheep" (after 1421) in Furnivall, *Political, Religious, and Love Poems*, 15.

"Of holynesse, of regnes, of victories, / Of love. . . . " With this maneuver Chaucer removes himself from the potentially hazardous arena of theological speculation. It is a discreet move, for medieval ecclesiastics and their allies were not always receptive to the notion of an author-narrator or author-character distinction, as the letters of Jean Gerson and Christine de Pizan would show a few years later in the "querelle de la rose." Nor is it, we might add, a distinction that the Narrator raises in his own defense against the God of Love, though something like it is broached when Alceste adduces the fact that the Narrator had only translated what others wrote, "as thogh that he . . . had himself it wroght" (F 371–72).

The shift to history is also a move that eases us into the fiction about to begin, for it motivates the presentation of the Narrator as bookworm, much as we have seen him in the first two dream-visions. Yet the extreme enthusiasm for written tradition evinced here might well give us pause, might well generate some suspicion, if we take seriously both the lesson of the *House of Fame* and the implications of the opening movement of the *Legend*. The relativism expressed in both places suggests that books simply cannot bear the epistemological load placed on them here. Such a conclusion is supported by the trial scene further on in the Prologue. The God of Love's angry response to *Troilus* and to Chaucer's translation of the *Roman de la rose* shows the extent to which "meaning is in the reader," as a proponent of contemporary affective stylistics might say. At the same time, Alceste's defense of the Narrator-poet challenges any easy assumptions about the motivation of critics (F 350–61) or of authors (F 362–72). Envy, stupidity, complaisance, or sheer opportunism may play a role. Alceste shows that assorted subjective and circumstantial factors may affect the production and reception of texts. Given all this, it becomes difficult to accept the Narrator's confession of "feyth and ful credence" in books as a sincere Chaucerian credo, and I shall show in the next chapters that the treatment of tradition in the legends justifies our suspicion here. It is worth noting, too, that while F remains fairly subtle, G text is quite overt in broadly hinting its subversive intention. There the Narrator claims he will translate "many a story . . . / As autours seyn," but caps his couplet with the arch warning "leveth hem if yow leste!" (G 87–88).

The Narrator begins as reader, but his concerns soon shift to authorial ones with the introduction of the daisy, which alone can lure him from his books. The intensity of his devotion to the flower triggers an apparent crisis of confidence: "Allas, that I ne had Englyssh, ryme or prose, / Suffisant this flour to preyse aryght!" (F 66–67). With this, the poet (whether Narrator or Chaucer is immaterial) bursts out of the naïve-scholar persona like Superman from a phone booth, for these words, although imitated in part from Boccaccio's *Filostrato*, inaugurate a thirty-line passage of striking self-awareness and poetic power. Doubting his ability to do poetic justice to his emotion or its object, the Narrator abases himself before the memory of his predecessors, the great love poets. (They are not named, but a list might include Ovid, Dante, Petrarch and possibly other *stilnuovisti*, Boccaccio, perhaps Chrétien de Troyes, Marie de France, and, among Chaucer's contemporaries at the French court, Deschamps, Froissart, and Machaut.)

> But helpeth, ye that han konnyng and myght,
> Ye lovers that kan make of sentement;
> In this cas oghte ye be diligent
> To forthren me somwhat in my labour,
> Whethir ye ben with the leef or with the flour.
> For wel I wot that ye han her-biforn
> Of makyng ropen, and lad awey the corn,
> And I come after, glenyng here and there,
> And am ful glad yf I may fynde an ere
> Of any goodly word that ye han left.
> And thogh it happen me rehercen eft
> That ye han in your fresshe songes sayd,
> Forbereth me, and beth nat evele apayd,
> Syn that ye see I do yt in the honour
> Of love, and eke in service of the flour
> Whom that I serve as I have wit or myght.
>   (F 68–83)

Will the Narrator-poet survive in the English tradition as an important and original author, or merely as minor and derivative? Implicit in this agony of influence is the problem of whether such vulnerability to precursors supplants or taints one's own passion. What is the relation of rhetoric and desire, books and nature, tradition and the individual talent?

Help is at hand, again, in a fideistic resolution. This allows the Narrator to transcend the dilemma of originality versus imitation by shifting responsibility to the daisy, which, as his muse, controls the Narrator's creativity:

> She is the clernesse and the verray lyght
> That in this derke world me wynt and ledeth.
> The hert in-with my sorwfull brest yow dredeth
> And loveth so sore that ye ben verrayly
> The maistresse of my wit, and nothing I.
> My word, my werk ys knyt so in youre bond
> That, as an harpe obeieth to the hond
> And maketh it soune after his fyngerynge,
> Ryght so mowe ye oute of myn herte bringe
> Swich vois, ryght as yow lyst, to laughe or pleyne.
> Be ye my gide and lady sovereyne!
> As to myn erthly god to yow I calle,
> Bothe in this werk and in my sorwes alle.
>
> (F 84–96)

It is a perfect example of self-reflexive subversion, for while the central question in the passage concerns the poet's talent and whether or not he is a world-class maker, the intensity and virtuosity of the passage answer this question unequivocally in the affirmative, showing us what it modestly pretends to deny. It is, after all, about as genuinely modest as the ending of *Troilus,* where, as Talbot Donaldson commented, Chaucer manages to transmute the modesty topos "into something close to arrogance."[20] The poet is even confident enough to rupture his own fictional illusion, for he refers to "this work" when the work has not yet been generated in the narrative.

The richness of this passage, and indeed of the entire Prologue, is such that discussion of it will appear in other connections further on. I use it here to note that the passage serves to jolt the Prologue from readerly into writerly concerns, the narrative persona from scholar to poet. That is where the balance rests throughout the Prologue, whose narrative is about the trial, defense, and expiation of a poet, a well-known and popular poet with a very considerable body of work behind him. The Narrator as poet is not only defended by Alceste, but he is sufficiently confident to defend himself (F 455–74), and with a great deal more dignity than Alceste's de-

---

20. "The Ending of *Troilus,*" in *Speaking of Chaucer,* 95. For studies of a passage of somewhat similar "problematical virtuosity" in Dante, see Terdiman and Hawkins.

fense allows. He concedes nothing to the God of Love but claims, contrary to the accusation, that he has in fact furthered the cause of love in both *Troilus* and the *Roman* translation. But his defense does no good, and expiation will be required. It is to write "a glorious legende / Of goode wymmen, maydenes and wyves, / That weren trewe in lovyng al hire lyves" (F 483–85). From this long dream of a prologue, the G text has the poet awake in the penultimate line. F has no awakening; instead its final couplet blends book and dream, tradition and subjectivity, in the act of composition:

> And with that word my bokes gan I take,
> And ryght thus on my Legende gan I make.

Yet both endings culminate in an assertion of authorial power. Both include a proud possessive designation of the text to follow, both include the minimal sentence "I make" as last assertion, both place the verb "make" in key position as last word in last line. What this confident author (whether Narrator or Chaucer is, again, immaterial) goes on to show us is that as reading writer, as writing reader, he has entered into the literary tradition far enough to be able now to put his mark upon it, to rework it and rewrite it to his own far-from-simple ends.

MAKING A LEGEND

It is possible to write about the *Legend of Good Women* as a series of negatives, absences, or denials. We might say that the Prologue is not one, because at nearly six hundred lines it is far too long for a prologue; that it is too self-sufficient—indeed, that it is a fully developed dream-vision narrative, which the legends appear to accompany almost as an afterthought or appendix; that its blatant fictionality fails to provide any of the factual, occasional, or analytical material normally expected in a prologue. We might speak of a heroine who is not one: Alceste, absent from the lives (although admittedly the text is incomplete), and in any case badly compromised, as I shall argue later, by her association with the God of Love. We might speak of a gallery without portraits, for not one of the women included in the *Legend* is given a physical description. We might speak of a hagiography without saints, and of good women who are far from unequivocally good. We might mention the denial of poetic worth that is co-opted into the poem itself by its fictional critics. And finally there is the absence—not absolute, of course: perhaps "diminished presence" would be a better phrase— of the *Legend* itself in the received Chaucer canon, as discussed in the Prolocutory above.

I want to concentrate here on one of these negativities, which forms a juncture of reading and writing: the hagiographical matrix deprived of saints. Chaucer was not the first to compose a collection of lives or portraits of legendary or even real women. He had been preceded in this by Ovid, whose *Heroides* (c. 10 B.C.E.), aside from being the generic model, also provides a possible model for ironic treatment of the subject. He was preceded too by Boccaccio (*De mulieribus claris*, 1361), and by the authors of *Nonnenbücher*, collective biographies of the members of a convent, usually written by one of their number. Curiously, though, no one had compiled a collection of lives of female saints, nor would this be done until Osbern Bokenham assembled his legendary nearly a half-century after Chaucer's death. Chaucer's *Legend* is thus a curious sport in the evolution of the hagiographical genre. Not itself hagiography, it is nonetheless generated by hagiography and the secular gallery of women. It borrows enough from hagiography to provoke a fifteenth-century clerical reader, Bokenham, to model his own (at that point unique) all-female hagiography on the *Legend*, yet its courtliness recommended it to the noble and middle-class reader of the day.

That Chaucer had substantial respect for hagiography is evident from the fact that he has Alceste cite, in her list of the Narrator-poet's exculpatory achievements, a life of Saint Cecelia (the *Second Nun's Tale*) and a translation of a homily, thought to be by Origen, on St. Mary Magdalene (F 426–28).[21] There is also the child-martyr legend told by the Prioress, which has a good deal in common with hagiography, particularly with the lives of Sts. Hugh of Lincoln,

---

21. The translation is lost, but John McCall notes the resemblance of Mary in the homily to the heroines in the *Legend*: "She is the faithful woman, of course, true and piteous, forsaken and ready to die at the sepulchre of her beloved Lord—less violent but with no less resolution than Cleopatra at the shryne [*sic*] of Anthony" ("Chaucer and the Pseudo Origen," 501). He also suggests that the flexible, vivacious, and sympathetic Narrator of the homily "may have been as valuable a model for the later Chaucerian narrators as Mary Magdalene was for the later heroines" (502). See, too, Janet Cowen, "Structure and Tone," on the hagiographical matrix of the *Legend*.

William of Norwich, and Herbert of Huntington, all of them adolescent victims, supposedly, of Jews. In the *Merchant's Tale*, Proserpina adduces Christian martyrs among the good women who confute traditional misogyny (IV.2283). The same tale may also contain verbal echoes of particular lives. The departure of wedding guests recalls a similar passage in some versions (although not Chaucer's) of St. Cecelia. In the unforgettable wedding night scene, the young May is "broght abedde as stille as stoon" (1818), while in the *South English Legendary*, St. Lucy is tied to a bed in a brothel where a thousand men rape her: "& evere heo lai as stille as stoon" (line 110). The Miller promises to "tel a legende and a lyf" (I.3141), his cynical abuse of generic terminology falsely reassuring the Host that his story will be fitting and proper. Laurel Braswell has shown that some anti-fraternal material in the *Wife of Bath's Prologue* and *Tale* and the *Summoner's Tale* can be traced to Jacob da Voragine's immensely influential thirteenth-century *Legenda aurea*, possibly via the *South English Legendary* or via liturgical readings (for which both the *Legenda* and the *Legendary* were often substituted). And of course there is St. Thomas à Becket looming silently over the *Canterbury Tales* as éminence grise and (as an Aristotelian would say) final cause of the pilgrimage. In *Troilus*, when Pandarus comes to his niece with love tidings and bids her dance, she replies that she ought rather to pray in a cave and read "holy seyntes lyves" (2.117–18); and if Criseyde's hyperbole here sounds slightly sanctimonious, the irony redounds less against hagiography than against herself. In the *House of Fame*, the Eagle swears "by Seynte Clare" (1066), a disciple of St. Francis and founder of the Poor Clares, perhaps introduced to hint at the parody of Franciscan super-rationalist scientism that is offered in the Eagle's lecture on natural philosophy.[22]

Noticeable in all these instances is an element of irony associated with the hagiographical reference.[23] This is so despite, indeed alongside, the obvious devotion indicated by the Origen translation

22. Several other hagiographical oaths, from the *Tales*, are briefly discussed by Ruth Cline, showing that "the choice of oaths was not entirely haphazard."

23. This is consistent with Ann S. Haskell's observation that, in the *Canterbury Tales*, "the saint is often used for Chaucerian irony" (2), particularly when its incongruity functions as contrast with the narrative. She correctly adds, though, that each hagiographical reference demands a separate and contextual study.

(and, of course, by numerous places in the *Canterbury Tales*, most explicitly the Retraction). In fact, I would maintain about these references or allusions, as I shall argue about the *Legend* itself as a whole, that the hagiographical matrix frames Chaucer's ironic project, that the notion of holiness stands as foil to the events and persons he portrays. It is not disrespect for hagiography but, on the contrary, precisely respect that enables the secular poet to use the genre as a touchstone, albeit a distant and unobtrusive one.

To be able to incorporate the apparently alien hagiographical consciousness into a courtly, classicizing work, a work moreover informed by contemporary issues in skeptical philosophy, is no Chaucerian perversity but rather the product of real familiarity with hagiography. When we understand the nature of hagiography, we may come to view it as after all less alien to Chaucer than we might have thought, for there is within hagiographical tradition ample room for both conscious invention and skepticism. High-medieval hagiography was a profoundly intertextual genre, to which Oriental and Western folktale, classical myth and legend, travel and adventure story, romance, political propaganda, doctrinal instruction, history, and biography all contributed. If the broad plot outline of a given life was fixed, its treatment was not, and successive compilers, editors, translators, and redactors felt free to add their version of incident, character, dialogue, description, and local color. They often did so quite overtly, justifying their creativity and poetic license with an aesthetic firmly based in an otherworldly notion of truth. One instance of this aesthetic occurs in the *Life of St. Gregory*, written by a ninth-century monk at Whitby:

> It should offend no one at all that the ordering of these events is irregular, for in that I am governed by the clear light of Holy Scripture. . . . And neither should anyone be offended if any of these deeds were actually done by some other of the saints, since the holy apostle, through the mystery of one body with its members the saints, by comparing it with the living body has so brought them into union that we should attribute to each member the works of the other in turn. . . . Therein we know that all of the saints are through charity of the body of Christ, whose members are in common. Hence if any of these things which we have written were not of that man . . . we should little doubt that they too should be in so great a man; for that holy man in his foreordained wisdom clearly teaches that with all

living things what is discovered in one should always be attributed to others. (Trans. C. W. Jones, 118)

A similar justification appears in the twelfth-century metrical *Life of St. Malchus* by Reginald of Canterbury, who, acknowledging discrepancies between his account and that of St. Jerome, urges the reader to believe the earlier version. Yet, he continues, since all things are common in the body of holy faith, what belongs to one belongs to all and vice versa. It would be wrong to believe the saint anything other than full of virtues, so that however much virtue we have attributed to Malchus himself, we do not deviate from truth (C. W. Jones, 214). Nor has this criterion been forgotten in our own day, for as Laurel Braswell observes, "the Bollandists still maintain after three centuries of hagiographical research and publication, [that] the *ratio* of saints' lives is the presentation of a sublime ideal in the sense that legend, like poetry, discloses a higher degree of truth than history itself" ("Chaucer and the Art of Hagiography," 210).

With respect to reception of the material by its transmitters, many a monastic hagiographer was willing (or his critics were) to question or dispute some of the more lush extravagancies of tradition. In the twelfth century, Guibert, abbot of Nogent, constructed a theological argument to refute the claim of the monks at St. Medard to possess the Savior's tooth (*Pat. Lat.* 156). Another text, Walter Daniel's life of Aelred of Rievaulx (1167) was attacked by some members of its first audience for the improbability of some of its material.[24] That St. Margaret of Antioch was swallowed and regurgitated by a Satanic dragon, which she then killed, is challenged by Simeon Metaphrastes[25] and by Jacob da Voragine (c. 1230–c. 1298), archbishop of Genoa, who called the episode "apocryphum et frivolum" (401). The compiler of the *South English Legendary* provides an apologia for his doubt about the motif:

> Ac this netelle ich noght to sothe · for it nis noght to sothe iwrite
> Ac wether it is soth other it nis · inot noman that wite
> Ac aghen kunde it were · that the devel were to dethe ibroght

24. See discussion of Walter Daniel in Heffernan.
25. The skepticism of Metaphrastes is mentioned in Francis Mack's Introduction to the thirteenth-century *Seinte Marherete*. Metaphrastes was once thought to be a source for *The Second Nun's Tale*, but Sherry Reames has proved otherwise.

For he nemai tholie nanne deth · i nemai it leve noght
And also i neleove noght · that is mighten were so stronge
A so holy creature · inis wombe avonge
Ac to sothe it is iwrite · that in a monnes like
The devel to this maide com · and fonded hure to swike.

(165–72)

But I don't relate this as truth, for it isn't written (intended) as truth. Whether it is or isn't true, I know no one who knows. But it would be against nature for the devil to be killed; because he can suffer no death, I can't believe it. Also I don't believe that his powers were sufficient to swallow such a holy creature [as Margaret] into his belly. But it is written as truth that the devil shaped like a man came to this maid and tried to tempt her.

It seems, then, that Chaucer might have found the saint's legend another case in point demonstrating the inextricability of "fals and sothe compouned" (*HF* 2108). As text, it is as subject as any other to the vagaries of textual transmission. But "God forbede but men shulde leve / Wel more thing then men han seen with ye!" (F 10–11): the letter is not the last word, nor is literality the final meaning.

What is a "legend"? Most literally, it is that which is to be read (*legenda*). This will seem pointlessly obvious—mere translation— unless we recall the context in which the material so designated was to be read.[26] It was to be read aloud, in church, as part of liturgy during the nocturnal office in an annual mass commemorating the anniversary of a holy person's death. The "legend" was originally a tributary biography or memorandum compiled by the local archivist from community memory and testimony as to the *gesta, signa et virtutes* (deeds, signs, and powers of holiness) of the deceased. If the saint grew more famous, the church or abbey more prosperous, then the service might become longer and more elaborate, the "legend" more fully detailed. The word was in no way opposed to history, in no way implied fictionality. A collection of martyrs' lives would be a "passionary": a collection of non-martyrs' lives (e.g., holy hermits, church functionaries, or unusually pious women) would be a "legendary," but this distinction collapsed fairly early on.

26. This and the next paragraph summarize material in Charles W. Jones, Aigrain, and Vauchez.

In the early Christian era—the period of persecution (through the third century)—with the exception of the scriptural saints the Virgin Mary, John the Baptist, and the Apostles, only martyrs were venerated as saints. Nor were these martyrs officially, that is, juridically, canonized. Holiness was manifested in the martyr's perseverance, death, and miracles, which were proclaimed by the martyr's community and local church. Canonization—the word first appears early in the eleventh century—was a privilege appropriated to itself by the papacy for the first time only in the late tenth century. Subsequently, it became an important aspect of Gregorian centralization, and in the twelfth century the papal bureaucracy began to assert that its approval was a necessary precondition to public veneration. Naturally, papal control of canonization extended to the accompanying liturgy and devotion. Equally naturally, the procedure of inquiry became very lengthy, very bureaucratic, very politicized, and very costly. Although there was a tradition, especially in England, of sanctifying clerical opponents of royal power, England's candidates for sainthood never managed to succeed under Pope John XXII (1316–34). During the Great Schism, though, the rival popes were quite generous in granting favors to their allies, so that England fared much better at the hands of Rome; and, as observed earlier in this chapter, such ecclesiastical politics were the medium in which the diplomat Chaucer swam.

What all this suggests is some flexibility in the concept of sainthood as well as in the generic notion of the legend. Such flexibility may help to account for the ease with which some medieval poets appropriated the vocabulary of hagiography for their love poetry. The rhetoric of the religion of love certainly feeds into Chaucer's use of the legend; the title, after all, under which the work was evidently known and by which it is called by the Man of Law is "the Seintes Legende of Cupide" (61). The reader of Chaucer's *Legend* has already seen the rhetoric of the religion of love at work in *Troilus*. What he or she sees about it there is its inadequacy as a guide to conduct and, sub specie aeternitatis, its falsity. The Prologue to the *Legend* apparently sets up the work as a palinode to *Troilus*: according to the God of Love, as a corrective to the romance's portrayal of the faithless Criseyde. In fact, though, as I hope to show in later chapters, that apparent purpose is reversed, so that the *Legend* winds up, in very winding ways to be sure, reasserting the same point about love that is proclaimed in the finale to *Troilus*.

The title of Chaucer's *Legend*, then, invites—even virtually forces—the reader to feel its daring and its dissonance. It is a parody, yet not one that depreciates the thing parodied. Rather, the thing parodied—a collection of saints' lives—is a silent presence by which the all-too-secular lives narrated in the poem may be measured.[27] *Parodia*, we recall, means literally a song or reply sung to the same tune as the original, or in a similar manner, or with similar words. The terms coined by Gérard Genette in his study of transtextual relations are helpful here, specifically Genette's fourth category, hypertextuality and hypotextuality. Hypotext is anterior; hypertext, linked to it as a derivative text that is not commentary, can serve as a way of investing old forms with new meaning. Following Genette, Linda Hutcheon severs parody from comedy, ridicule, or humor. Parody, she argues, is repetition or imitation with a difference, a form of transcontextualization "characterized by ironic inversion, not always at the expense of the parodied text," "a method of inscribing continuity while permitting critical distance" (6–7, 20, 32). Such a concept of parody helps us to understand why there was a good deal of room during the high and later Middle Ages for levity apparently at the expense of ecclesiastical, liturgical, or even scriptural authority: I might cite the well-known belching-joke "cor meum eructavit," the feasts of the Ass and of the Boy Bishop, and the Middle English "Cockaygne" poem by way of illustration. These humorous phenomena are far from genuinely iconoclastic— Hutcheon comments that parody reinforces, "its transgression is always authorized" (26), and this is its central paradox. But they do indicate the sort of flexibility I have in mind.

There are, therefore, several ways in which the "legend" rubric is by no means sarcastic. One of them is that hagiography offers a

27. A similar concept of parody is elaborated by Edmund Reiss, who distinguishes parody from satire in that "the ideal is not contained or fully reflected in the given, as in satire. Rather, when we call up the ideal, we are aware of the gap between it and the given. . . . [Parody] insists that we see [the given] in terms of something that is adequate" (27). Thus the Wife of Bath, for example, is a parody of the ideal of woman. Reiss goes on to take a scriptural-exegetic position that is both too narrow and not necessary to his concept of parody. Curiously, he does not mention the *Legend of Good Women*.

culturally normative array of exemplary women. In Chapter 2 I take up the question of why Chaucer wanted such an array. That he is asked for it by his own fictional character (the God of Love) is not, of course, an adequate answer, and I propose that his generic/formal choice relates to the moral and aesthetic purposes of the work as a whole (if we may speak of an apparently unfinished work as a "whole"). Another reason for hagiography is that it does show women suffering and dying as a consequence of love, and so does Chaucer. In basic plot, therefore, his stories do parallel those of hagiography, and open up the possibility of bringing into play different or competing concepts of love. *Cupiditas* and *caritas* are part of the Augustinian legacy that enriches the *Legend of Good Women*, and other aspects of that legacy will be discussed in later chapters.

There is a saint in the *Legend of Good Women*, but it is not a woman. It is the daisy, the modest English flower that is prayed to as "the clernesse and the verray lyght / That in this derke world me wynt and ledeth," as "maistresse," muse, "gide and lady sovereyne," and "erthly god" (F 84–94). It is the daisy whose "blisful sighte" wins all the Narrator's "reverence." It is only the daisy whose name receives the etymological treatment popularized by Voragine's *Legenda aurea* and duplicated by Chaucer in the Prologue to his life of Saint Cecilia: for "wel by reson men it calle may / The 'dayeseye', or elles the 'ye of day' " (F 183–84; not in G). Even without etymology, however, the daisy's name carries hagiographical weight, or at least it does so in French, because its French name, *marguerite*, is that of a well-known saint much venerated in England, Margaret. This equivalency was acknowledged in the *"marguerite* poems" of Chaucer's French contemporary and influence (for *Book of the Duchess* particularly), Guillaume de Machaut,[28] and in his stanzaic "Legend of Seynt Margarete" (1430), John Lydgate calls the saint "this daysye, with leves red and white." "Marguerite" also means "pearl," and in versions of St. Margaret that etymologize her name, this is the interpretation always given, for like the pearl, Margaret was little, round, and white: little in humility, round in perfection, white in purity. Of

28. Wimsatt, 28, 60–61. Because of this inherent relation of the daisy with St. Margaret, it is gratuitous to look further afield to account for its intercessionary role, as do Lisa Kiser (*Telling Classical Tales*, 47) and Robert Burlin (40) in identifying the daisy with the Blessed Virgin Mary.

course, a daisy too can be described as little, round, and white, and this commonalty of qualities assists my argument. Besides his explicit etymology, Chaucer also avails himself of the traditional one, although he does so only imagistically, by giving Alceste a white crown made "of o perle fyn, oriental" (F 221).

The hagiographical treatment of the daisy is continued when the God of Love refers to the flower as "my relyke" (F 321: the image is not present in G). This is a technical term denoting a part of the saint's body, item of his or her clothing, or object touched by or associated with the saint.[29] The relic is invested with such intense metonymic or synechdochic power that it is capable of miracles and becomes itself the object of veneration. During the high Middle Ages there was much dispute about the possession of relics. They were in demand by secular and ecclesiastical authorities alike; there was a significant international market in relics; and competition for relics led not infrequently to their theft from one establishment for pious transfer ("translation") to another. The remains of Margaret herself were believed to have been removed several times before arriving at their final resting place in Montefiascone, north of Rome. According to Osbern Bokenham, Margaret's foot was in a priory near his place of birth (he does not specify the town), while the great toe and heel to this foot were at Reading Abbey (*Legendys*, 135–43). Edward III was particularly devoted to relics. He was, in W. M. Ormrod's words (855), "heir to one of the largest relic collections in England," visited numerous shrines annually, and generously funded their coffers. Richard II has been described as "probably the most genuinely pious of the later medieval kings of England" (Ferris, 212). He was especially devoted to the cult of Edward the Confessor. He also strove mightily to have his great-grandfather Edward II canonized, but without success, despite the popularity of Edward's cult and shrine at Gloucester. Eros's possessive jealousy about relics thus reflects not only his tyrannical character, but also a genuine social phenomenon of religious life, one with special domestic and indeed courtly-political resonance for an English audience.

I wrote a few pages earlier that literalism is not the last word, but here I want to make it my last word. If *legenda* is that which is to be

---

29. On relics, see Brown, *Cult*; Brown, "Relics," Hermand-Mascard, and Geary.

read, what better title could there be, what more modestly boastful title, for a text in which the poet asserts his talent, reputation, and independence? He knows that his work has been read and discussed and will continue to be read and discussed. In appropriating this generic title, he proudly tells us so.

2

Women, Nature, and Language

> Here we see another good illustration of the original sin of
> all metaphysics, the attempt to read real or alleged features
> of language into the world.
>
> John Searle, *Speech Acts*

That the *Legend of Good Women* is above all a collection of stories, an
experiment in short narrative, Robert Frank reminded us nearly two
decades ago in his rhetorical study of the poem. The reminder
usefully warns against an approach to the *Legend* that is especially
tempting in a period of renewed interest in literary theory and
Chaucerian poetics, and one to which numerous scholars have
succumbed: I mean the temptation to concentrate on the Prologue
as a poetic credo, while ignoring or minimizing the legends. The
Prologue is a poetic credo, but not a freestanding one. It introduces
the legends that follow, and its fiction motivates their production. If
that fiction constitutes a statement of poetic principles, then the
poetry it generates can be seen as the manifestation of those principles. I believe that Prologue and legends are related as theory and
practice. The legends exemplify a theory of literary production,
which is defined in the Prologue in a variety of indirect ways.
Whether we call this theory a poetic or an aesthetic, it includes a
great deal more than what we now consider proper to either aesthetics or poetics. I shall call it an aesthetic of nature.

The other dimension of what follows begins as an addendum to
Frank's reminder. It is the observation that the *Legend of Good Women*
is above all a collection of stories about women. One is led, then, to
ask why Chaucer should have chosen, as the test, demonstration,
or praxis of his aesthetic of nature, the literary representation of
women. The answer closest at hand is that that is what some of his
important sources had done. The trouble with answers closest at
hand, though, is that they often do little more than defer the question. In this case, that there were antecedents is no sufficient an-

swer, for we should then have to interrogate Ovid's *Heroides* about its representational strategies, and likewise Boccaccio's collection *De mulieribus claris*. And the answers would differ from case to case, for we cannot assume identity of purpose among exemplars in a diachronically dispersed generic or representational tradition. My aim, therefore, is to problematize the obvious, which always seems less problematic than the obscure, but which—as Roland Barthes showed in *Mythologies* and elsewhere—constitutes the ideology-laden language of a culture.

NATURE, LANGUAGE, WOMEN

I want to begin *in res medias*, with a passage from the Prologue that, like so many of Chaucer's rhetorical flights, crystallizes, in minia-ture, the issues and meanings of the whole work. They are issues of language, nature, and women, and their imbricated relations create a densely textured, multilayered textual fabric. The *mise en abîme* I have in mind is the description of the spring season, lines 125–52 in the F text. The passage opens with a short, vivid dramatic scene or *enargia*: the warfare of winter against earth, and the rescue of earth by the sun.

> Forgeten hadde the erthe his pore estat
> Of wynter, that hym naked made and mat,
> And with his swerd of cold so sore greved;
> Now hath th'atempre sonne all that releved,
> That naked was, and clad him new agayn.
>   (F 125–29)

This elaborates an earlier passage from the *Book of the Duchess*:

> Hyt [the erthe] had forgete the povertee
> That wynter, thorgh hys colde morwes,
> Had mad hyt suffre, and his sorwes;
> All was forgeten, and that was sene,
> For al the woode was waxen grene;
> Swetnesse of dew had mad hyt waxe.
>   (410–15)

The struggle of personified seasons in the amplified *Legend* version recalls the marvelous passage in *Sir Gawain and the Green Knight* (fitt 2, stanzas 1–2) describing the progress of the seasonal cycle. In both places, personification conveys a sense of dynamic purposiveness in nature. But personification of natural process is a rhetorical device fraught with ideological implications. It carries a sense of that "commerce twixt heaven and earth," that "traffique" whose loss John Donne would lament some two and a quarter centuries later in "The First Anniversary." It is a kind of mutual transferability that lets us believe we observe ourselves writ large in nature, and nature writ small in our human selves. The trope is a rhetorical consequence, one might say, of the theory of correspondence between microcosm and macrocosm, that series of interlocking metaphorical registers that was the foundation of traditional political theory, natural philosophy, and medicine. This ideology found perhaps its clearest practical expression in the sixth-century *Etymologies* of Isidore of Seville, with their intense desire for connection between word and meaning, word and thing. *Amor* (love) is derived from *amus* (hook) because love entraps us like a hook. The spider is called *aranea* because it is generated from air; and so on. The history of correspondence as a basis for language theory or sign theory extends from Plato (especially the *Cratylus*) through Augustine, Anselm, and Aquinas.[1]

The *paronomasia* in the penultimate line of the passage—relieved/re-leaved—is more obvious in G's version, where the mention of greenery in the last line ("And clothed hym in grene al newe ageyn" [G 117]) becomes a fairly blatant hint.[2] Now pun, or *paronomasia*,

---

1. It is interesting to note, about Isidore, that the correspondence cannot be merely imagined, it must really be there; this is why Isidore denies the etymological relation of Latin *animum* (soul, spirit) to Greek *anemos* (wind): because a fetus has a soul already *in utero* and therefore a soul cannot be wind. For Augustine, Anselm, and Aquinas, see Colish. In *Dante, Chaucer and the Currency of the Word*, R. A. Shoaf treats "the assumption that word and thing do tally," attempting to define "a late medieval poetics of reference." The theory of correspondence was under attack in the fourteenth century, and Chaucer was sufficiently a man of his time to have withdrawn, in his poetic practice, from the full allegorical implications of the theory: see Delany, "Undoing Substantial Connection" and "The Politics of Allegory," both in *Medieval Literary Politics*.

2. A. C. Spearing notes of this pun that we cannot be absolutely certain it is one, because *re-leave* is not attested in the *OED* until the seventeenth century, and the vowel sounds in the two *releves* would be slightly different (*Criticism*, 9–10). I think we can press our dependence on the *OED* too far: words circulate orally long before they are canonized in writing, and many a pun depends on a neologism that may or may not eventually enter the mainstream. As for differing vowel sounds, Frederick Ahl shows (55) that this was no obstacle to Latin poets in their wordplay, and I doubt it was to medievals either.

does in small what allegory does on a larger scale: it holds in equilibrium two lines of interpretation. Here, the wordplay duplicates linguistically the two-level operation of the little allegorical scene to which it belongs. In this sense, the pun itself is a metaphor, not by virtue of its content, but by virtue of its method, its structural and functional resemblance to the larger construct; that is, its ability to balance two levels of meaning.

In another way the wordplay operates thematically, its method and its content recreating the stable instability of nature that is the explicit content of the passage: the equilibrated alternation of the seasonal cycle. Finally, the polysemous word—the signifier with multiple signifieds—represents a condition of plenitude. It does not destroy the relation of words with things but rather fulfills it, literally fills it full, as do Isidore's multiple etymologies for a single word. In doing so, language is once again true to nature, for nature was created as full as it possibly could have been. We may observe the principle of plenitude at work in both microcosm and macrocosm, in nature and in language. In multiple ways, then, this tiny bit of equivocal language imitates equivocal reality. Through this use of language and others noted above, we begin to see that the Prologue is developing a concept of language as itself resembling nature, language perhaps as an aspect of nature. The implications of this concept for the poem as a whole, and its relation to the literary representation of women, will become evident further on.

Already, then, the nature of language and of the linguistic sign is inscribed as a subtext in some of the rhetoric Chaucer has used in the short passage from the *Legend* quoted above. It was a problem that also occupied philosophers of language throughout the Middle Ages. Is language a natural phenomenon or is it arbitrarily consensual? Is a word *signa dei, flatus vocis,* or some compromise? The controversy—recorded in Plato's *Cratylus*—was carried, during the thirteenth and fourteenth centuries, in competing theories of modist and terminist grammarians. Jan Pinborg describes the modist approach as follows: it assumed

> that language, thought, and things are isomorphic with one another: the elements of any one of these three systems correspond to the elements of both the others in their internal relations. . . . According to this "modistic" analysis words are endowed with an immutable meaning, derived from the original imposition of words to signify

something specific, which can be influenced by context not at all, or only to a strictly limited degree. . . . The *modistae* tried to bridge the gap between words and objects by various kinds of entities . . . partaking both in the nature of signs and the nature of objects. And so, unavoidably, they ran into the trouble of all picture-theories: the construction of "bridging" entities could go on ad infinitum since there is no real tertium comparationis between objects, concepts and words. In the years after 1300 these difficulties caused considerable tension which gradually undermined the theory. (21–22)

The work of terminist or nominalist opponents of this approach—scholars like Jean Buridan, William of Ockham, Pierre d'Ailly, and Johannes Aurifaber—has received far less attention than that of the modists. Nonetheless, from what has been done, it is possible to deduce that the essence of the anti-modist position was to empha-size the truth-value of propositions and to reject the existence of "modes of signification" as something distinct from signifier or signified. Terminist theory "therefore displayed what has been called a contextual approach, that is, it attended to the precise function and reference the term actually had in the proposition analyzed" (ibid.).

That Chaucer was no scholastic could not impede his awareness of the general problems of signification, any more than it could hinder his absorption, in broad outline, of the epistemological spec-ulation of his day (see Chapter 1). Both as practicing poet and as reader of Augustine, Chaucer had to confront the nature of signifi-cation. Moreover, one of the most important works of medieval literature and one of Chaucer's most fertile sources—the *Roman de la rose*—poses the problem of signification both implicitly and ex-plicitly. The implicit method occurs, as Daniel Poirion points out, in the first part: Guillaume de Lorris's use of codified courtly language, and his use of dream (which signifies the allegory, which signifies a truth). Jean de Meun, on the other hand, uncomfortable with both allegory and courtly love, exemplifies the *crise de signification* that French literature would experience during the thirteenth century. This is accomplished most obviously in the famous discussion of Reason's use of the word *coilles* (testicles) in her account of Saturn's fall (*RR* 6871 ff.). "Voilà une souriante leçon de philosophie de langage!" comments Poirion, a lesson in which is evident "ce courant nominaliste qui se caractérise par l'opposition entre *res* et *vox*" (173).

The poetic proposed in Chaucer's Prologue and exemplified in the legends plays with notions of language and meaning, as I want to show in my exegesis of the passage at hand. That the text of the poem hovers in the space of what Jacques Derrida has called *différance* may account for the difficulty scholars have had in reading and interpreting it. One finds in the poem the play of differing/deferring/deference between—on one hand—the ideals of a pristine, stable, absolute, and paradigmatic *langue*, and—on the other—the realities of fallen, contingent, infinitely variable *parole*. The signifying system or code in which this disjunctive play occurs may be language, ethics, literature, love, beauty, nature, or the human body. In the *Legend of Good Women*, it is all of them. This play of *différance* destabilizes the poem, producing an aura of uncertainty about meaning and the status of language that affects content and structure, narrative and rhetoric.

For the text resists classification. It is hard to pin down, unusually hard even for a text within a corpus well known for its ambiguities. On the one hand, it expresses a longing for "the naked text" (G 86), a phrase to be more fully glossed in Chapter 3. Here it may mean a text bare of rhetoric, a text faithfully translated, a text devoid of gloss, or a text completely transparent to meaning. On the other hand, the actual linguistic surface of this text could scarcely be more elaborately draped, displaying as it does the techniques of classical rhetoric, metaphysical speculation, formulas of courtly love, and a range of ironic devices, including pun and, as we shall see further on, obscenity. A puzzling text, then, as rich and as self-contradictory as the three entities, the ones named in the title of this chapter, that it unites. Let us return now to nature, women, and language.

The passage I have chosen continues with another little dramatic scene, another scene of conflict, but this time between the small birds and their old enemy the fowler:

> The smale foules, of the sesoun fayn,
> That from the panter and the net ben scaped,
> Upon the foweler, that hem made awhaped

In wynter, and distroyed hadde hire brood,
In his dispit hem thoghte yt did hem good
To synge of hym, and in hir song despise
The foule cherl that, for his coveytise,
Had hem betrayed with his sophistrye.

(F 130–37)

Here the opponents are types of nonrational and rational life: or, to replace that Aristotelian formulation with a Christian one, creatures without and with souls. We know how fond Chaucer was of dovetailing the activities of avian and human species: the *Parliament of Fowls* reminds us of it, as do the opening of the *Canterbury Tales,* and the *Nun's Priest's Tale.* The present birds have escaped the fowler's nets and traps, but he has frightened them all winter long and destroyed their young. We would scarcely expect a Chaucerian bird to turn the other cheek, and indeed these gloat in triumphant self-assertion, for their survival is the trapper's failure.

Who, or what, is this fowler? Satan, B. G. Koonce proposed, basing his interpretation on scriptural exegesis. The art historian Meyer Schapiro, though, writing on the bowman and bird motif in the plastic arts, grouped it with a "large class of medieval images of the hunter and the beast," many of which have secular rather than religious significance. I consider a secular source for Chaucer's fowler more likely than a scriptural-patristic one.[3] But whatever its origin, the figure of the fowler can be understood only contextually and diacritically: what he is and what he is not, what he is for and what he is set against. Here he is set against the birds.

The simplest relation of fowler to birds is that of hunter to victims. It is easy enough—too easy, I think, with our post-Romantic and ecology-conscious sensibilities—to take the bird-victims' side and to deplore the hunter's pursuit. Yet such a response can scarcely have been desirable or even imaginable to a society that not only lived in part by the hunt but elevated it to a fine art. The theme emerges elsewhere in the Chaucerian corpus as well. If rapacity is

3. Specifically, the well-known story of the churl and the bird, in which a greedy churl tries to outwit the bird but is himself outwitted. This story is told in Peter Alfons's *Disciplina clericalis* (available to Chaucer in Latin, French, and English), in several French tales, and in a short poem, "The Churl and the Bird," attributed to John Lydgate. In *Disciplina clericalis,* the story (#22) is followed up with the moral that not all books are to be believed, a theme that brings Peter's version into closer relation with Chaucer's *Legend* than the other versions.

part of the natural order, as the *Parliament of Fowls* suggests it is, with its aristocratic predators in Nature's park; if the sexual power struggle is a principle of nature, as the presence of Pluto and Proserpina indicates in the *Merchant's Tale*, then the relation between fowler and prey in the *Legend*'s Prologue has anticipatory and persuasive power. It invites us to see the battle of sexes waged in the legends as a permanent condition of postlapsarian life. Men will victimize women, it is their (fallen) nature to do so; and if social structures encourage or enable that victimization, they too are consequences of the expulsion from Eden. It is, as Tennyson would later phrase it, "nature red in tooth and claw," and in Chapter 5 I shall look more closely at the Chaucerian representation of these "facts" of life and of nature. Nonetheless, this view of man as predator (more recently articulated by Susan Brownmiller in *Against Our Will: Men, Women, and Rape* [1975]) should not be interpreted as justification for rape: any sin, after all, is equally the consequence of our fallen nature. Rape was considered a sin and a crime, punishable in the ecclesiastical sphere by excommunication, in the civil by various penalties, depending on time and place and provability, but in England in the fourteenth century including "loss of life and of member." It is possible, as I have suggested elsewhere,[4] that Chaucer's personal experience with *raptus* in 1380 gave him a particular awareness of the subject, reflected not only in the *Wife of Bath's Tale* but in the legends of Lucrece and Philomela.

Yet our birds are no silent victims. They turn the tables in derogatory song, as surely as May turns the tables on January in the *Merchant's Tale* with the ready reply guaranteed her and all women by Proserpina. It is through language that—Proserpina assures us—women will always prevail, or at least survive: "For lak of answere noon of hem shal dyen" (IV.2271). It is through language that the victimized women in the *Legend* also eventually triumph, their suffering memorialized and perhaps transcended through the works of art that tell their stories and renew their lives to posterity. Ovid had already opened the way to such a perspective when he wrote, in the *Ars amatoria*—apostrophizing a list of abandoned women including Dido, Phyllis, and Ariadne—that what ruined

4. In "Strategies of Silence in the Wife of Bath's Recital," *Exemplaria* 2 (1990): 49–69, and reprinted in *Medieval Literary Politics*.

them was a lack of art: "Defuit ars vobis; arte perennat amor" ("Art was lacking in you; love endures by art" [3.42]). The art he means is, of course, the *technē* of loving; yet it is also the *technē* of poetry, and particularly his own poetry, which the ever-assertive Ovid was never loathe to advertise: in the present passage one notes the strong *dicam* (I will say) in the line preceding the one cited, and the obvious echo of Horace's monument *perennius aere*. An ambiguity similar to Ovid's surfaces in the opening line to Chaucer's *Parliament of Fowls*—"The lyf so short, the craft so long to lerne"—where "craft," although soon glossed as love (4), nonetheless is easily mistaken for poetry, especially if one recalls another Latin commonplace, "Ars longa, vita brevis."

That it is not their own language that accomplishes the permanence of women's stories but someone else's—many others, Virgil, Ovid, and Chaucer among them—suggests again the necessary intermediacy that is art or tradition. The poets are, by and large, men; but in Chaucer's fiction the memorialization is a woman's idea. Alceste motivates the poetic language that commemorates these literary lives, just as in the *Merchant's Tale* Proserpina motivates the argumentative language women use to facilitate their real lives. In both cases a woman generates language on behalf of women.

Is it sheer coincidence that these female figures, Alceste and Proserpina, linked in a similar relation to women by way of language, also share several other elements in their stories? Both travel to the underworld. Both are companion to a powerful god who represents a force of instinctual nature (Eros and Thanatos respectively). In both cases the female companion has to mitigate the punitive force of the male deity she attends. Here, then, is another permutation of the woman/nature/language triangle: poetic language, inspired by women or about women, as a means to moderate (or sublimate) the effects of nature.

There is still more to our birds, though, for these are poet-birds. They have a natural song based on experience and on instinctual desire, with which they are able to insult the fowler. The fowler, on the other hand, has technology: the panter and the net. He also has a complicated moral life, partly the consequence of his participation in a complicated social life, for his motive is said to be "coveytise," the profit motive. He is trapping birds not to eat but to sell. His relation to the birds is neither aesthetic nor strictly natural: he neither appreciates their song nor hunts them for biological susage-nance. From the fowler's point of view, the birds are a commodity. They have no immediate use-value but only exchange-value on the market, where they may be bought as food, as pets, as bait for larger birds, as a source for feathers, and so on. The birds are, for the fowler, mediated and distanced by a socially determined system of value within which they are signs and therefore to be exchanged. We shall return to this notion of signs and exchange later on in connection with women.

If such is the fowler's view of the birds, they too have their special view of him. From a bird's-eye view, the fowler has "sophistrye" and "craft." What is meant is the fowler's *techne*: the special skills and tools he possesses that enable him to follow his profession. Yet these are curious words for Chaucer to have chosen here, and curious qualities with which to endow a "cherl," an undereducated rural working man, for they are linked to advanced verbal skills both oral and written: sophistry to the philosophical argumentation that formed an important part of university training,[5] craft to poetic making. "Sophistry" in particular also has a much older ancestry; it goes back to Plato (as so much does in medieval culture), where it is intimately linked to the notion of the hunt. In the *Sophist*, a philo-sophically inclined visitor from Elea, instructing Theaetetus on the sophist's nature, develops the predatory image at length (secs. 219–23). In these sections, and in the two following, both professions are also considered in their economic light. The Eleatic's conclusion is that sophistry can be defined as "the chase after young men of wealth and reputation by an art of appropriation by conquest, effected by hunting, of an animate quarry inhabiting the dry land, when the quarry is man, and the hunting done by the persuasion of an individual, paid in current coin, and carried on under a pretext of imparting education."

That Chaucer has chosen these heavily freighted words for his fowler should alert us to the language theme. If the birds are natural or intuitive singer-poets, what sort of wordsmith might the fowler represent? Is he perhaps a hostile critic or censorious patron, or a

5. On sophistry and sophisms in medieval university life, see Gilbert, "Richard de Bury," 241–48.

heavy-handed ideological poet? Or ought we rather to see him, more simply and more generally, as an abuser of verbality in any genre? Louis Marin wrote of narrative itself as a trap, although this is not a trail I want to follow here. Nonetheless, the vocabulary of sophistry and craft bespeaks a long-standing mistrust of the rhetor, as well as mistrust of rhetoric as a technique of disguise, hence entrapment. If, in my reading of hunter and birds, the fowler's technology represents the snares of rhetoric, then the scene offers another connection with the stories to follow, where a male lover lays verbal traps for his "bridde" (woman/bird). Plato too made this connection:

> ELEATIC: Then I suppose you have never remarked how a lover
>   gives chase.
> THEAETETUS: Why, what of him?
> ELEATIC: He actually lavishes presents on his quarry.
> THEAETETUS: Very true.
> ELEATIC: So we may call that type of persuasion the *art of love*.
>   (*Sophist*, secs. 222–23)

In Ovid's *Ars amatoria*, the hunt is a constant structural metaphor for love. Perhaps picking up Plato's lead, Ovid also uses the vocabulary of the hunt for the rhetoric of love: Cydippe is captured by words (*verbis capta* [1.458]); the mind is trapped (*deprendere* [1.619]) by flattery; poetry is recommended to women as a way of attracting prey (3.329–48), as is writing (3.467–98): these are among the ways "we [men] are caught" (*capimur* [3.133]). Later, a relationship among language, hunting, and sexuality would also be discerned by John of Salisbury, who, in *Metalogicon* (1159), wrote of sophistry that it "disguises itself as all the disciplines, and . . . lays its traps for everyone, and catches the unwary. . . . [If abused, sophistry] will play the adulteress, who betrays her blinded lovers by exposing them to errors and leading them to the precipice" (4.22).

Lisa Kiser (*Telling*, 67) adduces two further passages: one from Walter Map's *De nugis curialium*, which links bird-trapping and sophistry, and the following lines from the *Roman de la rose*, in which the nearly triumphant lover warns others that though many women are like birds deceived by word traps, the older woman is likely to be suspicious even of lovers who swear by all the saints who are, will be, and were ("Les sainz qui sunt, seront e furent" [21458]). The lover operates through simulation,

ainsinc con fet li oiselierres
qui tant a l'oisel come lierres . . .
li fos oiseaus de lui s'aprime,
qui ne set respondre au sofime
qui l'a mis en decepcion
par figure de diction.
(21461–70)

as a fowler does,
who lures the bird . . .
the silly bird approaches
not knowing how to respond to the sophism
that has deceived it
by a figure of diction.

As with so much in Chaucer, the figure is overdetermined.

However we read the fowler, he is as much a philistine as the God of Love will shortly prove to be with *his* critical sophistry and all his craft of love. And the fowler is as cleverly defied in bird song as Eros will be defied in the ironical legendary whose making escapes his control. Are they, Eros and the fowler, to be condemned? Yes and no, depending on what view we take. In their defense it can be observed that, from a normative medieval perspective, neither erotic nor economic compulsion is entirely avoidable in the world as we have it: such is Jahweh's curse on Adam and Eve. We might therefore want to see fowler and birds as a necessary dialectic in nature—much like men and women. We might want to see them as two kinds of artist in confrontation: the trained, sophisticated/sophistical rhetor with his elaborate nets, limes, and traps, versus the intuitive, naïf, spontaneous singer who blurts out love and hate. We might even want to see these as two aspects of the same artist, like the two brothers in Sam Shepard's play *True West*. One of them, a well-paid professional scriptwriter in suburban Los Angeles, lacks a compelling story to tell; the other, an ill-educated wanderer, can recount his fascinating experience in the desert but cannot write it up. Eventually the two change places: the scriptwriter abandons his house and typewriter to go on a pilgrimage to the desert in search of material, inspiration, and his "real self," while the wanderer moves into the house, learns to type, and sells scripts. It is, in short, about the integration of book, experience, and dream in a writer's work, a theme familiar to Chaucerians.

It remains only to add that our birds do not only produce a song of hatred. They are also capable of "clere / Layes of love, that joye it was to here" (F 139–40), songs in praise of springtime and Saint Valentine, who lets them choose their mates (F 145–47). These simple, contrasting songs reflect the double reality of the birds' merely instinctual lives. As nature is dual and contradictory, so is our experience of it, and so must art be if it is to be faithful to nature and to life. But how much more ambivalent and nuanced must be the *lai* of the human artist if he or she is to maintain a similar "troth" with nature. Nature is the given—and yet nature is not all, for the opening lines of the Prologue have already warned us that there is more to it than meets the senses. Nonetheless, fidelity to nature is at least where one starts to tell the truth, and part of the truth is the "troth," the connections, bonds, or promises that are present but invisible, possible but unachieved, once felt but now lost.

The power, and the danger, of the God of Love, is that he aims precisely to break a representational troth, the bond between signifier and signified. Demanding an unbalanced representation of women, which is really misrepresentation, Eros requires the poet-Narrator to falsify experience in the name of a specialized literary tradition. Much like the discourse of Pandarus, although in another register, the god's command can only cut language off from its mooring in reality. He will effect a divorce rather than a marriage. The image of woman that Eros proposes is simply a massive synechdoche, taking the part for the whole or taking one (ideal or good) woman for the entire sex. It substitutes a rhetorical device for reality. Of course, there are good, faithful, and true women, but there are also bad and faithless women, and then there are most women, whose goodness is mixed with error of various kinds and degrees. To let the individual stand for the sex is a standard tactic of misogyny, which Christine de Pizan would denounce some twenty years later in her *Livre de la cité des dames*. As a defense of women, essentialism destroys itself. To argue that women are by nature good is to accept the conceptual foundation for the opposite view: that they are by nature bad. Either position is reductive, and therefore false. Chaucer's intent, I suggest, is to occupy the orthodox middle ground, neither misogyny nor courtly adulation. As Henry Fielding would more cynically put it some centuries later, in *Tom Jones*:

The finest Composition of human Nature, as well as the finest China, may have a Flaw in it; and this, I am afraid, in either case, is equally incurable; though, nevertheless, the Pattern may remain of the highest Value. (Book 2, ch. 7)

To return to my exegesis, here are the last lines of the passage at hand:

> And therwithalle hire bekes gonnen meete,
> Yeldyng honour and humble obeysaunces
> To love, and diden hire other observaunces
> That longeth onto love and to nature;
> Construeth that as yow lyst, I do no cure.
>   (F 148–52)

The last three lines contain a favorite Chaucerian device, the "deliberate mystification" as Talbot Donaldson christened it, or coy evasion that tells all. Sexuality belongs to nature and therefore to love. No love poetry that omits it can claim to be realistic or complete. The coy remark above hints at this perspective, and we ought not to expect that the tales to follow will be purged of lust or sexuality. As I show in Chapter 3, the steady current of sexual wordplay in the legends keeps this dimension of natural experience firmly before us.

Finally, a curious thing happens in the very last line of the passage. We, the audience, are suddenly kidnapped into subjectivity, in several senses. The reader becomes the subject (topic) of poetry, incorporated into the line as "you." The reader is urged to act (to become grammatically a subject) and specifically to construe something (to exercise personal subjectivity). What are we to construe? The antecedent of "that" is indefinite, referring both to the reported action of the birds and to the coy verbal formulation in which the report is couched. When the poet reaches out in the imperative mood to shake us into judgment, he forces us to realize that there is an author. This author can choose rhetorical tactics and now separates himself from his composition in order to designate it as "that."

With the command to construe, Chaucer abruptly reinserts us into history, specifying a textual procedure that bore important contemporary meaning. To "construe" is to translate a text literally and grammatically, word for word rather than meaning for meaning, and a "construe" is a text so translated. About the relative merits of these two methods there was much debate in Chaucer's day, for between about 1375 and 1395 the Wycliffites were engaged in their translation of the complete Bible out of the Vulgate's Latin into the vernacular: as Margaret Deanesly put it, "a great undertaking, and no one had done such a thing before in England" (*Significance*, 4). Was it lawful to translate Scripture at all? Would ordinary people benefit or would they be spiritually endangered by difficult or shocking episodes? Should the massive project rely on strict construal of the Latin, or should Latin grammar and usage be adapted for ease of comprehension? Even more significant, ought the text to be accompanied by a gloss—accumulated authoritative exegetical commentary (as, say, Richard Rolle's translation of the Psalter was accompanied by parts of the gloss of Peter Lombard)— or might it legitimately be confined to "the bare text"? An allusion to the problem of method occurs in the *Friar's Tale*, when the fiend refers to controversy over literal versus interpretive understanding of a biblical passage (1 Sam. 28:7–20):

> Somtyme we . . .
> . . . speke as renably and faire and wel
> As to the Phitonissa dide Samuel.
> (And yet wol som men seye it was nat he;
> I do no fors of youre dyvynytee.)
>   (III.1506–12)

A first version of the "Lollard Bible" was completed probably in 1384, the year of Wyclif's death and not long before Chaucer began to work on the *Legend*. Construal was the method chosen. As a construe, this first version maintained a Latinate vocabulary, word order, and grammar. But the method produced a stilted translation that impeded rather than facilitated comprehension: it was, in short, a failure. In the 1390s, therefore, a second, more fluent and colloquial version was undertaken. Its General Prologue (1395–96) summarized many of the relevant scholarly and interpretive questions and stated the principles of the new project.[6]

---

6. The history is given, together with several of the relevant documents, in Deanesly, *Lollard Bible*. Some of her conclusions are questioned or disproven by Anne Hudson in *The Premature Reformation*. The portion of the General Prologue that is significant to my purpose is printed in Hudson, *Selections*, as Text 14. Also see

With all its freight of contemporary meaning, there is an irony to Chaucer's demand for construal, for that method can produce nothing beyond the literal. Who is so austere a reader of poetry as to want to practice mere construal, or indeed who is capable of it? The inevitability and the limitation of subjectivity are constantly before us in the rest of the poem; as Chapters 3, 4, and 5 will show, we find that no encounter, whether with texts or with persons, can produce pellucid meaning. Our construal is always tainted with interpretation. In the present locus, only subjective interpretation can carry us beyond the literal to wonder what "hire other observaunces" might be, or why the poet should choose to mention them.

For these reasons, I hear the tone of Chaucer's "Construe that!" as resembling the tone in which Canadians, displaying a raised middle finger, often told their prime minister, "Tax this, Brian!" Given the newly published Wycliffite construe, hyperscholarly and unusable as it was, there is a distinctly snide edge to the remark, which cuts at the removedness of some scholar-theorists from social reality and practice, even from their intended popular audience. And, since the object of construal here is that most experiential of things, a kiss, the remark crystallizes the problem crucial to the legends: less *how* to translate human interactions—especially sexual ones—than the very possibility of doing so. It is fitting, I think, that this poem, which is so deeply about ambiguity and ambivalence, should have been influenced by the preeminent English intellectual figure of its day, John Wyclif, in both positive and negative directions. The inadequacies of construal, so recently demonstrated for all to see, gave way to something less pure, more realistic. That tension between original purity and present reality is at the core of the *Legend*, whether language is the immediate concern, or women, or nature. In Chapter 3 we shall see how this tension is tightly focused in the single image—also drawn from the Wycliffite project—of "naked text."

Returning to Chaucer's birds, then, perhaps we may read the poet's imperative as a prod to interpretive method. We are not to lose ourselves in delight at the marvelous poetry we have just read.

Schwartz, who sheds considerable light on the Wycliffite project, although his study is mainly about Reformation controversies. See also Blamires and Jeffrey on Chaucer and Wycliffism.

On the contrary, we must now contemplate this fabrication with critical intelligence. And how exactly do we wish to engage it? This is no mere rhetorical question, for the problem of construal versus interpretation will soon be illustrated by Eros and Alceste. It will motivate production of the work itself, a penalty arising from Eros's pedantically literalistic construal of the Narrator's previous works. Rejecting all but the most superficial reading of text and of behavior, denying the need for any interpretation (gloss) of either, Eros upbraids the Narrator:

> Thou maist yt nat denye,
> For in pleyn text, withouten nede of glose,
> Thou hast translated the Romaunce of the Rose,
> That is an heresye ayeins my lawe. . . .
>   (F 327–30)

Is the Narrator a misogynistic lout, as Eros woodenly asserts? Or is he merely a gullible fool, as Alceste explains in her contextualizing interpretation? Do we construe the legends as boring, sentimental tales, or do we interpret them on other levels? Are these "good women" to be pitied, or condemned, or both? The history of *Legend* scholarship in this century shows how live an issue construal has remained.

Women, nature, and language overlap especially strikingly in the passage I have just examined, but prominently everywhere in the Prologue. Central to this convergence is the daisy, which is at once flower, object of erotic devotion, female poetic muse, poetic topic, linguistic equivalent to (Saint) Margaret, and "remembraunce" (F 530) of Alceste. Nothing distracts the bookish narrator from his studies, he says, except devotion to the daisy. Although his protestation of inadequacy undercuts itself in its virtuosity, what one can believe is the Narrator's lament for his own belatedness, addressed to his famous precursors, the great love poets:

> For wel I wot that ye han her-biforn
> Of makyng ropen, and lad awey the corn,
> And I come after, glenyng here and there,
> And am ful glad yf I may fynde an ere
> Of any goodly word that ye han left.
>   (F 73–77)

The central conceit is of reaping and gleaning grain. This agricultural image also evokes the figure of a woman, the scriptural

gleaner Ruth, which in turn evokes the question of literary tradition, authority, and interpretation already addressed in the opening
lines of the Prologue. And there is the triple pun in line 76 on the
word "ear," again uniting nature, language, and woman as ear of
corn, audience's ear, lover's ear. The passage evokes tradition in an
even more practical way, for a very similar concatenation of themes
and imagery occurs in Ranulf Higden's famous encyclopedic world-
history, the *Polychronicon*. Its presence there suggests direct influence on Chaucer, and a widespread acceptance of the language/
nature/woman connection. Higden too begins with belatedness
and inadequacy, then moves to Ruth and gleaning:

> Yif after the travaille of Hercules, . . . a pigmey bosketh hym to
> bataille and array hym to fighte, who myghte thanne leve to laughe?
> Also who wolde not schoute to skorne, yif I pipe with an otene reed,
> and unhighte so noble a matire with grisbaitinge, gruntynge and
> whistelynge, after so noble spekers that sownede at the beste . . . ?
> But ich have wel in mynde what Booz seide to Ruth that was schame-
> fast, and lase up the eeres after his ripe men, "No man," he seide,
> "the schall wratthe." . . . Therefore . . . I schal entre in to the feeldes of
> oure forme fadres, and folwe the rype men, yif ich may any wyse
> leese and gadre me som eres that rype men schedeth and skapeth of
> here hondes. (1.1)

Higden was already a famous author when he was summoned to
the court of Edward III in 1352. His book is another of the massive
fourteenth-century compilations whose usefulness to Chaucer, although probably significant, has not been fully investigated yet. I
have in mind also Bersuire and the *Ovide moralisé*, about which more
below.

Lastly, there is the courtly fad of leaf and flower, twice introduced as occasion for poetic making:

> In this cas oghte ye [lover-poets] be diligent
> To forthren me somwhat in my labour,
> Whethir ye ben with the leef or with the flour.
> (F 70–72)

> But natheles, ne wene nat that I make
> In preysing of the flour agayn the leef,
> No more than of the corn agayn the sheef;
> For, as to me, nys lever noon ne lother.
> I nam withholden yit with never nother;
> Ne I not who serveth leef, ne who the flour.
> (F 188–93)

Furthering the language-nature connection, Jesse Gellrich has noted the possible play on "leaf" as page of a book, and "flower" as rhetoric (212). Beyond rhetoric, though, there is an underlying idea, or even ideology. Flower and leaf, corn and sheaf: courtiers may set them in competition, but in nature they are part of a single organism. To insist on one or the other is at best an innocuous pastime. At worst, though, it might indicate a taste for verbal or intellectual structures that are unnaturally rigid, unnecessarily divisive. This idea allows us to look forward to the legends to come. Good women or bad women, dark or fair, slim or plump: should the one be "lever or lother" than the other? Is any woman all bad or all good, or do the two aspects of personality coexist as closely as corn and sheaf?

WOMEN, NATURE, LANGUAGE

A piece is missing. It is a piece of rhetoric, a metaphor so deeply embedded in Western culture, so absolutely taken for granted, that it is virtually invisible. Nonetheless it is this missing piece that enables the connection of theory to practice—that is, of Prologue to legends—and of the aesthetic of nature to the literary representation of women. This link is the equivalency of woman with nature. This is so ancient and omnipresent a turn of thought and of language that only with difficulty can it be treated simply as metaphor. It has become what P. N. Medvedev and Mikhail Bakhtin called an "ideologeme."

"Is female to male as nature is to culture?" Anthropologist Sherry Ortner asks this question in the title of her well-known essay and the answer, she claims, in most cultures is "Yes." She cites three reasons for this phenomenon. First, women's reproductive capacity; second, women's social role as family nurturer and socializer of children; third, the "feminine" personality structure that is a consequence of social arrangements, particularly division of labor and family structure.

While Ortner's evidence comes mainly from the tribal societies that constitute her field of specialization, the idea itself is by no means limited to these societies. In ancient Greece, for instance, gender difference was intimately linked with agriculture and with writing: as Page du Bois writes, "For the Greeks, writing is like plowing is like sexual intercourse," and women are "tablets for inscription, fields for sowing and writing, assuring the scriptural, agricultural and sexual reproduction of the polis" (45, 47). Since my interest here is the analogy itself rather than its socioeconomic determinants, I shall confine myself to noting its amazing longevity through the most drastic metamorphoses of social life. Wolfram von Eschenbach's *Parzival* gives us the startling image of earth as a virgin grandmother raped by her grandson Cain (9.464), and the femininity of nature was an accepted topos among the Chartrian humanists of the same period. We learn from Annette Kolodny that "Mother Earth"—a slogan in the battle for People's Park in Berkeley, 1969—was a recurrence of the "land-as-woman symbolization in American life and letters" (ix, 3–4), and Susan Gubar brings the metaphors full circle with her discussion of places in modern and contemporary literature where woman is likened to page or text. I choose these moments—classical, medieval, and modern—as representative of what would otherwise be an unwieldy list of references. To transfer these data, then, to the *Legend of Good Women*: the literary representation of women can serve as test case for an aesthetic of nature, because woman has traditionally been thought to bear a far more intimate relation to nature than man does, a relation so close as to border on equivalence.

Women and nature, then; but where does language fit, the third component of my argument? Here anthropology can help again, for it is Claude Lévi-Strauss's exposition of the exchange of women that links women to language through the notion of the sign. Insofar as women represent value, they become signs. It is not, however, simply as "a thing of worth" that Levi-Strauss uses the term "value," although women's reproductive capacity certainly renders them valuable in this sense. Like language, they are full of "meaning" in their ability to generate other signs: more people, the wealth of the tribe. But the value represented by women, according to Lévi-Strauss, is rather a social function, the prohibition of incest. This rule has the same purpose as language: communication and integration with others. Rules governing marriage and non-marriage are "a means of binding others through alliance," so that "the relations between the sexes can be conceived as one of the modalities of a great 'communication function' which also includes language." Thus "Women themselves are treated as signs, which are misused when not put to the use reserved to signs, which is to be communicated" (493–96). Although the exchange of women is no longer as important as it once was, the remnants survive, as testified in these words to an old jazz classic:

> As a silver dollar goes from hand to hand,
> A woman goes from man to man.

In the Middle Ages, though, the exchange function of women was still a very prominent aspect of marriage mores, including dowries, property settlements, and family or political alliances made by marriage. Chaucer himself, as guardian of marriageable young aristocrats and bourgeois, personally profited from the marriage market of his day. The socioeconomic realities of marriage, especially the exchange value of women, are an important theme in the *Canterbury Tales*. Obvious examples are the Merchant's sardonic praise of a wife as a more durable gift than "londes, rentes, pasture, or comune, / Or moebles" (IV.1313–14) and Alison of Bath's commodification of her own sexuality as a response to society's commodification of women. Less obvious, perhaps, is Chaucer's description of the other Alison, the young wife of the *Miller's Tale*. In a long series of natural images—animal, avian, and botanical (I.3233–70)—there intrudes the following dissonant couplet:

> Ful brighter was the shynyng of hir hewe
> Than in the Tour the noble yforged newe.
> (3255–56)

Coinage of the gold noble had been introduced only in 1344, and it is not clear just how complimentary Chaucer means to be here. On one hand, the Tower mint maintained probably the purest standard (that is, the highest percentage of precious metal) in Europe, during a period when debased or alloyed foreign coinage was common; indeed during the 1390s the English noble would be counterfeited by Duke Philip the Bold of Flanders. On the other hand, John Munro notes that the gold noble had already been debased by 14 percent of its original weight within a few years of first issue, and after 1370 there was a continuing deterioration of English coinage (Munro, chs. 1 and 2). Relatively, then, the coin was "fine"; absolutely, it was flawed.

Why an intrusive money image—social, urban, man-made, technological—to disrupt this otherwise consistent set, if not to make the point that woman, like the coin, has exchange value: she does go "from hand to hand." In one sense, of course, she ought not to do so: that is in the promiscuous sense represented in the narrative. Yet in another sense, she must, for such are the demands of marriage as a social institution when a woman goes from her father's hand to that of her husband, her exchange value dependent on her father's income and status. Of this perspective we are reminded in the last lines of the descriptive passage:

> She was a prymerole, a piggesnye,
> For any lord to leggen in his bedde,
> Or yet for any good yeman to wedde.

Intertextually, though, the money-image was related to nature in the Chartrian discourse familiar to Chaucer. In a passage Chaucer had already imitated in the *Parliament of Fowls*, Alanus de Insulis has Natura define herself as God's vicar. She uses the imagery of numismatics:

> He appointed me as his substitute, his vice-regent, the mistress of his mint, to put the stamp on the different classes of things. . . . I obeyed the commander's orders in my work and I, to use a metaphor, striking various coins of things according to the mould of the exemplar, and producing copies of my original by fashioning like out of like, gave to my imprints the appearance of things imaged. (*Plaint*, trans. Sheridan, Prosa 4)

By way of Alanus's treatise, then, the coin-and-mint image came to Chaucer already integrated into a doctrine of nature, already spoken by a female figure whose fertility links woman, nature, and language in the metaphor of exchange.

It might be objected here that men as well as women were exchanged in medieval marriage; indeed, both of Chaucer's wards were young men. Yet this would be a superficial objection. One needs to ask with whom exchange is made, and for what. To the extent that men hold positions of social power (government, clergy, administration) and, in the main, own capital (land and other means of production), to that extent it is men with whom political alliances or property settlements are made. Hence woman remains, structurally, the exchanged item. Had women equal power and status with men, we would be able to speak of exchange of men and women, although this power and status would have to be general rather than exceptional. Two centuries after Chaucer wrote the *Legend of Good Women*, even Queen Elizabeth I knew full well that her best strategy to retain "maistrie" both personal and political, was precisely to maintain her single state.

Returning now to language, I note that an interesting feature of Chaucer's rhetoric in the *Legend* is an absence, one of the several mentioned in Chapter 1. Nowhere in any legend does the poet describe the lady who is its protagonist. This absence of physical description is especially striking because the blazon of female charms was so prominent a convention in the courtly literature that the Narrator has been ordered to imitate. In *Troilus* the deferral of physical description invests those descriptions with special force when they do finally appear in book 5. Here, the omission of physical description seems a clue to the poet's subversive intention. He refuses to titillate the reader with a conventional catalogue of female charms, or to fragment the natural human body and hand it over, in fetishized form, on a silver platter of rhetoric.

Yet if this refusal of the catalogue signals a poetic practice that Chaucer means to reject, it simultaneously implies what he wishes to endorse. I mean that sense of the proper use of goods that came to Chaucer from numerous late-classical and medieval sources. Here is one formulation, taken from Augustine's discussion in *The City of God* (22.17) of whether women's bodies will retain their own sex in the Resurrection:

> For my part, they seem wiser who make no doubt that both sexes shall rise. For there shall be no lust, which is now the cause of confusion. From those bodies, then, vice shall be withdrawn, while nature shall be preserved. And the sex of a woman is not vice, but nature. It shall then indeed be superior to carnal intercourse and child-bearing; nevertheless the female members shall remain adapted not to the old uses but to a new beauty, which, so far from provoking lust, now extinct, shall excite praise to the wisdom and clemency of God, who both made what was not and delivered from corruption what He made.

If the poet Jack Spicer is right that the desire for meaning is the desire for love, then the medieval poet's wish for "the naked text" is a utopian wish for the naked body too. (The wish, and the metaphor, are further explored in Chapter 3.) Text-as-language becomes analogous to woman, the two linked as versions of what Eugene

Vance suggests we think of as temporality. It is a wish infinitely deferred, as Augustine writes, to the time or non-time beyond nature when we will see naked bodies with no ill effect; when we will interpret everything aright, and meaning will be redeemed in the transcendent signifier. This, I propose, is what Chaucer too considers the best use of signs, whether these are female beauty, nature, or language: as good coin in the exchange between this world and the next. That his text juggles these registers of meaning may explain not only the silence of scholars but that of the text itself: unfinished, after all, like the *House of Fame* before it, which also dealt with the nature of language, textuality, and communication. To end where I began, with Barthes: "The disintegration of language can only lead to the silence of writing" (75). It is no coincidence, therefore, that I find a fit ending in the last chapter of the same text, *Writing Degree Zero*, entitled "The Utopia of Language":

> Feeling permanently guilty of its own solitude, [literary language] is none the less an imagination eagerly desiring a felicity of words, it hastens toward a dreamed-of language whose freshness, by a kind of ideal anticipation, might portray the perfection of some new Adamic world where language would no longer be alienated. The proliferation of modes of writing brings a new mode of Literature into being in so far as the latter invents its language only in order to be a project: Literature becomes the Utopia of Language.

For the medieval writer, necessarily mistrustful of utopia, literature could not be the site of utopia outright, not while there remained, in Catholic ideology, a "mystical society of universality" that did hold forth the ultimate possibility of transparent signification. At best literary language could acknowledge the utopian wish together with its natural failure, so that only in this restricted sense might one add to Barthes's conclusion the rejoinder: it always has been.

GENDER-MARKED WRITING

In "The Laugh of the Medusa," Hélène Cixous proposes "marked writing" as a term for gender-influenced work. She goes on to say that writing is "a locus where the repression of women has been perpetuated . . . and in a manner that's frightening since it's often hidden or adorned with the mystifying charms of fiction." I don't know that I would want to apply the word "charming" to the *Legend of Good Women*. It has always impressed me as far too strenuous a work to warrant that description, what with its narratorial egotism, its elaborated linguistic texture, its deaths and lamenting. Nor have critics generally responded in large numbers or with strong attraction to whatever fictional charms the work does offer. Conveniently for my purpose, Cixous speaks of fiction in the time-honored ambiguous imagery of clothing or adornment. This discloses a mistrust of fiction familiar to every medievalist, particularly to Chaucerians: we recall, for instance, the Parson's scorn for "fables and swich wrecchednesse" (X.34), as well as the agonized ambivalence of the Retraction. Cixous's metaphor of adornment implies the existence somewhere of a writing unmarked, unhidden, unadorned: a "naked text" as it were—and a utopian wish. Needless to say, such a manifesto carries its own ideological premises, which I do not accept.

What I would like to borrow from Cixous is the notion of "marked writing"—gender-marked—and to look at the *Legend* as an instance of it. Obviously the best way to explore the murky field of gender-linked aesthetics here is to compare the *Legend* with a similar text written by a woman—that is, a text with more or less the same variables except the author's gender. Such a text is at hand in Christine de Pizan's *Livre de la cité des dames*, composed about twenty years after the *Legend* (1405). Its author was, like Chaucer, a courtier-poet and scholar, and, like him, not native to the courtly milieu, for while Chaucer came to the English court from the London bourgeoisie, Christine came to the French court from the Italian urban intelligentsia to which her father had belonged. Both authors shared—besides similar social status—an intellectual background and ideological assumptions; they were largely self-educated and had read and been influenced by roughly the same set of authors (among them Boethius, Boccaccio, Matheolus, Scripture, assorted bits and pieces of medieval mainstream philosophy, Ovid and the *Ovide moralisé*, hagiography, French courtly lyric, and the matter of Troy). There is no evidence that the two writers met, but they probably knew of each other. They shared a patron in Henry IV, who invited Christine to England. She did not go, but her son did, and Henry became his protector at the English court.

Both works are written in the first person, and the stimulus for each of them is said to be the author-narrator's anxious confrontation with literary misogyny: Christine's reading of a misogynist text, the Chaucerian Narrator's trial for misogyny. Each text opens with an intensely self-conscious account of how the writer resolved his or her relation to the authoritative (but not uncontested) mis- ogynistic tradition; each results in a compilation of short biogra- phies of famous women. Both works purport to rewrite that tradi- tion in order to present a new image of woman, that of the good woman. That Christine actually does this, while Chaucer does not, strikes me as an interesting opportunity for speculation within the problematic of gender-linked literary production.

How does gender become relevant to these two texts? To begin with, the social mediation between biological sex and culture— gender—is strikingly and painfully evident in the position of the narrators. Chaucer's Narrator meets the misogynist tradition as a male poet accused of belonging to that tradition: he is accused of having written ill of women and love, of turning people away from love (F 320–40). He appears, therefore, as speaking subject, with a good deal of power in his speech. Christine meets the misogynistic tradition, represented by the work of the thirteenth-century cleric Matheolus, as a woman reader, whom that tradition defines as inferior to men, lacking the high moral and intellectual capacity required of a writer. She appears, therefore, as spoken object, justly deprived of speech. For Chaucer, the issue is what kind of writer to be, with the representation of women his test case. For Christine, the issue is the possibility of writing at all, with the representation of women offering role models of strength and virtue. For her, then, the stakes are much higher, and the questions are gender-specific.

The directive to rewrite woman as good comes to both authors in a dream-vision and from a female figure; yet the treatment and role of this figure and her instructions are very different in each case. An important aspect of the dream-vision as genre is that it can be seen as an externalization of the author's internal monologue; this is particularly true of the *consolatio* form deriving from Boethius. The *Livre de la cité des dames* is an instance of this form, while Chaucer's Prologue might be seen as a kind of inverted version of it, a *discon-solatio*, as it were, a vision bringing not comfort and rehabilitation to the poet but criticism and a penalty.

If we can read Chaucer's discussion with Alceste as externalizing part of the poet's inner debate about the meaning, reception, and worth of his own work, we note some gender-linked features in the treatment of the character. First, the externalization function is suppressed: we have to read it in. The female figure is not represented as an aspect of the poet's self. Instead, she is distanced, remaining woman-as-object: critic of the poet's work and object of his devotion, Other. Christine's female figure, on the other hand, is Lady Reason, explicitly portrayed as an aspect of the narrator's self: her own capacity for reason, as well as the personification of human reason generally.

Consequently, while Chaucer's Alceste is a deeply ambivalent figure, as I shall show in the next section of this chapter, there is no such ambivalence to Christine's Lady Reason. She gives no orders. She suggests and supervises and works alongside Christine, engaging in frequent tactful dialogue with her. The author-narrator is not struggling against herself, but rather, with Reason's help, for herself, for full integration of personality. It is after all herself she must rewrite, not, as in Chaucer's case, an Other.

This is why the two narrators confront the misogynist tradition, and tradition generally, with completely different strategies. Geffrey's skeptical fideism (see Chapter 1) allows him to give "feyth and ful credence" to authoritative texts, while limiting the truth-value of (merely subjective and empirical) personal experience. Skeptical fideism also permits him to resolve the "agony of influence" he undergoes in comparing his own belated talents to those of his predecessors, the great love poets (F 66–83). He is able to transcend his doubts by invoking the daisy-saint-muse as controller of his creativity:

> . . . ye ben verrayly
> The maistresse of my wit, and nothing I.
> My word, my werk ys knyt so in youre bond
> That, as an harpe obeieth to the hond
> And maketh it soune after his fyngerynge,
> Ryght so mowe ye oute of myn herte bringe
> Swich vois, ryght as yow lyst, to laughe or pleyne.
> Be ye my gide and lady sovereyne!
> As to myn erthly god to yow I calle. . . .
>
> (F 87–95)

Striking in this passage is the passivity inherent in fideism: the poet represents himself as an instrument played by a superior hand. His

intellectual posture can scarcely generate a frontal assault on tradition, for it is a posture of receptivity rather than of reconstruction.

As a woman writer, Christine can afford no such passive toler-
ance of tradition. If she were to give "feyth and ful credence" to all
old books, she would believe in her own inferiority and abandon
the role of writer. Her first task as a writer must be to enable herself
to work: to affirm woman's intellectual and moral capacity. She
must therefore select the texts she wishes to believe in, and polem-
icize against the others; this is accomplished in book 1 with the help
of Lady Reason. She must also develop, as Chaucer did, an epistemology on which to base her authorial stance; but it will be an
epistemology opposite to his. Rather than depreciating personal
experience, she asserts its value as a source of genuine knowledge.
"We have come," Reason says in her first speech,

> pour . . . te gitter hors de ingnorence qui tant aveugle ta meismes
> congnoissance que tu deboute de toy ce que tu scez de certaine
> science et adjoustes foy ad ce que tu ne scez, ne vois, ne congnois
> autrement fors par pluralite d'oppinions estranges. Tu ressembles le
> fol dont la truffe parle, qui en dormant au moulin, fu revestu de la
> robe d'une femme, et au resveiller, pour ce que ceulx qui le mou-
> quoyent luy tesmoignoyent que femme estoit, crut myeulx leurs faulx
> diz que la certainete de son estre. (1.2)[7]

> to take you out of the ignorance which so blinds your consciousness
> that you debate with yourself what you know as certain knowledge,
> and lend faith to what you neither know nor see nor understand
> except through the multiplicity of different opinions. You are like the
> fool that the joke tells about, who while sleeping at the mill was
> dressed up in women's clothing, and on waking—because those who
> were mocking him assured him he was a woman—believed their
> false assertions rather than the certainty of his being!

It is not simply her own experience that Christine brings forward as
a basis for knowledge. Constantly Reason urges her—and thus the
reader—to use personal experience against misogyny. Women are
said to show off at church? It would be strange if young, pretty, and

---

7. Quotations are from Curnow's edition; translations are mine. Through an
editor's error, footnotes in an earlier version of this material ("Rewriting Woman
Good," in Wasserman, 91) make it seem that I used the translation by E. Jeffrey
Richards (New York: Persea, 1982); however, the paper was written for a 1982
conference, before the appearance of Richards's book, and a comparison of our
versions will show the differences.

wealthy women were not seen there, but for every one such you will see twenty or thirty older women, soberly dressed. Women are supposedly self-indulgent? Just recall the drunk you saw the other day whose wife's utter sobriety compensates for his sins (1.10).

What then of textual authority? We have seen that Christine can scarcely afford fideism, but skepticism she can. Reason points out that philosophers differ among themselves: their words are not articles of faith, and they can err. Poets often speak figuratively or ironically, and some lie. So, "Chiere ami," Reason concludes,

> or te reviens a toy meismes, reprens ton scens et plus ne te troubles pour telz fanffelues. Car saiches que tout mal dit si generaument des femmes empire les diseurs et non pas elles meismes. (1.2)

> now return to yourself, take hold again of your good sense and don't trouble yourself any longer on account of such nonsense. Know that all evil spoken so generally about women vitiates the speakers and not women themselves.

Now Chaucer also understands the contradictory nature of written authority: it is what the *House of Fame* is about. Skepticism he shares with Christine, yet her skepticism does not pause at the fideistic resolution; it pushes through to faith in herself. "Experience, though noon auctoritee / Were in this world, were ryght enough for me . . . ": it is the Wife of Bath's stance and her revisionist methodology, but seeing it in the flesh (as it were) lets us appreciate its survival value above its solipsism; its corrective rather than its distortive effect. It is an epistemology—"the certainty of one's being"—which, for all its modest presentation in an old French jest—heralds renaissance individualism and the Cartesian *cogito.*

The God of Love asks Geffrey for propaganda. Although Geffrey will not provide it, Christine not only will but must. She has to rewrite woman good in order to provide herself with role models, with a line of mothers to think back through (to paraphrase Virginia Woolf). Christine also writes on behalf of other women: to keep them, she says, from despondency such as she had experienced upon reading Matheolus, to give sage counsel, to offer positive role models, and to influence men in favor of female education. Does Christine flatten out contradictions in her version of womanhood? She does. Does she skew the tradition, omit what is unsuitable to her purpose, rationalize aberrant behavior in the women she writes about? Certainly. Are her figures realistic, balanced, or contradictory characters? By no means. Xanthippe empties no pisspot over Socrates's head but is a loving and reverent wife. Medea kill her children? No children are mentioned in either of Christine's versions of Medea. Semiramis did marry her son Ninus, but only for reasons of state. Women invented virtually all the technology of civilization. Christine acknowledges the existence of individual bad women, but she has no reason to portray them; indeed, an evil woman is unnatural,

> monstre en nature, qui est chose contrefaitte et hors de sa propre condicion naturelle qui doit etre simple, coy et honeste . . . (1.8)

> a monster in nature, a thing wrongly made and outside its own natural condition, which must be simple, quiet and honest.

One does not know whether Christine would extend this attitude to men also, but in any case someone of the Chaucerian persuasion might be struck by the theological naïveté of this position. It seems to deny the decisive effects of Original Sin, in consequence of which evil is precisely an aspect of the natural human condition.

We have, then, two revisionary texts about women, but revising different representational traditions and in different directions. Chaucer revises the courtly tradition in disobedience to Eros; Christine revises the misogynistic tradition in cooperation with Reason. For Chaucer, to write in unambiguous praise of woman would be to reduce the natural complexity of reality. To write such poetry is punishment; it is to be set right again, rendered complex again, by irony. For Christine, it is the clerical-misogynist tradition that distorts reality, reducing the natural complexity of women by effacing their goodness. To read such poetry is punishment, and the proper balance is restored by a necessarily one-sided completion of the picture. Christine does offer her crisis and its cure as representative and therapeutic; she does produce her text explicitly on behalf of women. The very image she chooses for her text—the city-fortress—is a clever extension of Augustine's cities of God and of man, but it also reveals the author's sense of the vulnerable and beleaguered condition of even the exceptional woman of her day.

If Christine writes as a woman in the *Livre de la cité des dames*, does Chaucer write as a man in the *Legend of Good Women*? I posed this question over a decade ago, in "Rewriting Woman Good" (now reprinted in *Medieval Literary Politics*), and I would stand by the conclusions I reached then. One does not have to be a man to endorse skeptical fideism, or to see nature as inherently contradictory, or to dislike formulaic and simplistic courtly verse. Nor does one have to be a woman to revise tradition in a humanist direction: Giovanni Boccaccio—Christine's countryman and her main source for the *Cité*—had taken an important step in that direction in *De mulieribus claris*, and the *Ovide moralisé* had contributed to the revisionary process with its moral-religious interpretations of classical characters. Yet the Chaucerian Narrator's role as daisy lover and as alleged misogynistic poet are clearly gender-defined features of the text. So is the issue he chooses to define and test his aesthetic of nature: the representation of women. At issue, I think, is less a specific intellectual position than a consciousness: relations to nature, love, tradition, oneself, the other sex; relations that are gender-linked so long as gender translates into privilege or exclusion.

EROS AND ALCESTE

The figure of the accused poet writing of his woes is a familiar one in the Chaucerian literary world. There is Ovid, exiled to icy Dacia for an offense against great Augustus; there is Boethius, imprisoned for treason; there is Guillaume de Machaut, forced to expiate in writing the antifeminism of an earlier work (cf. *Le Jugement dou Roy de Navarre*, 1349). Even the highly placed Richard de Bury claimed that he wrote to silence "the perverse tongues of gossipers" who accused him of curiosity, vanity, greed, and intemperate pleasure in books (Zacher, 63–64). Such oversupply of precedents is typical enough for Chaucer, even at those moments when we want to think he is most personal, most revelatory, most sincere. But whether contradictory or mutually reinforcing, experience and authority are a coexisting pair throughout Chaucer's work and, I do not doubt, his life. What I want to examine here is authority of another kind: that of the peremptory figures who appear to the poet-Narrator in order to accuse, to try, and to punish him for literary-ideological offenses committed against them.

Measured against the aesthetic of nature that emerges in the Prologue to the *Legend of Good Women*, the God of Love can only appear absurd in demanding a poetry that effaces contradiction or

nuance. His aesthetic, competing with that of the rest of the Prologue, is a prescriptive bureaucratic utopianism where women are
always true and good. His utopia, though, has nothing in common
with the one imagined by Augustine, but is its polar opposite, an
"eroticist unrealism" based on the maintenance of his own power.
This can scarcely surprise, if Chaucer's model is Ovid's imperious
Cupid as portrayed in *Amores* 1.2.19–34, a figure modeled in turn on
the emperor Augustus: as Eleanor Winsor remarks, "the triumphs
of Augustus become the triumphs of Cupid" (259). The issue of
sheer feudal-bureaucratic power is unabashedly to the fore in Eros's
address to the Narrator:

> [T]how [art] my foo, and al my folk werreyest,
> And of myn olde servauntes thow mysseyest,
> And hynderest hem with thy translacioun,
> And lettest folk from hire devocioun
> To serve me, and holdest it folye
> To serve Love. Thou maist yt nat denye,
> For in pleyn text, withouten nede of glose,
> Thou hast translated the Romaunce of the Rose,
> That is an heresye ayeins my lawe,
> And makest wise folk fro me withdrawe. . . .
> (F 322–31)

Instead, Eros asks for tales of "clene maydenes . . . trewe wyves . . .
stedefaste widewes" (G 282–83) in imitation of classical and Christian authors, tales of women "trewe in lovyng al hire lyves" (F 485).
He asks, in short, for propaganda. It is from the standpoint of a self-
interested courtly bureaucrat afraid of losing influence that the
Narrator is accused of being anti-love and anti-woman, in short, a
misogynist.

It is interesting that Christine de Pizan, about fifteen years later (in
1401, in her correspondence in the "querelle de la rose"), would also
denounce the *Roman de la rose*. We may speculate whether she did so
for the same or for opposite reasons. Christine's critique is based in
what she conceives as the misogyny and immorality of the work: its
warnings against marriage, its "revelations" of women's tricks, its
blunt sexual language, its portrayal of joyful non-marital fornication
at the end. Chaucer's Eros might also deplore some of the *Roman*'s
negative portrayals of women's wiles, but he could scarcely be of-
fended by much else. One wonders whether Chaucer has given Eros

a cannier understanding of Jean de Meun's ultimately orthodox religious attitude than the deity is usually credited with: that Eros hates the work not only because of its misogynistic passages but also because it is too moral or even moralistic. Such appears to be the import of the following lines from G, immediately after the passage about the *Roman* cited above, but missing in F:

> And thynkest in thy wit, that is ful col,
> That he nys but a verray propre fol
> That loveth paramours to harde and hote.
> Wel wot I therby thow begynnyst dote,
> As olde foles whan here spiryt fayleth;
> Thanne blame they folk, and wite nat what hem ayleth.
>
> (G 258–63)

The offense pinpointed here is not misogyny but alienation of affection in general.

As for *Troilus*, there is no ambiguity. Eros's sentiment is the same in both versions, though F adds an unobtrusive little homonymic play on the syllable "seyd":

> And of Creseyde thou hast seyd as the lyste,
> That maketh men to wommen lasse triste . . .
>
> (F 332–33)

> Hast thow nat mad in Englysh ek the bok
> How that Crisseyde Troylus forsok,
> In shewynge how that wemen han don mis?
>
> (G 264–66)

The God of Love is no frivolous reader, we see: he takes literature as ethically exemplary. His confidence in the real effectiveness of literature—that it will change the behavior of masses of readers—can only strike us as it must have struck Chaucer, as another piece of utopian-bureaucratic comedy, consistent with the pedantry already noticed. Although he grossly overestimates the powers of art, nonetheless Eros understands *Troilus* very well, probably better than the gentlemanly spark of Chaucer's day who might consult it for amorous guidance. Eros is not exactly wrong, then, but his reading is a narrow one. To take the lesson of *Troilus* is not necessarily to trust individual women less, but rather to invest less trust in the project of erotic love as redemptive act. In this sense the Narrator-poet is even guiltier than charged.

Besides being a bureaucrat, the God of Love is a philistine. In G, repeating the agricultural imagery of earlier portions of the Prologue, he says:

> Let be the chaf, and writ wel of the corn.
> Why noldest thow han writen of Alceste,
> And laten Criseide ben aslepe and reste?
> (G 529–31)

The irony is that Troilus himself had thought of Criseyde as another Alceste. Enraged at his sister Cassandra's prognostication that "Diomede is inne, and thow art oute" (5.1519), Troilus accuses Cassandra of falsehood, adding,

> "As wel thow myghtest lien on Alceste,
> That was of creatures, but men lye,
> That evere weren, kyndest and the beste!"
> (5.1527–29)

It is worth noting here the little escape-clause "but [unless] men lye"; its relevance will become clear further on. In any case, Eros's question does have an answer. The answer, of course, is that Criseyde is so much more interesting than Alceste: so much more complex and realistic, so much more natural, we might say, in her will to survive than Alceste in her will to die. But Eros, single-minded as always, intent only on what affects himself, is blind to aesthetics or psychology.

Last but not least in the list of Eros's flaws is the near-blasphemous assurance he gives near the end of the Prologue: "Ne shal no trewe lover come in helle" (F 553), Dante and the Church to the contrary notwithstanding. There is something here—only the lightest hint (or anticipation, depending on chronology)—of the Wife of Bath with her single-mindedness, her false doctrinal reassurances, her revisions of doctrine in the interest of eroticism.

And so, to mediate the God's anger, there steps forth Alceste. If, as V. A. Kolve has proposed, the *Legend* is a quest to discover the identity and meaning of Alceste, then we must, I believe, take a broader view than the strictly iconographical to yield the full range of Chaucerian meaning. Together Alceste and Eros form a Mercy/ Justice pair, perhaps to be seen as an extension of the *sapiential/ fortitudo* polarity discussed by Ernst Curtius (ch. 9). Eros and Alceste are not unlike Theseus and Hippolyta in the *Knight's Tale* (a version of which is mentioned in F 420) or Arthur and Guinevere in the *Wife of Bath's Tale*: the ruler enforcing law, his wife diverting it.

The parallels may be instructive. When we consult the place in the *Knight's Tale* where Hippolyta, Emily, and other ladies successfully intervene to deter Theseus from enforcing the death penalty on Palamon and Arcite (who have wittingly courted capital punishment), we find it followed by two speeches by Theseus that evoke the *Legend*. In the first, Theseus reminds himself of a lord's obligation to mercy, in an internal monologue ("softe unto hymself" [1773]) which is a shorter version of Alceste's lecture on good rule. In the second, spoken aloud ("al on highte" [1784]), Theseus offers a sardonic praise of "the god of love, a, benedicite!" (1785) who can reduce two such noble gentlemen to such desperate straits. "Who may been a fool, but if he love?" (1799). Theseus also ridicules the fact—"yet the best game of alle" (1806)—that Emily, the bone of contention, knows nothing of her self-styled lovers' love or even of their existence. Without dismissing love (for Theseus acknowledges that he, too, was once Eros's servant [1814]), he shows how foolish love—and love's servants—can be. So that besides introducing an orderly system of justice tempered by mercy, Theseus also introduces a comic and naturalistic perspective on the conventions of courtly love.

More complex is the role of Guinevere in the *Wife of Bath's Tale*, for her intervention achieves the eventual pardon not of a lover but of a rapist. This is done in contravention of the law of the land ("cours of lawe . . . the statut tho" [III.892–93]), which makes rape a capital offense. The law has been brought into play by the maiden's relatives or neighbors protesting the knight's "oppressioun" (889). Evaluation is complicated by several factors, most prominent among them the question of narrative viewpoint. Is Guinevere disloyal to her sex in helping to save a member of her class? Is the law too harsh? Is Arthur a henpecked husband? Without attempting to cut through this Gordian knot, I mean simply to observe that female intervention—the manifestation, apparently, of mercy—is no straightforward matter here but problematic in the extreme.

Alceste's intervention combines salient features of the other two. Like Hippolyta's, it is associated with a distancing of the conventions of courtly love, for she defends the poet against Eros's accusations, and her penalty generates an ambiguous portrait of erotic passion in the legends. Like Guinevere's, it discloses an ambiguous position for the intervener, although this may not be evident at first. Alceste's role is a strong one, but she is rhetorically tactful. Like the good fairy in "The Sleeping Beauty," Alceste cannot rescind a penalty, but she can mitigate it. She remonstrates gently with her lord about due process of law. She lectures on the duties of godhood and of good rule (F 342–411). She brings out extenuating circumstances for the offending poet, also balancing his dossier by citing his works that do praise love. Alceste is the complete lawyer and courtly advisor—and no less a virtuous, attractive woman. What takes place is a rather interesting reversal of stereotypical gender roles, which has the effect of exculpating the poet even as he is charged with misogyny. We are given a male deity who is narrow-minded, selfish, and temperamental, with a female advisor who is balanced, objective, and controlled. It is as if Chaucer intends to prove that he can indeed portray a good woman—when he wants to.

In context of our exploration of the *Legend* as "marked writing," the significance of Alceste in the trial scene resembles that of Penelope invoked in Hades (*Odyssey* 11). The two figures are already, in Chaucer's mind, a "natural" pair, possibly because he could have found them linked in the headnote to a medieval commentary on Ovid's *Epistulae ex Ponto*. Chaucer mentions them together in *Troilus* (5.1778), the *Man of Law's Tale* (75), and the *Franklin's Tale* (1442–43). Of six references to Penelope, she is linked with Alceste in three; and in four references to Alceste outside the *Legend*, she is linked with Penelope in three. Chaucer has in mind, apparently, the two women's capacity for wifely self-sacrifice: Penelope waited twenty chaste years for the return of Odysseus, Alceste volunteered to die in place of her husband, Admetus. That there is no story of Penelope among the nine extant lives is perhaps a clue to Chaucer's ironic intention in the *Legend*, for the figure of Penelope reached the Middle Ages as the most unambiguous example of female virtue that a genuine vindicator of the sex could use. She occupies the choice first position in Ovid's *Heroides*, Chaucer's major source for the *Legend*. On the other hand, silence is not a strong argument in the case of an unfinished work, and we do not know how Chaucer might have ironized even Penelope. Ovid—as ever, deflating the epic viewpoint—managed to present a wife who, while certainly chaste, is nonetheless reproachful to her husband, deeply resentful of the war and the adulterer who caused it, suspicious about the reason for her husband's delay, and occasionally sarcastic.[8]

What I propose in comparing these two female figures is not similarity of character but rather similarity of strategic function. In the *Odyssey*, in Hades, the shade of Agamemnon makes the strong misogynistic claim that all women are evil, tainted by the misdeeds of one woman, his own wife, Clytemnestra. It is a more or less essentialist position, allowing one to stand for all. Agamemnon's position can be refuted by the existence of a single good example. This example, the polar opposite to Clytemnestra, is, of course, Penelope, whose memory frames the misogynistic passage: before it in information about her provided by the shade of Odysseus's mother, afterward in Agamemnon's own praise of Penelope. Yet few women can be either a Clytemnestra or a Penelope. Most women occupy a middle position on the spectrum of female virtue, and of this we are reminded in the procession of female shades, the wives and daughters of great men, that comes up after Odysseus's mother has spoken. The poet thus asks us to see that neither he nor his hero is misogynistic. Implicitly, he asks us to make the same judgment about other values represented in the *Odyssey*, such as monogamy, female chastity, the double sexual standard, monarchy, and patrilineal transmission of property and rule. These values are not considered misogynistic or anti-woman; they are, rather, "natural" and good. Women may be very good, very bad, or a mixture of good and bad. Outright essentialist misogyny is displaced onto the embittered Agamemnon, while (or in order that) the hero's value system can be represented as the moral, "natural," and deity-supported one. We might note a similar strategy in the *Aeneid*: the hero's decision to abandon Dido is to some extent displaced onto the god Mercury. Mercury appears to the hero in a dream, urging a hasty departure with the essentialist misogynist comment that "semper varium et mutabile femina est" ("woman is always variable and fickle" [4.569–70]). We will come back to this episode in Chap-

---

8. Howard Jacobson discusses the anti-Odyssean countertradition of the promiscuous Penelope, which would certainly have been known to Ovid but not to Chaucer, 246–49.

ter 5, where I will show that Chaucer's treatment of it extends the Virgilian direction.[9]

In its broad structure, the Homeric strategy is duplicated (although I infer no direct influence) in the *Legend*. The God of Love accuses the Narrator of misogyny: he has represented all women by a single treacherous one (Criseyde). His charge against the poet is refuted, albeit implicitly, when the poet has his accuser shown up by an archetypally virtuous female character. Yet few women can be either Criseyde or Alceste. Most of them occupy the middle range, as represented in the legends themselves. The poet thus asks us to see that neither he nor his Narrator is misogynistic. Nor, by extension, are the values represented in the *Legend*: the battle of sexes, victimization and suffering, obsessive desire. These, if not absolutely moral, are the natural, inevitable conditions of human morality. Their transcendence in a doctrine defined and transmitted by a partially gender-exclusive institution (the Catholic Church, in which women could not be ordained) is also not to be viewed as misogynistic but as a moral absolute. Both poet and Church understand the complexities of created nature, including human nature. Real misogyny, or at least its reductive essentialist method, is displaced onto the God of Love.

How good, really, is Alceste? I find her a deeply ambiguous figure, whose kindness is limited by her loyalty to the angry God of Love. Her defense of the Narrator-poet is scarcely what any of us would wish for ourselves, for she refutes the charge of malice with that of stupidity: "this man ys nyce. . . . Hym rekketh noght of what matere he take . . . he kan nat wel endite" (362–414). She cites to the Narrator's credit not only works like the *Book of the Duchess*, the *Parliament of Fowls*, and the story of Palamon and Arcite, which might legitimately be seen as conducing to love (although not without considerable ambivalence in the latter two), but also a series of religious works that can surely only compound the poet's sins in the

---

9. The example from the *Aeneid* is, however, a weaker analogue than the *Odyssey*. Dido is not as overtly malevolent as Clytemnestra, so that she does not participate in quite as pronounced a moral polarity. Also, that the antifeminist statement is couched within the hero's dream rather than in an experiential encounter makes it possible to read it, and the dream itself, as a manifestation of the hero's own wishes. This is the direction developed by Chaucer in his version of the story of Dido and Aeneas: he eliminates even the dream, forcing us to rely only on the hero's statement that he has had a dream.

eyes of Eros, for these works portray real holiness, not erotic "holiness" in the religion of Cupid. Alceste's compromise penalty also leaves a great deal to be desired. It requires the Narrator not only to retell stories of good women, whose goodness is defined as truth in loving, but to

> telle of false men that hem bytraien,
> That al hir lyf ne do nat but assayen
> How many women that may doon a shame. . . .
>> (F 486–88)

This resolution is as shortsighted as Eros's original accusation, for it only reverses the terms of offense. Instead of the treacherous woman and suffering man, we are to have treacherous men and suffering women. It is scarcely an edifying prospect, and, if we bear in mind the debilitating eye-for-an-eye morality of the *Reeve's Tale*, little more than an example of sexual "quiting." Indeed, its effect is blatantly misogynistic, for once we introduce "false men" into the structure of female goodness, the "good" woman will almost inevitably be an abused woman, faithful despite the atrocities done to her. Clearly it is not mainly happy women Alceste has in mind but suffering ones who wind up affirming the model of masculine power and feminine weakness all over again. Their suffering—indeed their death—is precisely the index of their truth, a perspective more succinctly shown in the G prologue than in F, in Eros's indictment of the poet:

> For to hyre love were they so trewe
> That, rathere than they wolde take a newe,
> They chose to be ded in sondry wyse,
> And deiden, as the story wol devyse;
> And some were brend, and some were cut the hals,
> And some dreynt for they wolden not be fals;
> For alle keped they here maydenhede,
> Or elles wedlok, or here widewehede.
>> (G 288–95)

Although this passage does not appear in F, its tenor is confirmed by Alceste in the passage cited above, and in the legends themselves. Plainly, Alceste belongs to Eros, and she does not transcend his laws.

Nor did she in some earlier representations. Chaucer cannot

have known Euripides's *Alcestis,* but the tonal kinship is suggestive of a not entirely dissimilar sensibility. The tone and meaning of the play are controversial among classicists. The play, produced in 438 B.C.E., was last in a tetralogy that would normally have ended with a satyr-play. The drama, while full of pathos, gives full weight to the ambivalencies of its situation. Apollo opens the play by setting its action in the context of the violent Olympian familial politics that have resulted in the imminent sacrifice of Alceste. Before she dies, Alceste requires her husband to promise that he will not remarry. The couple's two children make an appearance on stage, and the boy is given short speeches. At Alceste's funeral, there is a vicious quarrel between Admetus and his father, in which the son castigates the father's selfishness in refusing to die for him, and the father the son's cowardice in being reluctant to die. Heracles appears in his traditional burlesque role, denounced by a servant as an insensitive, brawling, intrusive guest. He is at first unaware of the death of his hostess, playing an inquisitive role very like that of the Chaucerian Narrator in the *Book of the Duchess.* When he returns Alceste, she is veiled in order to intensify the final recognition through the long scene known as "the Teasing of Admetus." It is, in short, an emotionally, socially, and tonally complex work for all its brevity (about 1,160 lines) and simplicity of plot.

There are a few other minor classical references that cannot be entirely ruled out as possibly having come to Chaucer's attention in some form, whether gloss, quotation, or florilegium. Plato, in the *Symposium,* refers briefly to Alcestis, "Pelias' daughter . . . the only person who was willing to die for her husband, though he had a father and mother living, and the affection which love inspired in her was so surpassing that it made them appear mere strangers to their son, and his kindred in nothing but name" (sec. 179c)—a critique consistent with that of Euripides. The first-century Greek writer Apollodorus tells the story in his *Library* (1.9.15)—with the interesting twist (apparently a more archaic version) that Kore, or Persephone, sent Alcestis back from Hades in rejection of such a sacrifice. Ovid mentions the story, without Alceste's name, in the *Ars amatoria* (3.17–20), and such a reference would certainly have been glossed in medieval commentaries on the *Ars.* Indeed, the story, with names, is summarized in a commentary on a text having nothing to do with Admetus or Alceste. The text is Ovid's *Epistulae ex Ponto;* the lemma is the first phrase in book 3 ("Aequor Iasonio"), and the gloss includes the story of Alceste, who endured death for her husband ("quae pro viro suo mortem sustinuit" [Hexter, 115]). Another first-century writer, Musonius Rufus, cites the story of Admetus and Alceste to illustrate the strength of the marriage bond (Foucault, *Care,* 159).

But there are several stronger possibilities. The figure of Alceste survived in mythographical compendia, so that, as Winthrop Wetherbee asserts, "its meaning was largely determined by the moralizations conventionally associated with it in mythographic tradition" (142). What were these associations? Kolve, with admirable succinctness, summarizes the tradition through Fulgentius, the Vatican mythographers, and Boccaccio (172); like him, Wetherbee focuses on the collections of Fulgentius and the Vatican mythographers, for whom Admetus represents the human mind, Alceste spiritual courage. If we limit ourselves to these sources, it is easy enough to conclude that Chaucer's portrait of Alceste is unequivocally a positive one.

Another well-known compendium offers a rather different approach, one far more congenial with the Chaucerian worldview than the others, and with the advantage over others that it is known to have been used by Chaucer elsewhere.[10] I refer to the mid-fourteenth-century *Reductorium morale* of the Benedictine Pierre Bersuire, a friend of Petrarch's in Avignon. At the end of his prologue, Bersuire tells the story of Admetus, Alceste, and Hercules. The story is glossed as an allegory of the good wife, whose perfect love of her husband causes Jesus to lead her out of purgatory into heaven, and also as an allegory of the virgin martyrs who preferred to die for their God rather than to live physically but perish spiritually. This interpretation is used by D. W. Robertson to support his contention that numerous incidents in the *Legend's* Prologue "all point to the same concept: the Christian ideal of marriage" (378); Kolve too, following Bersuire, emphasizes the Christian-redemptive possibilities of the Alceste story.

Yet the spiritual interpretation is only part of Bersuire's commen-

10. Meg Twycross summarizes the case for Chaucer's use of Bersuire (1–14). It is significant for my purpose to note that Steadman's argument for the influence of Bersuire relies on Chaucer's use, not of the narrative, but of the interpretation. The Chaucerian locus in question is *Knight's Tale* 1959. Twycross also discusses *HF* 135–36.

tary, for amidst his doctrinal exegetics, the Benedictine author moves into a long comic digression deploring the lack of faith of modern women:

> Nowadays it stands against many women that they not only would not die so that their husbands might live, but they even wish them dead so that they themselves might remarry. There are many who assert they would die for their husbands if necessary, but if the necessity arose, would not wish to suffer anything for them. This is shown in the story of a young woman who claimed she would rather die than her husband. To test this her husband said that death would come within three days to take him. When she said she wished to die for him, the husband took a live chicken and plucked it and hid it, along with himself, in a closet, forbidding his wife to show Death (who was to arrive very soon) the hiding-place. When he let the plucked chicken out, the wife thought it was Death himself and, frightened, began to scream: "It isn't me, it isn't me you're looking for!" And she revealed the place where her husband was hiding. Seeing this, the husband crept out of the closet rebuking his wife for her false promise. He killed the chicken and ate it, saying to his wife that she would not eat of this Death since she didn't wish to endure it for him. There are infinite other examples, such as [the one about] the wife whose husband tested her love by pretending to be dead. When he was carried in his bier under a tree, the branches lifted the bier-cloth. He immediately arose and his wife pretended to be very happy. Then it befell that the man really died. She, fearing he might once again revive, wouldn't let him be carried by the same path, so that he shouldn't be resurrected by the branches as before.[11]

Alceste is not criticized in Bersuire's text, but her story is associated with a strong critique of women conveyed in comical, indeed nearly fabliau-like, sketches. Besides a skeptical attitude toward women, the other aspect of Bersuire's treatment that Chaucer might have noted with interest is the virtual frenzy of interpretation accompanying many of his narratives of gods and heroes. "Vel si vis

11. From *De formis figurisque deorum*, ed. Engels (1966), 54–55. My translation. This text is chapter 1 of book 15 (*Ovidius moralizatus*) of Bersuire's massive *Reductorium morale*, which in turn is only one of several encyclopedic compilations he perpetrated during his lifetime. Engels recapitulates the extremely complex bibliographical history of the "Ovidius." Chaucer is likely to have used this version of Bersuire, i.e., the later and fuller "P" (for Paris) text rather than the earlier "A" (for Avignon) version, also published by Engels (1960) under the same title, and rather than the *Libellus*, an epitome of Bersuire. However, as Engels remarks, there is "un ample choix" (xvi, 1966). On the *Libellus*, see Eleanor Rathbone.

dic . . . vel si vis exponere iste moraliter . . . vel dic e contrario" are among the formulae littering Bersuire's text. Of course, if the book were effectively to fulfill its purpose as a handbook for preachers, it would have to display a wide variety of applications. Yet for an author as attuned as Chaucer to the vagaries of communication both oral and written, and to the subjectivity of interpretation, the flurry of alternatives might have seemed at once bizarre and para- digmatic: bizarre when placed against an imagined or desired norm of univocity—the "naked text"—but paradigmatic of the real condi- tions of textual transmission and interpretation.

Despite a variety of possible classical and medieval sources for Chaucer's version of Alceste, we need to recall, as Robert Payne emphasizes, that Alceste is a fictional figure; moreover, that Chau- cer, by this point in his career, felt free to rewrite the classical tradition, because his fiction was as valid as any other. He is a producer of fiction like others, as Alceste herself points out, who compose "Ryght after hire ymagynacioun" (F 355). Quite aside from attitudes in the sources, there is ample reason for Chaucer to offer an ambiguous portrait of Alceste. She is a woman, a natural crea- ture: how could she escape the mixed motives humanity is doomed to? Even Hercules, who rescued Alceste from the underworld, is far from a univocal sign: he will play a bad role in the story of Hyp- sipyle, as Jason's best friend and go-between.

Moreover, Alceste is a woman whose love—like that of the secu- lar "saints" portrayed in the legends—leads her to suicide. The problem of suicide is one that Chaucer had already addressed openly in the *Book of the Duchess*, at a point when the Black Knight's obsessive sorrow leads the Narrator to anticipate a possible impulse to self-slaughter. In a passage that names, as negative examples, several of the protagonists of the *Legend*, Chaucer has his Narrator intervene in impeccably orthodox Christian and Stoic-philosophical terms:

> "A, goode sir," quod I, "say not soo!
> Have som pitee on your nature
> That formed yow to creature. . . .
> Ne say noght soo, for trewely,
> Thogh ye had lost the ferses twelve,
> And ye for sorwe mordred yourselve,
> Ye sholde be dampned in this cas
> By as good ryght as Medea was,

That slough hir children for Jasoun;
And Phyllis also for Demophoun
Heng hirself—so weylaway!—
For he had broke his terme-day
To com to hir. Another rage
Had Dydo, the quene eke of Cartage,
That slough hirself for Eneas
Was fals—which a fool she was!
And Ecquo died for Narcisus
Nolde nat love hir, and ryght thus
Hath many another foly doon; . . ."
(714–37)

Even if Alceste's apparent motivation for suicide is not lust but charity, nonetheless, from a doctrinal viewpoint, this is misplaced charity, appropriating to oneself the right to decide the moment of one's death rather than leaving it to God or to nature, "the vicaire of the almyghty Lord" (*Parliament of Fowls* 379). Alceste could be seen as so subordinated to her husband that she does for him what everyone must do for himself, namely, die. Fulgentius etymologizes the names of the spouses in order to support his interpretation (1.22), so it will not be entirely gratuitous if I also analyze them, although not etymologically. I am struck by the homophonic similarity of the two names, which begin with the same letter, have the same number of syllables, and end with nearly the same syllable (Alcestis/Admetus). In the late-fourteenth-century or early-fifteenth-century *Libellus*, "Admetus" is miswritten as "Almetus," so there seems to be a scribal tendency for the names to become even more similar.[12] Is her devotion so voracious that she would become a version of her husband, not allowing his separate submission to the process of nature? With or without the analysis of names, from a Christian perspective Alceste in her will to substitute herself for another is as sinful, albeit more subtly so, as any of the women in the legends, and as arrogant as Eros, her lord and companion.

12. Liebeschütz, 125. Nicole Loraux comments on the "recoil" effect of Alceste's death. In Greek terms, a fine death, showing courage and endurance, was considered essentially masculine. Alceste thus becomes "manlike," while Admetus is feminized: "He is driven to become the mother as well as the father of their children, and condemned to live henceforward cloistered like a virgin or chaste as a bride [Alceste has extracted this promise from him before she dies—S.D.] inside the palace, which his wife has left to join in death the open spaces of manly heroism" (Loraux, 29).

This is why Alceste is finally the instrument of a double bind for the reader. Does the Narrator deserve the punishment he gets? If yes, then it is because he wrote ill of women and judges them badly; because he was, in short, a misogynist. If no, then Alceste is wrong to assist in the punishment. She proves a misogynistic point: that women lack courage and independence but are best suited to act as agents of men's judgment. This lets the Narrator off the hook, but it implicates the poet.

My last comment on Alceste as she appears in the *Legend* is to observe that she is obeyed in form but not in spirit. Her instructions are to produce a propagandistic work, but the result is far more complicated and nuanced than that, as I show in Chapters 3, 4, and 5. The movement of Chaucer's poem, then, is that of a double subversion. It is a movement we see again in the *Wife of Bath's Prologue* and *Tale*, where a female and apparently prowoman speaker winds up undermining her own case in a variety of ways. Here, the directive to rewrite woman good is supposed to subvert a traditional antifeminist representation of woman (that is, Chaucer's pre-*Legend* representation, as Eros sees it). But the actual response is to subvert that directive in accordance with an aesthetic predicated upon the inherently contradictory nature of nature. Hence the legends assert not unitary faith and goodness, but contradiction. They do so indirectly, to be sure, but just as inevitably and "naturally" as birds in spring defy the fowler's "sophistry."

3

The Naked Text

Dieser Einfall für den Schluss ist geradezu entsetzlich, verzeihen Sie mir, lieber Dr. Strauss—, Sie haben diesen Brief in keinem guten Moment geschrieben. Denken Sie die Höhe der Stimmung, die mühsam erkommen ist, vom Anfang des Vorspiels an, immer höher, in die herrliche Oper hinauf, dann im Kommen des Bacchus, im Duett eine fast mystische Höhe. Und nun, wo die nötige Coda nicht mehr als ein Moment sein darf . . . nun soll solcher Quark wieder sich breitmachen (auf dem *breit* liegt der Ton).

Hugo von Hofmannsthal to Richard Strauss, 1916[1]

This inspiration for the end is truly atrocious, if you will excuse me, dear Dr. Strauss—, you did not write this letter in any fortunate moment. Consider the lofty atmosphere that we have been striving so hard to reach, rising ever higher from the beginning of the overture to the glorious opera, then the entrance of Bacchus, reaching in the duet almost mystical heights. And now, where the necessary coda need not last more than a moment . . . now this bilge is to be spread out again (the emphasis is on *spread*).

In 1969 an anthology of "recent American poetry in open forms" was published under the title *Naked Poetry.* The phrase, borrowed from the Andalusian poet Juan Jiménez (1881–1958), was intended, wrote the editors, Stephen Berg and Robert Mezey, to express "what we feel about the qualities of this poetry as no technical label could do." The qualities—or at least the formal features—of the poetry chosen for the collection are that it generally neither rhymes nor "move[s] on feet of more or less equal duration" (xi). Further, what interested the editors more than formal features were the "dreams, visions and prophecies" of the contributors, "the shapes

---

1. Letter from Hugo von Hofmannsthal to his collaborator Richard Strauss about their opera *Ariadne auf Naxos*, in Forsyth, 104–5; translation based on Forsyth's with some modification by me.

of their emotions." In short prose accounts accompanying their poems, the contributors found various ways to describe their work: Denise Levertov wrote of "organic" poetry, Robert Bly of "association," Robert Creeley (following Charles Olson) of "returning to poetry its relation with the physiological condition," Allen Ginsberg of "native sensibility" and "personal breath," Gary Snyder of work that communicates "straight from the deep mind of the maker to the deep mind of the hearer. This is what poets call the Poem."

The "nakedness" in the title refers, then, to two related things: a freedom from traditional formal and technical restrictions, and a more intense, sincere, or revelatory language than is believed possible in structured verse. The assumption appears to be that less structure enables a more honest revelation of feeling. It is a romantic aesthetic, and an essentially lyric (rather than narrative) aesthetic, but what interests me here is the shared conviction that a "naked" poetry is possible. For none of the contributors contemplate the idea of the rhetoric of their own stance, of its temporally conditional and conditioned nature, indeed of its artificiality. Even Ezra Pound acknowledged all this, while apparently rejecting it, in his "Salutation the Second," which appeared in *Poetry* magazine in April 1913. "Here they stand," he wrote of his poems,

>   without quaint devices,
> Here they are with nothing archaic about them.
> Observe the irritation in general:
> "Is this," they say, "the nonsense
>   that we expect of poets?"
> "Where is the Picturesque?"
>   "Where is the vertigo of emotion?" . . .
> Go, little naked and impudent songs,
> Go with a light foot! . . .
>   greet the grave and the stodgy,
> Salute them with your thumbs at your noses.
>   . . . go! jangle their door-bells!
> Say that you do no work
>   and that you will live forever.

Pound's naked verses, supposedly devoid of archaic devices, exhibit at the very least envoy, apostrophe, anaphora, personification, enargia, irony, and pun ("foot").

Taken for granted by the modern poets cited here is an idea of the natural as hitherto latent beneath a centuries-old accretion of poetic form, but now able to emerge in its pristine glory. And this unstated premise perpetuates one very ancient idea about language, while opposing another. It denies that rhetoric, form, and style are coterminous with language itself, and that they assist in expression; it asserts that they impede expression, serving as cover-up for emotion or truth. The interplay of these conflicting ideas about language, already adumbrated in Chapter 2, is what this chapter will explore, with Chaucer's *Legend* as its field.

NAKEDNESS

For a medieval writer, the desire for naked text is even more problematic than for a modern, complicated as it is by the intertextual nature of medieval poetic production. Nowhere is this more the case than with the medieval posterity of Ovid, Chaucer's major source for the *Legend*. "What difference does it make who is speaking?" Samuel Beckett's question, used by Michel Foucault to problematize the notion of authorship, can scarcely be more aptly applied than to the medieval conception of "Ovid"—a name designating not only a large number of texts by the Roman poet, but texts not even claiming to be composed by Ovid, texts known to be written by others, and yet constituting in their ensemble the "author-function" (to use Foucault's term) called "Ovid." If we limit ourselves to the *Metamorphoses* alone, the range includes the manuscript of a long classical Latin poem, usually transmitted with medieval marginal and interlinear glosses; Latin prose commentaries on the poem; a moralized condensation of the poem in Latin verse; excerpts from the original in florilegia; scattered episodes inserted as exempla in many Latin and vernacular poems or embedded in scientific treatises and encyclopedic compilations; a substantially amplified French verse translation of the original with naturalistic, euhemeristic, and Christian allegories added; and a Latin prose redaction incorporating several of the preceding, which in turn incorporate one another.[2] Such was the intertextual *embarras de richesses* confronting the late-medieval English poet in search of Ovid.

2. Because there is a vast bibliography on medieval Ovid, I refer the reader to the partial list in Delany, "Naked Text," 290 n. 2.

Small wonder, then, that in introducing his collection of tales drawn largely from Ovid's *Heroides* and *Metamorphoses*, Chaucer should attempt to clear a space for himself, a territory just wide enough to accommodate a narrative stance:

> For myn entent is, or I fro yow fare,
> The naked text in English to declare
> Of many a story, or elles of many a geste,
> As autours seyn; leveth hem if yow leste.
> (G 85–88)

What the "nakedness" of a text might mean to the Chaucerian Narrator is not necessarily a simple thing, as I have indicated in Chapter 2. Here I would like to come closer to this "nakedness" in order to feel its meaning to Chaucer, to derive some sense of the poetic project he seems to set for himself, and thence to observe the operation or non-operation of the concept in the legends.

"Naked" is the past participle of a transitive verb: to naken or to nake an object, meaning to make bare, to expose, to strip someone or something of covering or protection. It carries therefore a sense of agency: nakedness is a produced condition, requiring an act of intervention. This transitivity suggests further that nakedness is not necessarily a usual condition, still less a desirable one. Both aspects of the word appear in the Prologue, when in spring the earth forgets "his pore estat / Of wynter, that hym naked made and mat" (F 125–26), and the sun reclothes all "That naked was" (F 129). One might indeed nake oneself, but this would be an exceptional, even a deplorable circumstance, as in Chaucer's translation of Boethius: "O nice men! why nake ye youre bakkes? (as who seith, 'O ye slowe and delicat men! whi flee ye adversites, and ne fyghte nat ayeins hem by vertu, to wynnen the mede of the hevens?')" (*Consolation of Philosophy* 4. m. 7, 60–70). More typical is Hoccleve's usage, in his "Letter of Cupid" (1402), in which Eve is relieved of direct responsibility for having "made al man-kynde lese his lyberte, / and naked yt of Ioye" (stanza 51). So that we need first to sense the verbness of "naked," to hear that a naked thing is a thing that has been rendered naked, it has been impoverished, stripped of what had properly covered or adorned it.

Yet, paradoxically, nakedness is a natural condition: the pristine condition, after all, of the human race and the human individual. In the sense of originary nakedness, we find the images "naked as a needle," "naked as a worm" (*Romaunt of the Rose*, 454), "naked as my nail."[3] There seems, then, to be a certain multileveled quality to the word and the concept, a quality revealed in other Middle English usages. A "naked bed," for instance, is not a bed stripped of bedding but rather a bed in which one sleeps naked, the attribute of the occupant transferred to the bed; one might, with similar poetic license, speak of a "sorrowful" bed as one in which sorrow is experienced. And to be in one's "naked shirt" (*Romaunt*, 5446) is not to be entirely naked but to be naked under one's shirt, clad only in one's shirt. Here the almost-perceptible attribute of the wearer is transferred to the garment. But this creates a logical conundrum, for since it is a garment worn by the wearer, the wearer is no longer naked, and this disqualifies the qualifier.

In connection with language or textuality, the word has a long and equally complicated history. Rather than compile a lengthy list of references from classical and medieval literatures, I shall offer a few examples that best illustrate ambiguities particularly relevant to my argument about the Chaucerian project in the *Legend of Good Women*.

In dedicating *A Treatise on the Astrolabe* (1391) to "Lyte Lowys my sone," Chaucer promises to give the work "under full light reules and naked wordes in Englissh, for Latyn canst thou yit but small, my litel sone." Further on in the dedication he seeks pardon from a more "discreet" audience for his "rude endityng" and "superfluite of wordes," justifying both by the fact that the recipient is a child. Nakedness of language here refers first to the vernacular, secondarily to a simple and repetitive instructional style. Rhetorical simplicity was also, apparently, what Richard de Bury had in mind when, in *Philobiblon*, he wrote of poetry and its enemies:

> All the various missiles by means of which those who love only the naked Truth attack the poets are to be warded off with a double shield, either by pointing out that in their obscene material a pleasing style of speech may be learned, or that where the material is feigned . . . , a natural or historical truth is enclosed beneath the figurative eloquence of fiction (in Robertson, *Chaucer's London*, 181).

---

3. John Nichols notes (169) the pre- and postlapsarian connotations of female nudity in medieval art. He also observes that while the female nude is usually a negative sign, this does not include scenes of nursing, parturition, or sleep (170–71).

This would not be, however, the primary meaning for many of Chaucer's contemporaries. The translator of the C fragment of the *Romaunt of the Rose* (who may or may not have been Chaucer) has Fals-Semblant send his audience to "The nakid text, and lete the glose" (6556) in order to determine whether there is scriptural antecedent for mendicancy. The text is Holy Writ, most likely in Latin, and its nakedness refers to the absence of interpretive glosses. It is interesting that in the corresponding French passage, Jean de Meun does not use the imagery of nakedness, although he does have Faus Semblant emphasize the literality of his interpretation (*la lestre* [11262]; *selonc la letre* [11336]) and the image was available in Latin texts very likely to have been known by Jean.

The English translator has therefore inserted the image, and this usage is consistent with that of the Wycliffites or Lollards, concerned as they were with the direct apprehension of Scripture in vernacular translation and without accumulated exegetical glosses (see Chapter 2). Since the Lollards believed that truth does not inhere in one language more than another, and used this principle to justify their translations, they did not see the vernacular as any more inherently "naked" than Latin. A Lollard tract on translating the Bible shows that the absence of gloss, rather than the language itself, is the important thing. If, the tract says, a priest can no longer preach, one remedy is as follows:

> recorde he in the woke [week] the nakid tixt of the Soundaie Gospel that he kunne the groos story and telle it to his puple, that is if he understonde Laytne, and do he this every woke of the yeer and forsothe he schal profite wel. . . . If for-sothe he understonde no Latyn, go he to oon of his neightboris that understandith, wiche wole charitabily expone it to hym and thus edifie he his flock . . . [for] if it is levefful [lawful] to preche the naked text to the pupel, it is also lefful to write it to hem & consequentliche, be proces of tyme, so al the Bibil.[4]

It was exactly this lack of gloss that the opponents of scriptural translation opposed, because of its subversive potential. This is why, as Anne Hudson observes, "The naked text in the ploughman's hand was a much more dangerous and a much more readily

---

4. Buhler, 175. This translates a sermon by Grosseteste, who uses the phrase *nudum textum evangelii*. The tract is also printed in Deanesly, *Lollard Bible*, 439–45, with the cited passage on 442.

available weapon" (*Lollards*, 155) than a sermon explained by the preacher. In several tracts, Jean Gerson, chancellor of the University of Paris, argued that such translation would be likely to sow heretical deviations. If the Bible "were badly translated or presumptuously understood, contrary to the exposition of holy doctors[, it] would be better to be completely ignorant of the matter." The "sowers of heresy, and enemies of truth" have already, he complains, infected England, Scotland, Prague, Germany, "and even, shameful as it is to admit it, . . . France." About 1415, in his tract *On Communion*, Gerson wrote: "Now this use of holy scripture by modern men, as if holy scripture should be believed in its bare text without the help of any interpretation or explanation, is a kind of use which is attended by grave dangers and scandals" (Deanesly, *Lollard Bible*, 104–6).

Nor were the British authorities unaware of the dangers of textual nakedness. When, about 1397, the Herefordshire squire John Croft was forced to renounce his heretical opinions, his renunciation included the promise to neither read nor own "English books extracted from holy scripture according to the bare text [*secundum nudum textum*], with evil intent, by certain persons commonly called Lollards, who oppose the Catholic faith and the doctrine of the Roman church" (ibid., 288). Another document (possibly as early as 1380 and possibly by Wyclif himself) attacks vain men who cite Scripture in the service of pride:

> And Poul seith, *Kunnynge makith a man proud*, that is nakid kunnynge withoute goode werkis, whanne it is medlid with pride veyn glorie and boost. Sich men semen to do goostli avoutrie with the word of God, for there thei schulde take of the Hooli Goost trewe undirstandyng of hooli writ by gret meknesse and hooli praier, to brynge forth very charite and goode werkis. Thei taken the nakid undirstondynge bi presumcion of mannes witt, and bryngen forgt pride veynglorie and boost, to coloure here synnes and disceive sutilli here negebours. (Ibid., 447)

Particularly interesting in this passage is the author's artful extension of the nakedness metaphor into a mini-allegory of adulterous engendering.

Nakedness, then, can be a good thing or a bad thing. It can connote simplicity, straightforwardness, honesty, naturalness, and eroticism; or it can connote unattractive lack or weakness, suffering,

degradation, poverty, or improper exposure. There is the nakedness of the lover in one's arms (*Romaunt*, 2571) and the nakedness of
the beggar on a dunghill (*Romaunt*, 6496). It is with the sincerity and
vulnerability of "my naked herte" that the narrator of Troilus invokes Venus (3.43); while Philosophy assures Boethius that evil
people are "naked of alle strengthes" (4. pr. 2, 10).

Such ambiguities in the word "naked" and its uses, the fact that it
is able to partake of meanings not only varied but contradictory,
makes it a sliding or polysemous signifier, linguistically in the same
arena as the puns discussed in the previous and present chapters.
Nor is it coincidental that in its Chaucerian uses this problematic
word should contain within its referential range the trio of nature,
women, and language discussed in Chapter 2, for the multiple
possibilities of the word, its very ambiguities, lead us again to the
ideological malaise noted there: the coexisting acceptance of, and
discomfort with, temporality in its various versions. In the *Clerk's
Tale*, Griselda's story combines the two axes of nakedness. As a
bride, she brings "feith, and nakednesse, and maydenhede"
(IV.866) to Walter; as a rejected wife, she is left nothing but her
smock:

> "Naked out of my fadres hous," quod she,
> "I cam, and naked moot I turne agayn. . . . "
> (871–72)

Her first nakedness is positive, her second negative; echoing the
Book of Job (1:21), Griselda aligns her trajectory to that of the human
condition both individual and collective. There was a time, "th'es-
taat of innocence" (X.325) as the Parson reminds his pilgrim audience, when nakedness was no cause of shame. On one level this
could be the moment of birth, on another, the prelapsarian condition, to which Augustine devotes a chapter, "Of the nakedness of
our first parents" (14.17) in *The City of God*. At either of those
originary points, "nakedness" would have only a single meaning; it
would be a univocal signifier. Such a condition will recur, Christianity promises, in the resurrection of bodies. Until then, the
nakedness of bodies can only be ambivalent at best, the nakedness
of nature temporary, and the nakedness of texts impossible, an
infinitely deferred utopian wish.

Whatever the phrase "the naked text" may have meant to Chaucer—whether a doggedly literal translation, or a work devoid of rhetoric, or a work so transparent in meaning as to require no interpretation—it must have been obvious to him even as he wrote it that he neither would nor could produce such a text. Few texts have come into a poet's hands, or left them, as elaborately appareled as Ovid's did Chaucer's. The wish is a quixotic gesture, and my use of this adjective is not accidental, for, like Don Alonso, Chaucer (or his poet-Narrator) is the willing victim of literary tradition, inspired and bound by it at once. His "credence / To bokes olde" is a leap of faith, and the *Legend*, like *Don Quixote*, chronicles (albeit on a different level) the collision between literary imagination and the exigencies of natural and social reality. Just how surely the desire for "the naked text" remains a pious but futile wish, a utopian wish, the rest of this chapter will show.

CLOTHING THE TEXT: THISBE

More prominently than other Chaucerian works, the *Legend of Good Women* foregrounds the carrying over of learning (*translatio studii*). In its opening lines and throughout, the poem poses the question of how the modern poet can or ought to use ancient material transmitted through a filter of grammatical and moral glosses, rhetorical amplification, and conflicting interpretation. What is the truth of such a mixed tradition, the weight of any given authority? What is it possible to know, and how may the maker judge? Although we are given no explicit answers, the answers are implied in Chaucer's poetic practice, which opts for heterogeneity of sources and multiplicity of meanings, hence suspended judgment: the very reverse, we may note, of a "naked text." I shall begin with the legend of Thisbe as my paradigm, and then turn to the other legends.

The Thisbe material came to Chaucer by way of Ovid's *Metamorphoses* (4.55–166) and a vernacular intermediary, the *Ovide moralisé*, a fourteenth-century French verse translation of, and moralized commentary upon, the *Metamorphoses*. The latter does not, however, give a straightforward translation of Ovid's tale of Thisbe. It offers instead a twelfth-century text, the Old French *lai* of Pyramus and Thisbe, inserted into the later work by its anonymous clerical compiler. It was not the only insertion, for as Paule Demats shows (ch. 2), this massive syncretic text also includes the *lai* of Philomela by Chrétien de Troyes, material from other Ovidian works (particularly the *Heroides*), material from earlier commentaries upon, or biographies of, Ovid, together with a variety of other sources such as Dares and Dictys, and Benoit's *Roman de Troie*.

For subsequent generations, the *Ovide moralisé* was a key text in *translatio studii*: a text located at the intersection of Latin and vernacular literatures, as Joseph Engels has remarked (81). Guillaume de Machaut transcribed whole sections of the *Ovide moralisé* into his *Voir dit* and other works. Christine de Pizan plundered it, especially for her *Epistre Othéa*; indeed, Campbell points out that for Christine, and doubtless for others, "Ovid" meant the moralization rather than the original Latin text. Chaucer too knew and used the *Ovide moralisé*, drawing on it, as I have shown elsewhere, for his distinctive portrait of Fame, as well as for several of his legends of good women.

In choosing the story of Thisbe, Chaucer joined an illustrious company of predecessors, contemporaries, and successors. A *lai* of Thisbe is one of the pieces performed by Gottfried's Tristan during his first appearance at King Mark's court, and a *lai* of Thisbe is mentioned in the thirteenth-century Provençal romance *Flamenca* (line 621). Either of these might refer to the extant text. A Latin prose version of the story was attributed to the influential grammarian Matthew of Vendôme.[5] Boccaccio includes Thisbe among his famous women, drawing from her fate the enlightened moral that parents ought not to interfere too rashly in their children's love. (There is evidence he too knew the *lai*.)[6] Several English poets, including Chaucer's friend John Gower, tell or refer to the story.

Later, in its best-known post-medieval incarnation, the story would become the subject of the "hempen homespuns" playlet in Shakespeare's *A Midsummer Night's Dream*. Arthur Golding—"Shakespeare's Ovid" and a prolific translator of French texts—seems to have known the *lai*, for at one point (*Met.* 4.84; Golding's

---

5. See Branciforti. On Matthew and academic uses of the Ovidian material, see Glendinning.

6. As in the *lai*, but not in Ovid, Boccaccio stresses the extreme youth of the protagonists and the fact that they fell in love as children. Also corresponding to the *lai* rather than to Ovid, Boccaccio attributes motivation to the parents, and has *luna monstrante viam* ("the moon showing the way") to Thisbe as she leaves the house rather than when she sees the lion.

line 104) he uses a word ("covenant") that appears both in the *lai* and in Chaucer's *Legend* but has no equivalent in Ovid. Shakespeare himself would have encountered the material through a verse translation published in the Elizabethan miscellany *A Gorgeous Gallery of Gallant Inventions*, as W. G. van Emden points out. The twelfth-century French version is surely the most touching of these medieval and Renaissance incarnations, for its author transformed the rather dry Ovidian narrative into a high-medieval Romeo and Juliet: a rhetorically extravagant tale of hot-blooded adolescent sexuality thwarted by parental obtuseness and culminating in a pathetic double death.

Chaucer's use of the French material in his version of Thisbe offers a revealing view of the poet at work, the ways in which not only his words but his attitudes, his conceptualization of the story, might be affected by its multilayered garments. The *lai* appears in all but one of the nineteen extant manuscripts of the *Ovide moralisé*. It also exists as an autonomous work in three anthology manuscripts. But since Chaucer is known to have used the compilation elsewhere in his *Legend*, I shall follow the principle of Ockham's razor in arguing for it rather than an autonomous version of the *lai*. Besides demonstrating verbal appropriations, I shall also suggest what use Chaucer made of the French moralization of Ovid's text.

Ovid's version is nothing if not succinct. In narrative terms we might call it bare, although it is far from "naked" rhetorically, as we shall see. Ovid opens with extreme narrative economy and rapid pace.

> "Pyramus et Thisbe, iuvenum pulcherrimus alter,
> altera, quas Oriens habuit, praelata puellis,
> contiguas tenuere domos, ubi dicitur altam
> coctilibus muris cinxisse Semiramis urbem.
> notitiam primosque gradus vicinia fecit,
> tempore crevit amor; taedae quoque iure coissent,
> sed vetuere patres: quod non potuere vetare,
> ex aequo captis ardebant mentibus ambo.
> conscius omnis abest; nutu signisque loquuntur,
> quoque magis tegitur, tectus magis aestuat ignis."
> (*Met.* 4.55–64)[7]

---

7. Text from Loeb Classical Library edition. Translation based on that of Frank J. Miller in that edition, with my alterations.

"Pyramus and Thisbe—he the most beautiful young man,
she most desirable of girls the Orient had—
occupied adjacent houses where, it is said,
Semiramis encircled the city high with baked brick wall.
Proximity made the first steps of their acquaintance, and
in time love grew. They should have come together under the
    marriage torch,
but their parents forbade what cannot be forbidden:
with equally inflamed spirit both of them burned.
There was no accomplice; they spoke by nods and signs.
But the more it's covered, the more a covered fire heats up."

In ten lines the hero and heroine are named, described, located, brought to young adulthood, and placed in a complicated relationship with each other and with their parents. A great deal is left out: the city is not actually named; there is no social context; the parents do not exist except far offstage as obstacles; no motive is offered for their resistance.

By contrast, the French author is at pains to establish a convincing social and psychological context for the story, and in this Chaucer follows him. The *lai* characterizes the fathers as "dui home renome / Dui citeain de grant hautesce" (4.230–32); Chaucer, borrowing narrative strategy and a key word, makes them "Two lordes, which were of gret renoun" (711). The *lai* also motivates parental opposition and, in quite a complex scenario (307–37), gives a realistic social setting for the action. A serf or servant notices the young people's behavior and reports it to Thisbe's mother, who promptly confines her daughter indoors. Simultaneously the fathers quarrel, ending communication between their offspring. Chaucer's scenario, less elaborate, nonetheless provides other characters, a social setting, and a motive for the parents' interference:

The name of everych gan to other sprynge
By women that were neighebores aboute.
For in that contre yit, withouten doute,
Maydenes been ykept, for jelosye,
Ful streyte, lest they diden som folye.
(719–23)

The class thrust of the French text (pinpointing a servant as the killjoy) is modified in favor of practical common sense and conservative morality. Sympathy for the lovers also begins to be modified, for the parental motive is not, by medieval standards, unreasonable. The danger of impetuosity is thus introduced as a theme in the Chaucerian text.

Ovid specifies no age for his lovers, but the French poet does, in order to deepen the pathos of his material. Love first touches his protagonists when they are only seven years old (301–4), and at the time of the action they are just fifteen. As their age increases, so increases their love: "Croist lor aiez et croist lor sens . . . / Croist lor amour, croist lor aez" (348–51). Chaucer too raises the question of age, imitating the French poet's parallel construction:

> And thus by report was hire name yshove
> That, as they wex in age, wex here love.
> And certeyn, as by resoun of hire age,
> There myghte have ben bytwixe hem maryage . . .
>   (726–29)

Ovid's narrative continues with the image of the cracked wall through which the lovers can speak:

> fissus erat tenui rima, quam duxerat olim,
> cum fieret, paries domui communis utrique.
>   (65–66)

Split it was by a narrow crack that had formed long ago when the wall common to both houses was built.

This crack becomes the path of love, but only for voice (*vocis . . . iter* [69])—the only form of intercourse available for the moment. Whether or not Ovid intended the hint of an obscene pun in his image of the narrow crack that is the path of love, it was certainly taken this way by other classical and medieval poets. It would not be unusual for the archpoet of urbane dalliance to signal in this way the erotic urgency propelling his characters: we have already got the idea from the repeated imagery of fire and cooking in the first ten lines. Whatever Ovid's intention (and I do not doubt for a moment it was playful), Juvenal appropriated the narrow crack as a symbol for female genitalia when he described Roman mimes who impersonate women so skillfully that "Vacua et plana dicas / infra ventriculum et tenui distantia rima" (you would guess that everything was empty and flat between the belly and that further narrow crack [3.97]),[8] while Alanus de Insulis, deploring the prevalence of homosexuality, incorporated Ovid's image into a triple homophonic sexual wordplay in the *De planctu naturae*:

> Non modo per rimas rimatur basia Thisbes
> Pyramus, huic Veneris rimula nulla placet.
> (metrum 1.53–54)[9]

No longer does Pyramus search out Thisbe's kiss through the cracks; the little crack of Venus no longer pleases him. (My trans.)

The *lai* poet amplifies Ovid's economical but suggestive statement about the wall in two directions. First, the crack becomes virtually another personage in his story: synonyms for it (*crevasse, pertus, creveure*) appear numerous times, it is apostrophized at length by both lovers, much is made of Thisbe's finding it and stuffing her belt through it as a signal, and the lovers salute the crack for the last time before they elope. Similarly, but with considerably more restraint, Chaucer dwells gently on the crack, giving us the word "clyfte" three times in seven lines (740–46) and once again (776).

Second, the French poet takes up the idea of sexual wordplay. This was, of course, a widely used rhetorical device in classical and medieval literature, not least in the troubadour lyric, with which this poet shares many other features of language and thought. Several examples follow. The first two are true puns, or *significatio*, making literal and grammatical sense on two levels of meaning. One comes from Piramus's lament of frustrated desire:

> "He Diex, come est la vie [vit] dure
> Cui longuement tel mal endure."
> (586–87)

---

8. This line is cited by J. N. Adams, who does not, however, give Ovid as a contributing source, although he does mention numerous other sexual uses of *fissa, rima,* and *tenui rima*. Nor does Elizabeth Thomas note this locus, although she adduces other of Juvenal's debts to the Piramus story. G. Karl Galinsky discusses humor in the *Metamorphoses,* including wordplay and other forms of wit (ch. 4), but he does not mention the "crack."

9. The image is long-lived, reappearing in Colette's *Claudine at School:* " 'Do you think it's wide, the crack?' asked Marie Belhomme innocently. Such guilelessness gave me a spurt of laughter. What could those two crack-observers be up to? The gawky Anais had opened her atlas and was interrogating me: 'What is known as a crack? A fissure, sometimes called in French a lézarde or female lizard. This lizard

> "Oh God, how hard is the life [cock]
> Of one who long endures such ill."

The other, using the same pun, is in Thisbe's speech urging Piramus to meet her outside the city walls:

> "Se trouverai le vostre cors.
> (Amis, ta vie [vit] est mes tresors.)"
> (812–13)

> "So I will find you/your body.
> (Friend, your life [cock] is my treasure.)"

The homophony of *vie/vit* enables another wordplay, not a true pun but nearly, when Piramus lists the symptoms of his unsatisfied desire:

> "Tisbe, por vos despent ma vie [vit]
> En plour . . . "
> (425–26)

"Thisbe, for you I waste/empty my life [cock] in tears . . . "

Here the image latent beneath that of tears is that of the weeping *vit*: "the expense of spirit," as Shakespeare put it. A last example again combines homophony and suggestive image, when Thisbe describes her sexual anguish:

> "Ains plus ne jour ne nuit ne fui
> Sanz plaie,
> Qui con plus dure plus s'esgaie."
> (763–65)

"So neither night nor day have I been without a wound, which the longer it lasts the wider it spreads."

Of course, the primary referent of the wound is love. Yet the image of this ever-present wound that spreads wider with time is strongly suggestive of the female genital. This association is helped by the homophony *com/con* (*m* and *n* are often interchangeable in Old French manuscripts, and *com plus . . . plus* is an idiom, but *con* also

---

should normally be found in a wall, but it is sometimes met with elsewhere, even in places completely sheltered from the sun'" (67–69).

means cunt). The play is also supported by the physical resemblance between a *con* and a wound, and by the partial homophony—certainly not lost on medieval poets schooled in Latin—of *vulnus* and *vulva*.[10] This wound, with its multiple erotic associations, ironically counterpoints the real and fatal wound that Thisbe will later deal herself. Examples of sexual wordplay could be further multiplied, but these will suffice to indicate the French poet's sensibility.

These puns were not lost on Chaucer either, for he adopted the rhetorical tactic of sexual wordplay to his own presentation of the Thisbe material, starting with the versatile crack. Its versatility is taken even further, for the Chaucerian association is not genital but anal. In nine lines describing the wall, we find the following cluster: "clove a-two . . . fundacioun . . . clyfte . . . clifte . . . clifte" (738–46). "Clyfte" meant distinctively the crack or cleft of the buttocks (see *Summoner's Tale* III.2145), while "fundacioun" (founding) is partially homophonic with "fundement" (anus); in combination with "clove a-two," it is hard to avoid the suggestion of buttocks here. The same association appears in a medieval French text that anticipates our bumper-sticker lore about which occupations "do it" where and how. The miller, it says, does it where the water spurts; the leatherworker does it where the skin cracks; and "le maçon sure le fondement."[11]

Further on in this passage appears the mini-cluster "thy lym and eke thy ston . . . ston" (765–68), in apostrophe to the wall. The primary meaning is "your lime and also your stone": the masonry kissed by the separated lovers. Yet "lym" is homophonic with the word we now spell "limb"—a well-documented synonym for the male genital,[12] and "stone" is a common euphemism for a testicle

---

10. The resemblance was turned to blatant comedy by Rabelais (*Pantagruel* 11.15) in an episode that, like the tale of Thisbe, juxtaposes a woman and a lion. Shakespeare also belabors the metaphoricity of the wound in "The Passionate Pilgrim," 9.

11. Gaignebet and Lajoux, 52, citing N. Dufail, *Propos rustiques et contes d'Entrapel* (Paris, 1842).

12. The *Middle English Dictionary* refers to the circumcision of a child's "limb" and to Adam and Eve hiding their "limbs"; see also *Piers Plowman* 20.194–95: "the lyme that she loved me for . and leef was to fele, / On nyghtes namely . whan we naked were." Chaucer surely relies on this sexual meaning when he has January boast that his limbs are able "to do al that a man bilongeth to" and that despite his white head his limbs are green (*MerchT* IV.1458–59, 1465); one notes further that the usual

(cf. *Nun's Priest's Tale* VII.3448). The phrase thus carries the latent meaning of "your genital and your testicle," and the kissing of stones becomes an obscene allusion to oral-genital contact. Lydgate, of all people, is able some three or four decades later to use a "lym and ston" pun to very nice theological effect, in, of all places, his *Life of Our Lady*. God, planning the creation of Jesus as a means of redemption for mankind, will build this palace "nother of lyme ne stone" but in a virgin (2.317). His creation, that is, will be not of masonry, and also not generated sexually.

A last cluster of possible obscene wordplay occurs in Thisbe's suicide speech:

> Thanne spak she thus: "My woful hand," quod she,
> "Is strong ynogh in swich a werk to me;
> For love shal yeve me strengthe and hardynesse
> To make my wounde large ynogh, I gesse."
>
> (890–93)

I read here a latent allusion to masturbation, an activity commonly treated in penitentials, confessional manuals, and some medical treatises (Jacquart and Thomasset, 152, 176). Now at this moment in the narrative, Ovid has Thisbe refer to her hand, to love, to strength and a wound:

> est et mihi fortis in unum
> hoc manus, est et amor: dabit hic in vulnera vires.
>
> (149–50)

> I too have a hand strong for one thing, and that is love (or: I too have love). This shall give me strength for the wound.

---

counterposition to white head is, as the Reeve reminds us, a green tail (*Reeve's Tale* 3878), and that the Latin *cauda* means both tail and penis.

To observe that the phrase "lime and stone" was a common one for masonry does not remove the possibility of Chaucerian pun. On the contrary, the "legitimate" usage would make obscene use of the phrase all the more comical. Moreover, the limitations of strictly dictionary-authorized interpretation are evident in the *MED*'s naïve gloss of "lym of love" as "the binding power of love" (p. 1055).

It is interesting to note that medieval sexual theory did not imagine the vagina as an absence. This is supported by the *Medieval Woman's Guide to Health*, ed. and trans. Rowland, which calls for a suppository to be "putte in her prevy membre," and by the Wife of Bath's reference to her "bele chose." In fact, medieval medicine saw male and female genitalia as reversals of each other—that is, as basically the same thing, but in mirror image. T. W. Laqueur traces the history, implications, and modern overthrow of this view.

The passage is full of possible sexual innuendo, but it says nothing about enlargement. The French does, in the passage cited above and elsewhere (463–64), and so does Chaucer, so that Chaucer's lines evidently conflate the Latin and French versions. It is interesting to note, too, that in another place Chaucer preserves the connection of Thisbe with "large woundes wyde" (*MLT* II.62–63).

In the last portion of the narrative, we again find Chaucer combining his sources. Where Ovid says that the lovers *statuunt* ("agreed," "decided" [84]) to elope, the *lai* has "Ensi ferment lor convenant" (280), which appears in Chaucer as "This covenant was affermed" (790). In Ovid, the lovers agree to meet *ad busta Nini* ("at Ninus's tomb" [88]). The French poet rephrases this as "la ou Ninus fu enterrez" (819), a formulation that Chaucer virtually translates as "There Kyng Ninus was grave" (785). In Ovid, Thisbe wears a cloak or ample garment; the French text changes Thisbe's covering to a *guimple*, or small throat veil (901ff.), a detail imitated by Chaucer. In Ovid, Thisbe does not swoon on seeing her dying lover; she does in the *lai* (1052) and in the *Legend* (872).

Ovid's tale ends with the metamorphosis of pale mulberries into dark, and with the fulfillment of Thisbe's wish that the lovers' ashes rest in a shared urn. In the *Ovide moralisé*, though, the end of a tale is never the end of the story, for interpretation is required in order to achieve closure. The naturalistic exposition need not detain us—it is an etiological fable about why the mulberry darkens as it matures—but the moralization poses as starkly as possible the full problematic of *translatio studii*. It combines ethical, doctrinal, and tropological readings of the fable, taking as its point of departure the joint burial of the two corpses. This is interpreted as a figure of Jesus's dual nature (*OM* 4.1178–96), and there follows a long amplification of Jesus's suffering and that of martyrs, whom we must imitate if we wish to be saved at the Second Coming (1197–1246). The marauding lion who frightens Thisbe is the devil, which threatens the pure soul; God, like the lovers, without flinching suffers death to rescue his beloved mankind (1147–67). In this way, a narrative that appears *ad litteram* to be a cautionary exemplum about rashness and lust is ingeniously transformed into a parable of holiness. The errant young couple become a symbol, first of humanity and divinity joined in Christ, then of humanity at large redeemed in Christ.

What might such an ending have offered Chaucer? I propose that the absence of obvious verbal parallels, such as can be shown for the tale itself, does not disqualify the moralization from a position of influence upon Chaucer's treatment of the Thisbe material. The relevance of the moralization lies in the opening it creates for tone and treatment—an opening already hinted at in Ovid, and enlarged in the Old French *lai*. It is the possibility of comic irony, of an antisentimental approach to a sentimental story.

The Franciscan moralist who composed the *Ovide moralisé* was doubtless innocent of ironic intention: I have no wish to implicate him in that regard. Nonetheless, the comically painful ingenuity of his interpretation—transmogrifying a pair of lustful adolescents into the figure of the Savior—can hardly have escaped the attention of an ironist like Chaucer. The inadvertent comedy of the moralization is well exemplified in large and in small: not only in the overall interpretations, but in a passage as short as the few lines telling us that the devil, disguised as a lion,

> defoloit
> Et coloit la vie et la guimple
> De la belle jouvente simple.
> (1257–59)

> trampled
> and tore up the life and the wimple
> of the lovely girl so simple.

This is, of course, unfaithful to the tale just narrated, for the lion does not attack Thisbe. Moreover, it is rhetorically ridiculous to link life and wimple in zeugma, as absurd an anticlimax as any to be found in *The Rape of the Lock*. The difference is that Pope uses zeugma masterfully, to expose the trivializing consciousness of his characters and the superficiality of their social life, while the compiler of the *Ovide moralisé* uses it awkwardly, to eke out his line and produce a rhyme.

The gap between text and interpretation looms so large here, the text so readily escapes its Procrustean bed, that the sophisticated reader can but smile. Are we, after all, to avoid or to imitate? And what, exactly, would we imitate? The interpretation tells us to imitate patience and chastity, but the fable shows us something else. To be sure, the compiler of the *Ovide moralisé*, like many other Ovid

translators and commentators before and after him, had his own
agenda, his own ideological aesthetic, which governed his procedures. John P. McCall observes that although such interpretations
"may seem strained and capricious, they are based on an old tradition. . . . Their real kin is the exemplum or fable of late medieval
homiletics in which moral or spiritual lessons were freely and ingeniously developed without any real concern for the obvious meaning of a story or text" (*Chaucer*, 13–14).

Yet this tradition was already on the wane in Chaucer's day, for
the allegorical sensibility had come under attack from several directions, not least—for Chaucerian purposes—from the Wycliffites.[13]
Fausto Ghisalberti reminds us that such "intransigent pietism" was
destined to fail as a method of interpreting the classics; indeed, it
was already a lost battle in the fourteenth century, for the Church
would meet the challenge of reform by co-opting humanism, asserting itself as the continuator of the Latin literary and historical tradition. A little more than a century after Chaucer's death, Erasmus
wrote in a letter: "No one raises loud protests against the work of a
certain Dominican"—he means Bersuire—"crassly stupid though it
is, which gives a Christian adaption—distortion, rather—of all the
myths in Ovid."[14] In his well-known Prologue to Gargantua (1534),
Rabelais would ridicule "the allegories squeezed out of [Homer] by
Plutarch" and other scholars, "For I believe them to have been as
little dreamed of by Homer as the Gospel mysteries were by Ovid in
his *Metamorphoses*." I think it likely that the hermeneutic difficulties
of the method would have been evident also to Chaucer even a
century and a half before.

With its contradictions, its puns and rhetorical excess, the *Ovide
moralisé*—*lai* and moralization together—strongly reinforces the
subtle comic potential of the original Ovidian narrative. But if Chaucer was open to a comic interpretation of the material, it is because
of his own aesthetic purpose in the *Legend*. As the next section of
this chapter will show, the tale of Thisbe is not the only one in which
irony, comedy, or wordplay appear. The general function of comic

13. But see also my "Undoing Substantial Connection" and "The Politics of
Allegory" in *Medieval Literary Politics*, and Smalley, *Study of the Bible*, 281ff.
14. Erasmus, letter to Maarten Lips, 1518, in *Correspondence*, ed. Mynors, 23–24.
Bersuire was not a Dominican but a Benedictine.

technique in the legends is to undercut the directive of Eros and Alceste, and to prove the fallibility of any effort to portray human beings as entirely good. The idealization of women proposed by Eros requires to be deflated. Humor, particularly the humor of subtle obscenity, is an effective way to do it—not least because it can always be disavowed by an "innocent" Narrator, blamed on faithfully followed sources or even on the reader's own interpretive bent (or bent interpretation).

The God of Love's rigidity and his monomaniacal inadequacy of critical method find their duplicate in the *Ovide moralisé*. In the fissure between *lai* and moralization lies the confrontation of twelfth-century courtly poet and fourteenth-century Franciscan ideologue, of the Ovidian spirit and the Catholic Middle Ages. Complacently and with utter lack of self-consciousness, the Christian moralization of classical fable slices through the question that occupied Chaucer throughout his creative life: how can one derive truth from contradictory texts? Chaucer's retraction to the *Canterbury Tales* shows that he never completely resolved that dilemma: despite the fideistic stopgap, he attained no permanent sense of the full autonomy of fiction such as would have exculpated his "endytynges of worldly vanitees." Nor was he able, by way of the allegorical exegesis practised by some others, to reduce those "vanitees" to subordinate status and explain away their moral difficulties. Those difficulties, inherent in human discourse of "fals and soth compouned" (*HF* 2108), mean that for anyone other than a single-minded allegorist, there is no "naked text." (If I might digressively add another unverifiable subjective hypothesis to the discussion about which Prologue antedates which, I would opine that Chaucer's use of the term in G bespeaks the younger poet willing to risk a phrase later discarded because of its patent incompatibility with the legends, and indeed with any literary production.) It is not only translation that is the problem, but the original text, itself draped in rhetoric, cultural context, intention. Or if we are to imagine text as a naked body, we can only think of it as Protean, capable of infinite incarnations. But as I wrote above in commenting on Cixous, such essentialist metaphors propose some pure meaning preexisting any concrete embodiment. We can do without them, and I suspect that Chaucer too had felt their limitation, although for other reasons than ours: his impulse would not be to write them off because they are metaphysical, but to defer them until the metaphysical can come properly into its own.

As the epigraph I have chosen for this chapter suggests, the problem did not disappear, although it certainly dwindled. Some scholars think the irony or ambiguity in *Ariadne auf Naxos* is the product only of an ill-fitting collaboration, but I see in its jarring juxtaposition of styles—heroic opera framed in commedia dell'arte—rather the problem of *translatio studii* in a nineteenth-century perspective. The work is an opera within an opera about the difficulties of producing serious art in a philistine age. A theater company are commissioned to perform a short classically based opera at the palace of an official, but at the last minute are required to render the opera more entertaining by mixing into it elements of their more frivolous repertoire. This specific self-referentiality strikes me as quite consistent with the stylistic mix. We know now that the conflict of ancient heroic versus modern cynical values already represents a distortion of classicism, which was far from univocally committed to the heroic outlook. Nonetheless that conflict, the perceived incompatibility of cultures, is built into the opera, which elevates irony into a compositional principle. The partners may have feuded about whether their piece should end on a serious or an ironic note, but the damage was already done.

For Chaucer, too, dissonance would register the collision of the tectonic plates of his intellectual world, and the form of dissonance I want to turn to now is sexual wordplay within the pathetic tale. This is a particularly difficult phenomenon for many modern critics to accept, particularly those reared in the German-influenced Romantic school of thought that emphasized "organic unity" and "harmony" as prime criteria for aesthetic value. The rupture of tone created by the presence of wordplay, especially sexual wordplay, in a serious moral work or an elegant romance (e.g., Chaucer's *Troilus*) constitutes unacceptable tonal ambiguity for some scholars, causing them to reject the cultural and textual evidence for wordplay in works of the highest moral intention and aesthetic achievement (cf. my article "Anatomy of the Resisting Reader" on this problem). Nonetheless it has become a commonplace, particularly since Robert Jordan's contribution, that medieval aesthetics was precisely not organic and harmonious in method but rather architectural, juxtapositional, accumulative. Moreover, our rigid separation of "high" and "low" cultures was not always valid in the Middle Ages, as has been shown by modern scholarship on the audience of the fabliaux, bawdy stories enjoyed by nobles, bourgeois, and artisans alike. Mary Carruthers points out that interlingual pun was essential to the medieval visual *artes memoriae* (137 and elsewhere): not only was wordplay shared by elite and vulgar, it was, as a habit of mind, especially cultivated by the elite. In short, therefore, modern standards of "consistency" ought not to be imposed on medieval texts; it means that the medieval author might expect an educated audience to operate on several cognitive levels during a reading (or listening) experience. These are some of the principles brought into play in considering the rhetorical method and ideological purposes of sexual wordplay in the *Legend*.

THE LOGIC OF OBSCENITY

In the *Remedia amoris*, Ovid writes that certain of his contemporaries have attacked his work, censuring his muse as a wanton (*proterva* [365]). The poet's response is to accuse his critics of envy, for even the greatest poets have suffered the attacks of the envious, but every poet knows the importance of fitting style to sense. By way of Alceste, Chaucer too accuses some of his critics of envy, "lavendere of the court alway" (F 358). The irony is, though, that Chaucer would respond to his critics precisely with wantonness, indeed, with obscenity, using it to administer a salutary moral lesson as to the nature of nature.

Obscenity has as ancient and continuous a pedigree as wordplay does, and in fact is one of its commonest forms.[15] Obscenity appears in classical tragedy. It was a prominent feature in Attic comedy, whence it was later transferred by Ovid to erotic elegy. It had an important place in Roman comedy and mime and in the poetry of Ovid, Catullus, Martial, and others. During the so-called "Dark Ages," anality and involuntary nudity appear as stock motifs in Merovingian literary humor. There is the fabliau-like short prose

---

15. Again, because of the wealth of material, I refer the reader to the list in my "Logic of Obscenity" (200 n. 3) and to more recent material documented in "Anatomy of the Resisting Reader."

narrative of Liutprand, bishop of Cremona, offered in Erich Auerbach's discussion of late-Carolingian mannerism; there is what Peter Dronke calls "bawdy double-entendre in Samson's efforts at
milling" in the ninth-century didactic poem *De sobrietate*, and the
tenth-century dialogue-poem on Jezebel, with a theme of sexual
depravity and language to match (78–80, 126); there are the plays of
the German nun Hrotswitha, with their occasionally risqué plots.
Latin "elegiac comedy" of the twelfth century was frequently
obscene. Homosexuality, often treated comically, was a frequent
topos in medieval clerical lyric and other genres, as Chaucer was
aware from his reading of the *De planctu naturae* of Alanus de
Insulis. One of the best-known debates on homosexual versus heterosexual love, the Anglo-Latin debate of Ganymede and Helen,
survives in many manuscripts, including one at Cambridge University where it is bound with the rhetorical treatise by John of Garland. Some troubadour poets used obscenity: it might be crude and
overt as with William of Aquitaine, or indirect and punning as with
Arnaut Daniel. Andreas Capellanus used obscene imagery and pun
in *De arte honesti amandi*, and French popular literature is full of
obscene humor in its fabliaux, songs, riddles, and jokes. The *Roman
de la rose* was considered by some contemporaries of Chaucer to be
pornographic in its forthright defense of vulgar anatomical terms
and in its allegorical representation of coitus. Even the French epic
does not escape the occasional grossity.

Like his other works, the *Heroides* of Ovid—a key source and
model for Chaucer's *Legend*—poses a sharp challenge to literary
decorum. Florence Verducci observes that "the wit and comic irrev-
erence" in Ovid's treatment of his seduced and abandoned heroines
have struck many readers as transgressive, obtrusive, or self-
indulgent: "capricious violations of an obligatory decorum" (4, 6).
Rather, Verducci proposes:

> The rule of Ovid's *Heroides* is the rule of indecorum, or wit in concep-
> tion no less than in language, a wit which is not his heroine's own but
> the token of the author's creative presence in the poem. Its dispas-
> sionate, intellectual, emotionally anaesthetizing presence is a con-
> stant reminder of how far we, in our sympathy for a heroine, have
> departed from the traditional view of her situation, and it is a con-
> stant goad to the dissociation of emotional appreciation from formal
> articulation. It is the medium by which our understanding of Ovid's

heroines becomes psychologized and historicized, the medium by which their speech becomes present as the empiric fact which inevitably overflows the confines of stable categories. (32)

My premise, like Verducci's, is that in the hands of an accomplished writer, rhetorical devices such as wit, wordplay, and obscenity have, like any other stylistic device, a logic of their own, an aesthetic reason for being. In the *Legend of Good Women*, that reason is to extend into poetic practice the aesthetic credo established in the Prologue to the poem. As a poet faithful to the contradictions inherent in nature, Chaucer has produced a series of legends perfectly integrated with the Prologue in their subversion of the reductive propagandistic task laid on the Narrator by Eros: to portray women as nothing but good. What the poet offers instead is a view of woman as no more and no less than a natural creature: a "maculate muse," to borrow Jeffrey Henderson's phrase. Slicing through the vapid formulae of courtly love with surgical astringency, dissolving the whitewashed version of womanhood that the Narrator has been ordered to produce, obscenity helps to reestablish what I believe Chaucer considered a healthier equilibrium: a more balanced, accurate, and "natural" view of women than could be provided by either courtly love or its inverse, clerical misogyny. Nature is not without its own balance; after all, the basis of medieval medical theory is the balance of humors in the body. We are reminded of this perspective when the Narrator cites the Aristotelian principle—"vertu is the mene, / As Etik seith" (F 165–66)—in describing the equilibration of danger (Daunger) and pity, mercy and justice (Ryght), innocence and courtliness (Curtesye) in the ultimately harmonious lovemaking and song of the small fowls. In this context, sexuality, sexual wordplay, and obscenity have their place. I am reminded of the paradoxically sanitizing function of Harry Bailly's anal and genital obscenities to the Pardoner (VI.948–55), the effect of which is to annihilate the Pardoner's attempt to bilk his fellow pilgrims. If we may speak there of the morality of obscenity, in the *Legend* we must speak of its aesthetic.

Edmund Spenser was doubly wrong, then, in referring to Chaucer as "well of English undefiled" (*Faerie Queene* 4.2.32): wrong with respect to foreign vocabulary, wrong with respect to "low" humor. Haldeen Braddy also erred in asserting that Chaucer's obscenity is

"hearty and robust, without snigger or leer" (216), for there is, in
the legends, plenty of snigger and leer. Perhaps Lord Byron had
noticed this, for he considered Chaucer "obscene and contemptible:
he owes his celebrity merely to his antiquity" (Spurgeon, 29). For-
tunately, we can do better than Spenser's adulation or Byron's
disdain by granting wordplay the honorable place it occupied
among classical and medieval rhetorical devices. In extending to the
rest of the legends the line of research begun in the previous section
with Thisbe, I shall first briefly indicate my findings, then specify
the "purple passages" in consecutive order through the legends
(omitting Thisbe), and lastly suggest some conclusions.

I have not considered as obscene those cases where sex is clearly
intended but coyly circumlocuted; therefore I shall not list such
common euphemisms for sexual activity as "grace," "ease," "labor," "refreshment," "dalliance," or "play." What I have looked for
is places where an anal or genital interpretation of a word, line, or
image is clearly not the first level of meaning, but where a sexual
innuendo is created alongside the literal and non-sexual sense,
usually by the presence of a cluster of ambiguous words or suggestive images. In a few cases an actual pun is produced that makes
coherent sense on two levels of meaning (*significatio* or *paronomasia*).
More often, though, the wordplay is homophonic (*annominatio*): the
sexual term has no coherent grammatical meaning in the sentence
but constitutes instead a free-floating referent or gratuitous association, with the effect, more or less, of an elbow in the ribs. A third
category relies less on language than on an image or situation that
provokes erotic associations. In all these categories, the terms are
primarily anal and genital, the latter referring to both male and
female organs and activity. Homosexuality appears, but not prominently, although to be certain of this we would require more familiarity with the language of gay subculture in medieval England than
is presently available. I found no outright scatology. This is somewhat surprising for a period when scatology was a staple of popular
humor; but our text is not a popular but a courtly production.

Skeptics in the matter of Chaucerian obscenity will naturally
welcome my assurance that not all occurrences in Chaucer (or in
other authors) of the words or images discussed here are necessarily sexual puns. "A word is known by the company it keeps,"

Hilda Hulme remarked, writing of Shakespeare (100).[16] All of my examples occur in clusters. Where we find one word isolated in a passage, there skepticism is at least legitimate, but where we find three, or ten, possible double entendres in a passage, we must perforce accept the probability of authorial complicity. There are also numerous non-sexual puns in the legends, which I shall mention in Chapter 5 in order to show that wordplay is very much part of Chaucer's deliberate rhetorical strategy.

In the first legend, that of Cleopatra, Chaucer devotes about a quarter of his brief narrative to a curiously detailed account of the battle of Actium. The passage contains these lines:

> And from the top doun come the grete stones.
> In goth the grapenel, so ful of crokes . . .
>   (639–40)

The stones will be used as weapons. Yet "stones" also means "testicles"; we recall Harry Bailly's words to the Nun's Priest: "I-blessed be thy breche, and every stoon!" (VII.3448). The grapnel, which is going in (to the water) is a small anchor with several "crokes." A "croke" is a curved segment or a bar with knobbed top; according to the *Middle English Dictionary*, the word is used "allusively" of the male genital.

Is it sheer coincidence that these two lines contain possible references to male genitalia? I think not. The context here is a military scenario sexually suggestive by virtue of its placement in the narrative, its verbal rhythms, its actual content of frenzied confrontational activity, and other aspects of its imagery. Nautical imagery, especially that of naval battle, is among the most enduringly popular images for sexual congress, from Attic comedy to Shakespeare and beyond.[17] John Fyler remarks that Chaucer recounts the battle

---

16. The same point about context is made by Archibald A. Hill, who attempts to establish some sensible guidelines for deciding what is wordplay. Yet a lot is left open to subjectivity, temperament, or interpretive bias in Hill's advice (adapting Ockham's razor) to multiply meanings only upon "need" and only when there is "contextual support." In "Anatomy of the Resisting Reader," I take up in some depth the questions of interpretive bias and tonal context.

17. Jeffrey Henderson lists nearly five pages of nautical wordplay from Attic comedy (161–66); Molly Myerowitz provides another list of scholarly references for "sea imagery in erotic contexts," especially Ovid (207–8 n. 20); Eric Partridge gives numerous examples (36 and glossary).

"in place of the wedding" (100)—the wedding having been dealt with in an *occupatio*—and it is an ironically appropriate replacement because of its sexual imagery. Here is the complete passage:

> And in the se it happede hem to mete.
> Up goth the trompe, and for to shoute and shete,
> And peynen hem to sette on with the sunne.
> With grysely soun out goth the grete gonne,
> And heterly they hurtelen al atones,
> And from the top doun come the grete stones.
> In goth the grapenel, so ful of crokes;
> Among the ropes renne the sherynge-hokes.
> In with the polax presseth he and he;
> Byhynde the mast begynnyth he to fle,
> And out ageyn, and dryveth hym overbord;
> He styngeth hym upon his speres ord;
> He rent the seyl with hokes lyke a sithe;
> He bryngeth the cuppe, and biddeth hem be blythe;
> He poureth pesen upon the haches slidere;
> With pottes ful of lyme they gon togidere;
> And thus the longe day in fyght they spende . . .
>
> (634–50)

The ships meet, up goes the trumpet, out comes the big gun, down come the stones, in goes the grapnel with its phallic crooks, the men press in. There is a pouring forth—of peas;[18] then a sticky white substance appears—lime, to be sure—and the opponents "go together." This last is a common synonym (says the *MED*) for copulation; indeed it is a calque for the Latin *coire*, the root of our present word "coitus." We find a contextual illustration in Higden's portrait of the barbaric Irish, some of whose ancestors were "vitio coeundi cum bestiis consuetissimos" (1.35); the modest Trevisa does not translate but gives "coeuntes cum brutis." We might well translate "go together" as "come together," maintaining the pun. The episode is summarized this way: "And thus the longe day in fyght they spende" (650). "Fyght" (fight) is homophonic with "fyked," past tense of "fykken," "to fuck," and if Saussure was right in observing that "nothing enters language without having been tested in speaking" (168), then we may and ought to assume that the word "fuck"

---

18. Scholars are not agreed whether peas or pitch would actually have been poured on deck in a medieval battle; both are called *pois* in French, and there is some precedent for both. See *Riverside* note to line 648.

(or a cognate), first attested in print in 1503, was already in oral circulation in Chaucer's day. While the secondary meaning would be ungrammatical here and so not a true pun, the homophony itself is the point, especially in context of the rest of the passage.[19]

The story of Cleopatra ends with the cryptic remark by the Narrator, "I preye God let oure hedes nevere ake!" A similar comment appears twice in *Troilus*, both times connected with lovemaking. The first locus is a sentence that Pandarus puts into Troilus's mouth in the fiction he concocts for Crideyde's benefit. Troilus, he says, was sleeping; Pandarus wakes him with a reproach of dullness; Troilus is then reported to have replied, "Ye, frend, do ye your hedes ake / For love, and lat me lyven as I kan" (2.549–50). I note here that the word is "heads," plural; and that Troilus is clearly contrasting his (loveless) condition with that of his uncle: "for love" means "because of love" and not necessarily because of its absence, and indeed we already know that Troilus considers Pandarus an expert in love. The second locus is 3.1561, where Pandarus coyly remarks to his niece that "som of us, I trowe, hire hedes ake." He is speaking on one level about himself, who, because of the rainstorm, has been unable to sleep well, but on another level he is making a mildly obscene jest (as he had Troilus do in the first locus). When we realize that in medieval medical anatomy, the tip of the penis was called the *caput virgae* (head of the penis), the comments in both *Troilus* and "Cleopatra" take on another dimension: it is a genital ache, the result of overindulgence. This usage is amply documented in medical literature, and in connection with another sexual metaphor it makes up an interestingly complex piece of late-medieval sex-gender lore. If men can be said to have two heads,

19. Ernst Curtius's section on *annominatio,* or homophony, shows that the device was highly recommended in the medieval *artes* and widely used in vernacular poetry (278–80). It is particularly profuse in Dante's *Commedia.* "Fuck" is rather a ghost word in Middle English. The 1503 attestation is from Dunbar, "Ane Brash of Wowing." The *OED* claims that the German word cannot be shown to be related to the English, yet it posits "a Middle English type, *fuken,* which is not found." The *MED* has several homophones with other meanings, one of which is "to flatter or deceive." If the obscene sense is admitted, this would produce a pun in Ballad 82 of Carleton Brown's *English Lyrics of the XIIIth Century* (Oxford: Clarendon Press, 1932): "Wymmon, war the with the swyke / That feir ant freoly ys to fyke" (25–26). A last remark in this digression: the Latin word for a priest's concubine was *focaria* (from *focus,* "hearth," hence "housekeeper"); "fuck" could thus be a back-formation from *focaria,* "fucker." But this still would not account for the apparent absence of occurrences in Middle English.

women can be said to have two mouths and two tongues (vagina as mouth, clitoris as tongue); this explains why men are more reasonable than women, and women more loquacious than men (Pouchelle, 311–12).[20]

The tale of Dido unfolds under the eye of Venus, the anti-hero's mother, and it is suffused with sexuality. All is "amorous lokyng" and "lusty folk," sighing and kneeling, pity and gentilesse. The bed is a primary *locus dramatis* and site for important conversations, confrontations, and laments. As if to underline the copulatory theme, the poet uses the word "prick" twice in the twenty lines just preceding the consummation of his protagonists' desire. Between these two occurrences appears the image of "the fomy brydal" (1208) of Aeneas's horse; so that the cluster is prick-foam-prick, with a possible homophonic play on bridle/bridal. Although "prick" as a noun would not come into documented literary use as a sexual term until the sixteenth century, nonetheless the verb—meaning to spur, prod, stimulate, or ride hard—was in Chaucer's day well enough known as a sexual metaphor to occur with obvious erotic meaning in the *Reeve's Tale* (4231) and in popular ballads (cf. Robbins, nos. 28 and 32). We may recall furthermore that if the word "die" were still current as a euphemism for orgasm (as it was in Chaucer's time), we would hear the heroine's name a little differently: "Die, do!"

Jason's treatment of Hypsipyle is both an economic and a sexual betrayal. The economic dimension is appropriate to this mythic hero whose quest was for the Golden Fleece—an item not only precious in itself, but glossed by at least one Ovid-commentator (whose work Chaucer knew) as *divitias temporales*.[21] Chaucer is able to turn the idea into a little negative exemplum of masculine sexual

---

20. The womb/mouth and "head" of penis are also profusely documented in Jacquart and Thomasset. For other uses of the head/penis image, cf. Thomas Gascoigne's mid-fifteenth-century "Theological Dictionary," 136. Here Gascoigne writes of the hideous genital effects of diseases caused by lechery; these include *caput virgae abscindere*. This is the well-known passage, incidentally, in which John of Gaunt is said to be a diseased fornicator. (There is no evidence he was diseased, and Gascoigne had political reasons to revile him.) Also cf. the fifteenth-century play *Mankind*, ed. Mark Eccles, *The Macro Plays*, EETS, o.s., 262 (1969), line 497.

21. This is the phrase of Bersuire in book 7 of his *Ovidius moralizatus*, 109. Bersuire goes on to add *et maxime divitias ecclesiae*, with Jason as (among many other things) *bonus praelatum* who wishes *ad ecclesias praebendas pervenire*. He was a Benedictine, so this defense of ecclesiastical wealth is not surprising. The *Ovide moralisé* (7.690ff.) gives quite a different interpretation.

economics. Jason bribes the queen's counselors so as to win her affection and her fortune; then he "tok of hir substaunce / What so hym leste" (1560–61). Now "substance" meant property or wealth, and Hypsipyle is a lady of substance. But the word also meant physical matter of a more intimate kind—semen, specifically—and this gives a true pun. As Michel Foucault points out, this equivalency, or "very pronounced ambiguity between the sexual meaning and the economic meaning of certain terms" (*Care of the Self*, 27) is already present in the Greek language; it would be carried forward in the medical works of Galen: "Thus, the word *sōma*, which designates the body, also refers to riches and possessions; whence the possible equivalence between the 'possession' of a body and the possession of wealth. *Ousia* is substance and fortune; it is also semen and sperm: the loss of the latter may mean expenditure of the former" (ibid.). In medieval times, the accepted medical and popular view of female sexual physiology was that female "semination" was required for conception to occur. This belief extended back to the Romans and would survive well into the sixteenth century.[22] We know that the emission of substance has occurred in the Chaucerian case, for we are told that Jason begat two children "upon" (another pun) Hypsipyle. I might add that, in *Troilus*, Chaucer had already exploited the word "substance" in a magnificent multiple pun that plays on the propertarian, philosophical, and sexual senses of two words. When Troilus tries to persuade Criseyde to elope with him, he argues that "folie is, whan man may chese, / For accident his substaunce ay to lese" (4.1505): accident and substance as chance and wealth, as physical properties and ontological essence, as involuntary ejaculation and semen.

In the legend of Lucrece, there is some suggestiveness in two places. During the rape, Lucrece faints and therefore "feleth no thyng, neyther foul ne fayr" (1818). If it seems odd to imply, as these lines do, that had she not fainted she might have felt something "fair"—that is, pleasurable—we may recall that no less an authority than St. Augustine had accused Lucrece of possibly experiencing "the pleasure of the act" (*City of God* 1.19). Moreover, if we read the cited line aloud, appreciating that "no" and "thing" are two distinct words, not combined into one as we pronounce it today, then "thing" emerges with a certain clarity and we recognize it as the common synonym for the genital.

Then, during her suicide, Lucrece carefully arranges her clothing as she falls, "Lest that hir fet or suche thyng lay bare" (1859). This covering is a classical topos, as Nicole Loraux points out (59). Chaucer imitates it from Ovid's *Fasti* (2.833–34), his main source for this tale, where Lucrece is careful to fall properly; he may have noticed it also in the *Metamorphoses*, where the sacrificed Polyxena takes care, while falling, to cover those parts that should be concealed and thus to conserve her chaste modesty (13.479–80). In the *Monk's Tale*, Chaucer has Julius Caesar cover himself while dying. There is nothing salacious in the passage, but there does not need to be, for the Narrator is quite explicit that Caesar covers "his hypes" in order to conceal "his privetee" (2715). With Lucrece, the heroine's impulse is modesty, but when the Chaucerian Narrator mentions first feet, then "or suche thyng," he sets in motion a train of upward associations in the reader's mind: associations not negated but affirmed in the Caesar treatment. Significantly, when Gower treats the Lucretia story, he clears up all such ambiguity, carefully specifying that when the heroine straightens her clothing it is so that nothing can be seen "dounward fro the kne" (Gower, *Confessio amantis* 7.5073).

I am able to locate only one outright sexual pun in "Lucrece": "The husbonde knew the estris wel and fyn" (1715). "Estris" means interior or hidden places, normally of a garden or courtyard, but figuratively perhaps of a human body. The same play appears in the *Romaunt of the Rose*, where Belacueil shows the lover "The estres of the swote place" (3626). The place is a hedged verger or little pleasure garden from which the lover has previously been excluded by Daungier (the lady's withholding of love). Now, however, he is given permission "overal to go" so that he is "raysed . . . / Fro helle into paradys" in the traditional courtly vocabulary of consummation or prolonged physical contact. The exegetical and lyrical tradition originating in commentary upon the *Song of Songs* would have prepared the way for such a parallel between lady and garden; Chaucer's understanding of this tradition is evident in the *Merchant's Tale*. The moralization of the Lucrece-story in *Gesta Romanorum* (#135), in which Lucretia is glossed as the soul "and the castle represents the heart, into which [Sextus, the devil] enters" also, in its use of body allegory, opens the way to the potential duality of "estris." (Robert Frank has suggested this as a possible source for Chaucer's version; see Chapter 5 below.) The Florentine politician and humanist Coluccio Salutati—a contemporary of Chaucer's—also made much of secret places in his short *Declamatio Lucretiae*, an exchange of speeches between Lucretia and her kinsmen just before her suicide. Part of their dissuasion consists in assuring the rape victim that she has protected her chastity "non solum in nominum oculis sed etiam in secretis domus penetralibus" ("not only in the eyes of men but even in the most secret chambers of the house" [79]). Chaucer may well have known this popular early work by Salutati, but the interesting point here is rather his displacement of secret inner places into a context (husband's knowledge) especially susceptible of sexual interpretation.

Moving on to Ariadne, we pick up the thread again (if I may borrow an image central to that legend): anal and genital obscenity, with a hint of voyeurism. Theseus is imprisoned next to a "foreyne" (1962), or toilet, belonging to Ariadne and Phaedra. There is no dramatic reason for this detail—it is original with Chaucer—except perhaps to titillate: for if the princesses from their quarters can overhear Theseus lament, does it not follow that he in turn must overhear them when nature calls?

Later, when Phaedra plans to help Theseus, there follows a passage of twenty lines loaded with obscene imagery:

"Lat us wel taste hym at his herte-rote,
That if so be that he a wepen have,
Wher that he dar, his lyf to kepe and save,
Fyghten with the fend, and hym defende. . . .
If that he be a man, he shal do so.
And we shul make hym balles ek also
Of wex and tow, that whan he gapeth faste,
Into the bestes throte he shal hem caste . . .
This wepen shal the gayler, or that tyde,
Ful prively withinne the prysoun hyde;
And for the hous is krynkeled to and fro,
And hath so queynte weyes for to go . . ."
(1993–2013)

The first line of this passage is, literally, "Let us taste him at his heart-root"; more idiomatically, "Let us test his character"—or feel or enjoy it. What is the object of this feeling, tasting, testing, or enjoyment? Heart has a well-established connection with lust and genitality, not least because, as a fourteenth-century medical hand-book points out, "the risynge of a mannes yerde cometh of a mannes herte" (Lanfranc, 174); and, as Chaucer reminds us in the General Prologue to the *Canterbury Tales,* some such connection holds even for birds. For Shakespeare, Eric Partridge glosses "root" unhesitatingly as "either penis or penis erectus" (176), and this meaning seems the likely one when, in the *Romaunt of the Rose,* the lover feels his "herte rote" (1026) affected by the memory of his lady's "every membre." Clearly, then, Princess Phaedra's project has strong genital overtones, and she goes on to speculate about the ups and downs of penile virility. If Theseus had a "wepen," and "if that he be a man," they will discover whether "he dar . . . Fyghten" in the place where "he shal descende." "We shul make hym balles" (2003), proclaims Phaedra—balls of wax and string, to be sure. But the word meant then exactly what it does now, its possible sexual referent providing the pun in a fifteenth-century lyric, "None but she my bales may bete" (none but she may amend my suffering / beat my balls / restore to health my balls).[23] In any case, the new balls will be cast into the minotaur's throat: another hint of oral-genital contact. The princess describes the labyrinth as "krynkeled" (convoluted); it has "queynte" turns: the first adjective imagistically allusive of, the second a possible synonym or euphemism for the female genital.

Eventually Theseus does outwit the monster, thanks to "His wepne, his clewe, his thyng" (2140). The repetition here is sus-picious, particularly since "weapon" and "thing" are well-known euphemisms for the male genital, and I suspect that, framed be-tween them, "clew" (ball) shares their meaning. A riddle illus-trates the popular understanding of the word "thing"; it is post-Chaucerian, but other texts demonstrate continuity of meaning:

> Thus my riddel doth begin:
> a mayde woulde have a thinge to putte in
> and with her hande she brought it to:

---

23. Robbins, no. 127. See also "For of my ploughe the beste stotte is balle" in Furnivall, *Jyl of Breyntford's Testament,* 36. Attributed by John Shirley (1366–1456) to Chaucer, the piece is an extended play on plowing as metaphor for sexual activity, with much emphasis on "ball."

> it was so meek, it would not do,
> and at length she used it so
> that to the hole she made it go.
> when it had done as she could wish
> Ah ha! quoth she, I'm gladde of this.[24]

The answer is "A maid went to thread a needle," but the point obviously depends on the audience assuming that "thing" refers to the male genital. It might, of course, in other cases refer to the female genital, as the Wife of Bath affirms in using the common French euphemism "bele chose" (III.447).

Philomela's appears to be the only story not undercut by irony, obscenity or tedious writing. To my mind it is written with genuine integrity and power. Perhaps Chaucer found this horrifying material too strong for irony, and in Chapter 5 I shall offer further discussion of it.

In Phyllis, several images suggest homoerotic and heterosexual copulation: Demophon is assaulted from behind by a wind that shoves so sore his sail cannot stand (2412); the sea pushes Demophon "now up, now doun" (2420), anticipating his later "doynge to and fro" (2471) with Phyllis; twice he is almost "at the deth," and Phyllis refers to "youre anker, which ye in oure haven leyde" (2501: cf. Cowen, "Chaucer's *Legend of Good Women*, Lines 2501–3"). There is also a syntactic ambiguity that lends a somewhat salacious tone to the following lines:

> [Demophon] doth with Phillis what so that hym leste,
> As wel coude I, if that me leste so,
> Tellen al his doynge to and fro.
>
> (2469–71)

Here I do not want to pinpoint only the "doynge to and fro," with its reminder of the old sexual in-and-out, but also the double take required to understand that the adverbial clause "as wel coude I" applies not to what precedes it ("doth," etc.) but to what follows ("tellen"). Even with different punctuation (always an editorial option) or with "And" instead of "as" (as in Skeat's edition), the ambiguity holds.

24. Furnivall found the riddle in an early seventeenth-century volume and printed it in *Love-Poems and Humourous Ones*, 21. The riddle is doubtless older than the volume.

In the last legend, Chaucer erroneously gives Hypermnestra's cousin and husband Lynceus the name Lyno, which is close to the Latin for whoremaster ("leno"). But since the reading "Lino" occurs in several Italian source manuscripts, and the *Ovide moralisé* has "Lynus" (2.4721 and elsewhere), we cannot assume this was other than an innocent mistake (although from his reading of Ovid, Chaucer would certainly have been aware of the meaning of the Latin word).

Probably the most obvious conclusion to be drawn from this brief study of sexual wordplay in the legends is that an interpretation of the *Legend of Good Women* that dismisses irony or humor simply ignores the linguistic facts. For too long the weighty authority of J. L. Lowes had a suppressive effect, encouraging scholars to see the work as little more than an occasional piece, a courtly jeu d'esprit. In the contest with Harold Goddard, whose monograph on the *Legend* Lowes aimed to refute, contemporary scholarship must, I think, belatedly offer the palm to Goddard. One might not accept all of Goddard's ideas on the poem—Eleanor Winsor offers a substantial critique (8ff.)—but his general interpretation and many specifics (e.g., the medieval ambivalence or negativity about several of Chaucer's "good" women) anticipated some of the recent scholarship on the poem. And to open the poem to irony—the play of language—is to open it to the play of critical theory, to treat it as a methodological field in which we can explore tradition and originality, textuality and the literary figuration of women.

I believe we also need to remember that Chaucer was a different kind of Christian than anyone can be today: a medieval Catholic. Between him and ourselves falls the long shadow of Calvinism, and even Catholicism has not been unaffected by it. The Puritan fact has decisively shaped many critics' notion of what it is to be a poet, a great poet, a moral Christian poet. But the universality for which Chaucer's religion names itself is not only geographical but also conceptual. Catholicism is large and inclusive (although in saying so I do not mean to exempt Chaucer or the clerical component of his culture from my own distrust of idealism and metaphysics). Catholicism makes a point of containing what look to us like impossible contradictions. Some of these are its basic mysteries, like the incarnation of Christ as Jesus, or the coexistence in one female body of virginity and maternity. With concepts like these at its base, small

wonder that Catholic culture in the Middle Ages generated a literary art so full of the verbal paradoxes and the disruptions of logic
and syntax that are the special consequences of wordplay; or, for
that matter, a sacred architecture that can incorporate images of
common, vulgar, and even obscene behavior (see Chapter 5). Moreover, Catholicism had means of interpretation that, as we have
seen, could turn nearly any text to the uses of instruction. This is
why it is clear, as Ralph Hexter writes, "that in the monasteries and
in the schools within their walls there was not the antipathy to eros
with which contemporary imagination credits them, nor even the
squeamishness many nineteenth- and twentieth-century scholars
have shown or felt compelled to show when dealing with certain
aspects of the classics" (25).

It is desire—Cupid, the god of love—who commands Chaucer's
Narrator to rewrite woman all goodness, patience, and faith. So
might any of us wish it to be about ourselves or our partners and
about love. Indeed, swayed by desire, we may well imagine it to be
so. Yet we learn eventually that besides desire there is nature, there
is experience, there is literary or rhetorical tradition, there is social
custom. The obscene language in the legends reminds us of these
other dimensions. Subtly, but stubbornly, it denies us the easy
utopian formulas of blind desire. Paradise can be had—but not
now. Adam and Eve went naked in the garden, but we do not. Our
language must be as veiled with its history, and with our intentionality, as our bodies with the garments that bespeak—precisely by
concealing—its history, its intentionality.

The desire for "naked text" has been explosively and notoriously
brought to our attention by the death sentence meted out by Islamic
orthodoxy to the novelist Salman Rushdie in retaliation for his
examination of that very problem in *The Satanic Verses* (1988). Islam
is far more strictly a textual religion than Christianity or Judaism.
The latter consider the revelation contained in their holy books to be
filtered through human perception and representation, hence receptive to, indeed, often requiring, interpretation of various kinds
(whether numerological, allegorical, historical, etc.). This indeed
was the problematic Augustine engaged in *De doctrina Christiana*,
where he writes that Scripture was translated "for the salvation of
peoples who desired to find in it nothing more than the thoughts
and desires of those who wrote it and through these the will of God,

according to which we believe those writers spoke" (2.5.6). Islam, on the other hand, considers its holy book, the Qur'an, an exact transcription of God's revelation to the Prophet Muhammad through the words of the angel Gabriel, and the only correct copy of Gabriel's dictation: "nought i-write with manis ynke," as Ranulf Higden put it (quoting "Mahometus"), "but with angelis hondes" (5.14). As the speech of God, the Qur'an is eternal and uncreated in its essence and meaning (though created in its linguistic particularity of letters and sounds). The Prophet himself is perfect. Hence there is no possibility of error or interpretation or disagreement—a position that ups the ante considerably: all the way, in fact, as shown by the extremists' will to murder Rushdie or any other "blasphemer." Islam veils its women but strips its holy text naked. This may seem paradoxical, but the link is the refusal of reality and of nature. The life-threatening presence of this apparent paradox marks the inadequacy of our metaphorization of text as body or body as text. In the end, a body is not a text nor the reverse. To insist too far on metaphor is to occlude reality, hence to risk sentimentalism; and in its extremest forms, sentimentalism kills. If we had any doubt about that, the Rushdie affair must lay it to rest. Rushdie shares more than a name with the famous Cordovan Aristotle-commentator Averroës (Ibn-Rushd, 1126–1198). Yet the medieval rationalistic Muslim survived his writing quite peacefully, whereas the modern one has been condemned to death for no more than the sin of historicizing. Never can it have been less merely rhetorical to wish a man a long life.

4

Different and Same

My indecision is final.
Samuel Goldwyn

In earlier chapters I have written about how Chaucer's poem uses the first two terms of its title, "legend" and "good." Chapter 1 proposed that the hagiographical legend is parodied (but not ridiculed) as hypotext to the *Legend*'s hypertext, present as a foil against which the Chaucerian personae play out their parts. Goodness, I suggested in Chapters 2 and 3, is problematized as a relative and temporal phenomenon, ever falling short of any absolutely ideal expression.

It is now time to turn to the third term in Chaucer's title, "women," and observe its treatment in the lives narrated in the main body of the poem, which, because of the length, richness, and intrinsic interest of the Prologue, tends to appear as an appendage to the Prologue. Formally, the collection of portraits is incomplete, breaking off in midsentence, and after only nine tales. Rhetorically, it might also be seen as incomplete because it lacks physical description of any lady whose misfortune is narrated (except Lucrece, who is said to have "yelwe her" [1747], as she does in Ovid's *Fasti* 2.763). To be sure, these ladies were generally not described in the traditional representations either: they are, after all, exemplary figures with moral and situational resonance irrelevant to specific appearance (other than general beauty). This is already, therefore, an imperfect and somewhat disappointing literary corpus, perhaps in its very imperfection formally miming a male, Catholic, and courtly writer's understanding of both women and language. It remains only to add that my metaphorization of text as body is no gratuitous modernism but has its precedent in medieval Ovid commentary and elsewhere. "Enides, id est Meleager, filius Enei . . . hanc fabulam require in corpore," advises one commentary on the *He-*

roides ("Oenides: that is, Meleager, son of Oeneus . . . look for this story in the body"). The lemma is from the epistle of Phaedra (*Her.* 4.99); the directive—similar to Chaucer's directives—sends the reader to "*Ovidius maior, Metamorphoses* 8.260 ff." (Hexter, 245 n. 54). The Ovidian text, then, is already a body in the commentary tradition, and some Christian instances of the text-as-body metaphor have been gathered by Carolyn Dinshaw. Yet whether Chaucer found the metaphor or reinvented it, it is one he was able to turn most effectively to his own investigation of gender, language, and morality.

DIFFERENCE: THE BALADE

One way in which the *Legend of Good Women* reshapes the title term "women" is by refusing rigid gender demarcation: blurring the lines, exchanging the roles. Chaucer's massive debt to Ovid in this poem has been acknowledged by virtually every scholar who has written on it, and Ovid does a good deal to even up the odds of gender. This is particularly true in the *Ars amatoria*, of which the third book aims at a female audience, and which, even in its first two books, stresses the importance of female desire and female pleasure, including foreplay and orgasm (e.g., 2.679–732). Woman may be the hunter and man the prey (3.558–60, 591, 669) as well as the more typical reverse. The *Remedia amoris*, sequel and palinode to the *Ars*, ends with the assurance that its therapeutic lessons will have cured both man and woman: "Carmine sanati femina virque meo." As for *Heroides*, not only are three of the epistles uttered by men, but portraits of female desire and initiative are prominent, and one of the epistles (9, Deianeira to Hercules) concentrates on the hero's adoption of woman's dress and labor.

Of the many formats through which Ovid was known to the high and late Middle Ages, one was the commentary on his works. We have already encountered (Chapters 2 and 3) prose and verse commentaries on the *Metamorphoses* in the *Ovide moralisé* and in the work of Pierre Bersuire, but all of Ovid's other works were commented on as well, and these texts tell us a good deal about medieval Ovid interpretation. They are all, for example, agreed that in the *Heroides*, Ovid, as self-defined *praeceptor amoris* ("love's instructor" [*Ars* 1.17], and not—as context makes clear—what Philip Roth might call a "professor of desire") expresses an intention that is genuinely moral and didactic: "per hanc monere ne qua stulte et illicite diligat, ne propter similem culpam similem penam incurrat" ("to warn [one] lest [one] love foolishly and illicitly, so that because of the same fault [as the characters, one] might not incur the same pain"). While this statement is from a comment on Epistle 17 (Helen to Paris),[1] the *accessus,* or introductions, to the commentaries make the same point. The scholia are equally sure that Ovid's moral was intended for men and women alike:

> Ethice supponitur: loquitur enim de moribus tam heroum heroidibus scribentium quam heroidum, idest matronarum, heroibus, idest viris, scribentium.[2]

> This is the ethical application: it tells as much about the behavior of heroines writing to heroes, as of heroes (that is, husbands/men) writing to heroines (that is, wives).

> Intentio huius operis est reprehendere masculos et feminas stulto et illicito amore detentos. (Huygens, 29)

> The intention of this work is to censure men and women enthralled by foolish and illicit love.

Nor is the Christian literary corpus without cross-dressing, so to speak. As Caroline Bynum has shown, the use of female imagery to describe God, Jesus, and even abbots was a well-established practice in high-medieval devotional writing, particularly among the Cistercians and including such authors as Anselm of Canterbury and Bernard of Clairvaux. Moreover, as James A. Brundage points out, canon lawyers from the twelfth century on "flatly rejected the postulate of female inferiority and insisted instead that men and women had precisely equal rights and obligations . . . both within marriage and outside of it" (67). Whatever Chaucer's textual in-

---

1. Hexter, 286, from the T2 (Tegernsee) commentary on *Epistulae Heroidum;* my translation, in which I have deliberately reproduced the genderless quality of the original. Further on Ovid commentaries and their literary influence, see Desmond's special issue of *Mediaevalia* on "Ovid in Medieval Culture," especially articles by Frank T. Coulson, Ralph Hexter, and Barbara Nolan.

2. Hexter, 223, from *accessus* to *Epistulae Heroidum.* Hexter comments that "from the very first words of the manuscript, students were presented with the idea that Ovid's purpose in the *Epistulae heroidum* was to castigate both men and women involved in foolish and illegal love affairs" (154).

spiration, I shall argue that his practice reflects both the medieval academic understanding of Ovid as ethical poet and the mixed messages about women contained in orthodox Christian doctrine.

Already in *Troilus* we have had a hero who, despite his valor on the field, becomes almost pathologically passive in his relationships with male friend and female lover. He is manipulated by both of them; he is seduced and abandoned; it is he who weeps and laments. In the *Legend*, commissioned by its fictional sponsors as a palinode to *Troilus*, Eros and Alceste require that this role allocation be reversed, back to what Eros defines as the "correct" version, and in five of the lives it is. These are the tales of Dido, Hypsipyle, Medea, Ariadne, and Phyllis, all abandoned. Of the remaining five heroines, two are raped—Lucrece and Philomela—while for three—Cleopatra, Thisbe, and Hypermnestra—there is no question of abuse or abandonment. In its self-reported genesis, then, gender role-reversal (from male to female suffering, from female to male malfeasance) is the intended point of the *Legend*, and if the issue is power, masculine power is shown at work in seven of the ten stories. Yet there is in the tales, as in the Prologue, a fragile and continually oscillating balance between the assertion and the undercutting of masculine prerogative, or between sexual equality and sexual hierarchy.

It makes little sense, I think, to try to decide whether Chaucer was or was not "woman's friend" (as the Scots poet Gavin Douglas put it in the early sixteenth century); I prefer here to look at the systems within which a late-medieval courtly writer was permitted to be women's friend, and the systems within which he was not so permitted. My argument will be that Chaucer both "is and is not" the friend of woman. I borrow the phrase "is and is not" from Salman Rushdie, who himself borrowed it from ancient Arabic storytelling. I use it in order to articulate a deep-rooted ambivalence about women that is a structural feature of late-medieval culture, providing a terminus ad quem beyond which even the most well-intentioned writer, male or female, cannot pass.

That the culture itself was divided on "the woman question" is evident from social fact and ideological theory. Socially, women were integrated into the work force in rural and urban communities, contributing their labor to the burgeoning European economy of the high Middle Ages and benefiting from the wealth they

helped to create. At the same time they were excluded from important arenas of social activity and influence: from universities, the
priesthood, and (with a few exceptions) government.

Ideologically, Christian myth performed a similar double take on
women. On the one hand, Christian ethics maintained the equality
of men and women with respect to grace, free will, and salvation.
"There is neither Jew nor Greek, there is neither slave nor free,
there is neither male nor female; for you are all one in Jesus Christ,"
Paul admonished (Gal. 3:28). On the other hand, the story of Eden
specifies several sorts of difference as permanent consequences of
the Fall. One is the difference between human beings and animals;
as Jahweh says to the serpent, "I will put enmity between . . . your
brood and hers. They shall strike at your head, and you shall strike
at their heel" (Gen. 3:15). Another is labor, and with it (according to
Catholic theologians) implicitly class difference, for Jahweh des-
tines Adam to "gain your bread by the sweat of your brow." And
there are also differences of sex and gender—that is, both biological
and social differences between men and women—for to Eve, Jahweh says, "I will increase your labor and your groaning, and in
labor shall you bear children. You shall be eager for your husband,
and he shall be your master." These differences are not correctable
historically, according to Catholic doctrine; hence utopianism,
which would erase the consequences of the Fall, is potentially
heretical.

My discussion begins with the apparently gender-blind balade
that is one of the poetic high points of the Prologue and appears to
adumbrate the question of gender role shortly to be raised by Eros.
The lyric praises a lady ("My lady" in F, "Alceste" in G); its catalogue
of ladies surpassed by the object of praise includes eight of the ten
figures treated at greater length in the poem proper (omitting
Medea and Philomela), as well as nine more ladies who are not
written about (but who might have been in a fuller version).

It is curious, therefore, that at the head of this catalogue of
women there stand two men. They are Absolon and Jonathan, in
the first and third lines of the poem. Two more men, Demophon
and Jason, are introduced in stanza 3, balancing the two men of
stanza 1 with approximate formal symmetry. What are these male
figures doing here, and how do they affect our response to the lyric?
They do so, I suggest, in two different and competing ways, de-

pending on our method of interpretation. One effect of their presence is to minimize gender difference; this occurs in a semantic register. The other is to reaffirm gender difference and female subordination; it occurs on the level of syntax. I shall begin with the former as the more usual way of reading a lyric.

Absolon, the son of David, is adduced as an exemplar of beauty for his "gilte tresses clere" (F 249; cf. 2 Sam. 14:25–26), and Jason was also distinguished for his golden hair, as Medea will later note (1672). In stressing the physical beauty of men—and particularly their golden hair, a primary desideratum for the aristocratic woman—the balade reverses conventional expectations. It makes a gender-blind point, reminding us that since physical beauty is not limited to women, neither are the attendant difficulties. Men have to take responsibility for their sexual attractiveness, to ensure its proper use, and to resist exploiting the power it confers: these are not merely the problems of femininity.

As for Jonathan, David's intimate friend, he embodies "frendly manere" (F 251; cf. 2 Sam. 18:1), again a quality that, while not exclusively feminine, tended in the courtly tradition to be associated with women largely through the example of Bel Acueil (Fair Welcome), one of the Lady's most important personified qualities in the *Roman de la rose*. The friendship of Jonathan to King David was both personal and political. It transcended family, for Jonathan has constantly to resist instigation to treason by his father, Saul. The example of Jonathan shows that loyalty, like beauty, is not the property of either sex, and therefore neither is disloyalty. (The legends themselves will amply demonstrate these principles.)

On a semantic level, then—considering only the associative or historical meaning of the men's names—the presence of these names in the balade minimizes sexual difference in the interest of moral egalitarianism. Far from "feminizing" the male figures by including them in this catalogue, the effect is, rather, to deconstruct gender (the social mediations of sex) by suggesting its irrelevance as an ethical category. This procedure is consistent with Christian ethics and eschatology.

But how gender-blind really is the balade? The moral life may well be gender-blind, but social life is not, and the balade manages to convey both aspects of that dialectic simultaneously. Looking now at the structure, or syntax, of naming in the balade, we find that it reasserts hierarchies that limit the moral egalitarianism of its references. This is because the names constitute a referential net-work, analogous to the acrostic sometimes concealed in the initial letters of the lines of a medieval poem and revealing the author's or translator's or recipient's name. In this case, we have a syntax, not of letters, but of names, whose relations within standard medieval theories of classification, both social and historical, carry the struc-ture of repressive ideology in this short and apparently innocent lyric. Let us first consider historiography, specifically the pro-foundly influential Augustinian representation of history.

One notes, first, that there are seven names in stanza 1. I shall attach a significance to this number only because it seems con-textually justifiable to do so. Seven is the number of historical periods in one of Augustine's historical schemes, the one he bor-rowed from hexameral millennialism: it represented history as a week of ages paralleling the week of creation. This theory appears throughout *The City of God*, most prominently and most dramat-ically in its final paragraph:

> The first age, as the first day, extends from Adam to the deluge; the second from the deluge to Abraham. . . . From Abraham to the advent of Christ there are . . . three periods. . . . There are thus five ages in all. The sixth is now passing. . . . After this period God shall rest as on the seventh day, when He shall give us . . . rest in himself. . . . Suffice it to say that the seventh shall be our Sabbath, which shall be brought to a close not by an evening, but by the Lord's day, as an eighth and eternal day, consecrated by the resurrection of Christ, and prefiguring the eternal repose not only of the spirit, but also of the body. (22.30)

Not only did Nicolas Trevet and Thomas Waleys comment on *The City of God* during the fourteenth century, but Ranulf Higden em-ployed the six-ages scheme as the organizing principle for his im-mensely popular and influential encyclopedic world-history, the *Polychronicon*: "In the whiche work, by the ensaumple of the firste worchere, that wroughte alle his werkes in sixe dayes and reste in the seventhe (for his doynge is oure lore), this werke I departe and dele in sevene bookes" (1.3). It was a common topos, and there can be little doubt that Chaucer was well aware of it. Despite these antecedents, this would be a weak argument were it not for other evidence that Augustinian historiography was very much on Chau-cer's mind here, as evidenced in the positioning of the seven names.

In accordance with its title, a second historical scheme structures

Augustine's great book. This is the parallel alignment, imitated
from Eusebius, of the cities of God and man. The development of
the city of God can be traced in the Hebrew and Christian Bibles,
while the city of man is manifested mainly in pagan/classical history, each phase of which is contemporaneous with and antithetical
to a phase in the city of God. We have, therefore, three major
cultural traditions to reckon with in the Augustinian periodical
schema: Hebrew, pagan/classical, and Christian. This periodization
is incorporated in the structure of the "nine worthies" topos, which
always includes three Jewish, three classical, and three Christian
heroes; it can be seen in Chaucer's *Monk's Tale* as well.[3]

This is the progression followed in the first stanza of Chaucer's
balade. We begin with three Old Testament figures; there follow
two classical ones; last come two Christian romance heroines,
Isolde and Helen. There is no reason to assume, as scholars have
always automatically assumed, that this "Eleyne" is Helen of Troy. I
propose that we think of her instead as "la belle Hélène" of Constantinople, eponymous heroine of an extremely popular French
romance of the fourteenth century.[4] The work exists in verse and
prose versions in several languages; it had, according to A. H.
Krappe, "un retentissement très considérable." Helen's story is a
variant on the suffering-queen saga, of which Chaucer's tale of
Constance is another instance. We might think of "La Belle Hélène"
as the hyper-Christian version, for it is framed in the struggle of
Catholicism against the Saracens; it features papal politics and,
besides the pope, includes hermits and priests as characters. The
heroine is daughter to a Roman emperor and niece to a pope; she is
named after the St. Helen, Constantine's mother, who found the
true cross, and her sufferings (which include the loss of a hand)

3. Lucifer provides an archetypal prologue to the series; Hercules (grouped with
Adam and Sampson) was often seen as a type of Sampson; the middle or pagan
section mixes "Assyrian" and Latin figures; and the modern instances should come
at the end, as Donald K. Fry has cogently argued. This is their placement in the best
group of MSS, including the Ellesmere.
4. A. H. Krappe gives a summary and discusses problems of origin and filiation.
He characterizes the tale as "un de ces interminables romans qui caractérisent le
déclin du moyen âge" (324) and concludes that "le poète inconnu était . . . un loyal
sujet des rois angevins, maîtres de l'Angleterre et de la plus grande partie de la
France" (353). A much more detailed resumé appears in the comparison of MSS by
Rudolf Ruths. As far as I am aware, the romance has not yet been edited. On the
evolution of the Helen cycle, see Linder, 84–85; and Mulligan.

equal those of many a saint. Her twin sons are Martin and Brice; the former becomes archbishop of Tours, while Brice becomes father to St. Brice, another archbishop. Given the unsavory reputation of Isolde, we might see the two heroines—courtly adulteress and saintly progenitor of holy men—as representing unredeemed and redeemed versions of womanhood in Christian literature.

There is, moreover, a specifically English component to the story, for Helen, like Isolde, marries an English king (Henry). Her son Brice also becomes king of England and of Constantinople, after making a crusade to Jerusalem. The progression of names thus asserts both *ecclesia* and *patria*, orthodox Augustinian historical periodicity culminating in a subtle compliment to the English monarchy. It is a stance, as Chaucer well knew, not always so easy to maintain as in the structure of a short lyric.

Of course there is no explicit textual assertion about how to interpret this Helen, Hélène, or even Elaine: all depends on our interpretive grid. If the Augustinian historical schema is granted, then Hélène fits. Two considerations persuade me of the validity of that schema in connection with the balade. One is the pervasive presence of Augustinian ideas and references throughout the *Legend*. The other is that the schema holds for six of the seven names, so that it seems to me the burden of proof is on those who would propose any other Helen than the one suggested here. Nevertheless, indeterminacy of this sort serves to highlight the role of interpretation, the necessary subjective activity of the reader. This becomes a prominent theme in the legends to follow, so that the balade is again paradigmatic of what it precedes: not only in content but in method.

Besides chronological structuring, a hierarchy of social values may be discerned in the placement of names in the balade. This social syntax reaffirms gender relations as a kind of subset to the doctrinal hierarchies already posited in the historical periodicity of the names. I used the metaphor "headed" earlier on, and I now want to literalize that metaphor, suggesting that the positioning of male and female figures at the start of the poem represents a "correct" organic structure resembling that of the traditional descriptive blazon of the human (not only the female) body. The blazon always begins with the head and works systematically downward. This is because what is highest is most important and therefore comes first.

In the human organism, the position of physical and conceptual primacy is filled by the head, seat of reason, the highest intellectual capacity. As in the body biological, so in the body politic: what is highest rules. As the head rules (or should rule) the body, so reason rules the passions, king rules state, and man rules woman.

Hence the balade opens with a man, expands to a man followed by a woman, and then gives a pair of men enclosing—constraining, if you will—a woman. The cluster of three names thus offers a tiny linguistic image of proper leadership and proper control. The poem opens also with the image of a head—Absolon's head of gilt tresses—as does the traditional blazon. It opens with three Old Testament figures representing temporal priority; they are, moreover, inseparably linked to monarchy, or headship of state. This power-packed opening movement is immediately followed by two examples of marital fidelity (Penelope and Marcia Cato), which extend the political principle into the domestic sphere.

The image of Esther is especially rich in this context, touching as it does all three areas of concern: state, marriage, and individual self-control. (Here I revert to a semantic mode of analysis.) The Book of Esther opens with an act of disobedience: Queen Vashti refuses to come forth at the command of her husband, King Ahasuerus. This misconduct carries potentially disastrous results:

> For this deed of the queen will be made known to all women, causing them to look with contempt upon their husbands. . . . This very day the ladies of Persia and Medea who have heard of the queen's behavior will be telling it to all the king's princes, and there will be contempt and wrath in plenty. (Esther 1:17–18)

The insubordination feared here is at once domestic and political: not only will other women follow Vashti's example against their husbands, but princes may do so against their superior the king. Royal advisors therefore urge that a "better" queen be found so that "all women will give honor to their husbands, high and low." The successful candidate is the Jewish maiden Esther, a paragon of obedience, tact, and modesty. Esther does assert herself eventually on behalf of her people, but always using feminine wiles: food, wine, appearance, tears. She achieves a writ of indulgence, the promotion of her deserving relative, and the death of her people's enemies. On every level—political, marital, ethical—Esther is represented as a model of proper female conduct. Her story reasserts the importance of gender-role difference (that is, of specifically feminine behavior); it reaffirms authority both sexual and social. Chaucer's *Clerk's Tale* and *Man of Law's Tale* adopt a similar narrative strategy of sexual politics.

If the first stanza of Chaucer's balade gives us images of headship, rule, and rational behavior, the second stanza shows what is to be ruled. It opens with the image of a body : "Thy faire body, lat yt nat appere, / Lavyne" (F 256–57). At its heart—that is, in its central line—passion appears: just where it ought to, for the heart is, in medieval medical lore, the seat of passion and particularly, though not only, of sexual passion. (We recall the opening of the *Canterbury Tales* with its birds pricked by nature in their "corages.") The "passyoun" here is that of Cleopatra, one of the most negatively charged figures in all medieval history and legend, as Taylor shows conclusively. Playing on the hagiographical matrix and the *passio* (suffering) of martyrs, Chaucer also avails himself of the already-acquired (and now predominant) subjective meaning of "passion" (cf. *OED*, s.v.). Death dominates this stanza as it does the natural body, for of the five ladies named, three were suicides and one was killed as a sacrifice. Moreover, all five are closely associated with warfare or family feud. One might add further that all these ladies are pagans, but I would not want to lean too heavily on the "spiritual death" notion. The figures in stanza 2 therefore lead us to consider the ways of irrational or excessive behavior both personal and social. In doing so, they contrast with the heavily charged onomastics of control in stanza 1.

Stanza 3 adds nothing to the dialectic of control and subversion already established, but illustrates it in a fairly pedestrian way: the feet, I suppose, of this small literary body whose structure does, after all, mime that of the conventional courtly blazon. (Nor is it necessary to apologize for etymological wordplay, a standard rhetorical device in classical and medieval literatures.)

In such subtle ways does the balade introduce the legends to come, not simply by naming several of the heroines to be represented there, but by showing, in its miniature poetic practice, the stress-ridden and paradoxical relations of men and women, reason and nature, eschatology and social life, form and content, syntax and semantics.

My analysis of the "Absolon" balade proposes a more schematic and more ideologically conscious poet than Chaucer is often conceded to be: a more medieval Chaucer if you will. As Georges Duby has shown in *The Three Orders*—his meditation on equality and hierarchy in high-medieval social theory—the thematic elucidated here became, after the twelfth century, absolutely central to conservative thought of the period. If the Chaucer portrayed here is less like ourselves than we thought, less different from his scholarly—indeed, clerical—contemporaries and antecedents, his work is by the same token all the more capable of revealing some dominant intellectual concerns of his day. Other of Chaucer's poems could be analyzed to disclose a similar pattern of first undercutting and then reasserting gender difference. *The Franklin's Tale* begins by inverting the traditional relation of husband and wife, but ends by affirming it. The knight Arviragus at first swears never to exert social or sexual control over his wife ("he, day ne nyght, / Ne shoulde upon hym take no maistrie" [V.746–47]). In the end, he must not only resolve her dilemma about honorable behavior, but threaten her with death if she breathes a word of it (1481–83). The Wife of Bath's recital allows its speaker, in her Prologue, to offer a radical critique of male appropriation of cultural production and to seize that right for herself. Yet it also lets her reaffirm both traditional textuality and traditional masculine fantasies about and behavior toward women, with her quotations that turn against themselves and her tale of a rapist who beats the rap.

The themes I have discerned in the balade resurface in the individual legends, to which I turn now and in Chapter 5 in order to indicate how they carry the dialectic of same and different, equal and subordinate.

GEOGRAPHIES OF DESIRE:
ORIENTALISM IN THE LEGEND

The construction of woman as Other would seem the obvious target in a work as fitly titled for that purpose as the *Legend of Good Women*. I have argued that the socio-literary construction of gender is what Chaucer aims to deconstruct—but not necessarily to reject—in his *Legend*, through a variety of rhetorical means and in the service of an ultimate (that is, a historically unattainable but nonetheless "true") genderlessness such as that offered by St. Paul in his remonstrance to the Galatians, or by Augustine in his vision of the Resurrection. Both have been cited above, but I repeat them here for the reader's convenience. The Pauline text says: "There is neither Jew nor Greek, there is neither slave nor free, there is neither male nor female; for you are all one in Jesus Christ" (Gal. 3:28). Augustine's statement, quoted in Chapter 2, is:

> For my part, they seem to be wiser who make no doubt that both sexes shall rise [at the Resurrection]. For there shall be no lust, which is now the cause of confusion. From those bodies, then, vice shall be withdrawn, while nature shall be preserved. And the sex of a woman is not a vice, but nature. It shall then indeed be superior to carnal intercourse and child-bearing; nevertheless the female members shall remain adapted not to the old uses but to a new beauty, which, so far from provoking lust, now extinct, shall excite praise to the wisdom and clemency of God, who both made what was not and delivered from corruption what He made. (*City of God* 22.17)

What I want to propose here, though, is another target than woman for the construction of otherness in the *Legend*: the foreigner, specifically the Middle Eastern, non-European Mediterranean or northern African foreigner, inhabiting what was called in Chaucer's day, and is still often called, "the Orient." I am indebted in this portion of my project to the provocative work of Edward Said, who distinguishes three meanings for the term "Orientalism." The first, the academic study of the Orient from whatever disciplinary perspective, is relevant to my discussion to the extent that it provides evidence for my reading of Chaucer. The second or "imaginative" meaning—"a style of thought based upon an ontological and epistemological distinction made between 'the Orient' and (most of the time) 'the Occident'" (Said, *Orientalism*, 2)—will accommodate most poets, including Chaucer. Further, I want to claim Said's third definition—"a Western style for dominating, restructuring, and having authority over the Orient" (ibid., 3)—for the fourteenth century, although Said (following Michel Foucault's notion of a discourse) locates the starting point of this meaning as the late eighteenth century. It is doubtful whether meanings two and three can really be separated: whether the ontological/epistemological uses of the Orient can exist without an accompanying and even generative material basis in colonialism (the Greeks in Asia Minor,

Romans in North Africa, etc.). The concept is "historically and materially defined" in the late Middle Ages—which, in the Crusades, certainly had its "institution for dealing with the Orient" (ibid.).

Although it is not possible here fully to display the medieval discourse on Orientalism, I hope at least to sketch its contours and to show its operation in a fourteenth-century English courtly poem about love and gender. As we shall see, the two versions of otherness—gender and geography—reinforce one another, although not necessarily in mechanical or predictable ways.

Let me begin with material and institutional definition: land, commodities, social organization.

Joshua Prawer has articulated the colonial character of the European military presence in Palestine—Outremer, the Holy Land, the Latin kingdom of Jerusalem, won by Europeans in the First Crusade in 1099 and reconquered by the Muslims in 1291. This presence had broader motives than the desire to salvage heathen souls and save one's own, even broader than the ambition of nobles and of ecclesiastical administrators to acquire fertile estates abroad or of the servile to gain their freedom there. The Orient included, for example, numerous Mediterranean port cities that opened "the Moslem hinterland to European penetration and inversely [brought] . . . a flow of Eastern wares to the European marts and fairs across the Alps" (Prawer, *Latin Kingdom*, 352) from as far away as India, Africa, and Southeast Asia. As a market, the Orient took textiles and clothing; furs and leather; pearls; timber; iron and tin; metalwork of various kinds, whether ornamental or armorial (along with wool, a British specialty for centuries); slaves (from non-Christian Slavic populations); and a great deal of hard currency. Pilgrimage was also, of course, major export business, especially lucrative for moneylenders, shipbuilders, seamen, hostelers, and suppliers. As resources, the Orient gave, as Lopez and Raymond show, oils; honey and wax; citrus and other fruits; wines; textiles (silks, brocades, cottons); ivory; glassware; dyes (used in painting as well as in the textile industry); grains; spices; and especially sugar.

Socially, institutionally, the Crusades had a profound effect on European society; even for the Church, they were more than a spiritual exercise. Christopher Tyerman writes of the lucrative crusade finance market, in which some ecclesiastical establish-ments had, by the thirteenth century, "emerged as major institu-tions of capitalist enterprise, acting as bankers and financiers as well as territorial empire builders" (206). The widespread desire to sell or mortgage in order to finance crusading created something like a real-estate boom in the thirteenth century, with what Tyerman calls "cut-throat competition" among lay and ecclesiastical pur-chasers to acquire available properties. The alienation of lands also created assorted problems for disinherited offspring and disen-dowered wives, who often had to pursue their rights in court.

There were other institutional consequences. A range of new taxes, with the necessary administrative apparatus (a layer of bu-reaucrats), came into being to support the Crusades. Privileges conferred upon the *crucesignatus* included exemption from interest, immunity from taxation and from court summonses, a debt mor-atorium, and protection for his family; neither were these privileges dependent upon immediate departure.

How important would or could the Orient be to an English courtier / civil servant of the late fourteenth century? Would it not seem remote to the point of utter irrelevance? And were the Cru-sades not already obsolete both as an ideal and as a military phe-nomenon? In fact, Aziz Atiya describes the fourteenth century as "the age of the later Crusade in its fuller sense . . . the real age of propaganda for the Crusade" (92, 94). This is because the military expansion of the Islamic Ottoman empire was taken very seriously indeed in Europe. As Thomas J. Hatton observes, "Europe buzzed with plans, preparations and half-hearted efforts to launch still another great expedition to the Holy Land. The need was real." If England was not directly threatened by Islamic expansion, some of its allies were. Although the major confrontations were to occur in the 1390s, there was nonetheless plenty of concern and action during the preceding decades, when Chaucer played an active, if minor, diplomatic role in his country's international politics, and when the *Legend* was composed. Certainly a very keen sense of East-West dynamic is revealed in the *Monk's Tale*, which has four of the five uses in all of Chaucer's work of the word "orient" (the other is in the *Knight's Tale*, 1494). Moreover, all four occur in context of Roman colonialism. Cenobia arouses the wrath of imperial Rome by conquering many kingdoms

> In the orient, with many a fair citee
> Apertenaunt unto the magestee
> Of Rome. . . .
>
> (VII.2314–16),

and Caesar's rival Pompey is no less than thrice characterized as a campaigner in the "orient" (2681, 2685, 2693), with Caesar himself "the conqueror, / That wan al th' occident" (2673–74).

Given the events of the day and Chaucer's role at court, it should scarcely surprise us that the poet incorporated into his work some consciousness of the East-West confrontation threatening Europe. Nonetheless, as is often the case with medieval authorial attitudes, and particularly Chaucer's, the question of specific response is not clear-cut.

Throughout the 1340s, there were battles against the Turks, chiefly by Italians. A key date in the Muslims' progress was 1353, when the Turks seized Gallipoli on the Hellespont and entered Europe. During the 1370s, they took control in the Balkans, and in 1389 they reached the Danube. All during the 1360s, there were appeals for military help from rulers directly threatened by the Turkish onslaught: from the king of Hungary; from Constantinople; from the king of Cyprus and Jerusalem, Pierre de Lusignan.

The latter toured Europe trying to organize a crusade; he visited the English court in 1363–64 (a time for which we have no records of Chaucer's whereabouts). Lusignan managed to organize a temporarily victorious attack on Alexandria in 1365, in which he was assisted by a company of English knights. This event was commemorated in *La Prise d'Alexandrie* by Guillaume de Machaut, whose poetry Chaucer knew well and often imitated. It appears also in Chaucer's own *Monk's Tale*, of which a stanza is devoted to

> worthy Petro, kyng of Cipre . . .
> That Alisandre wan by heigh maistrie
>
> (VII.2391–98),

and again in Chaucer's description of his Knight, who has participated in this battle and numerous others, both with and against the Muslims, from the 1340s through the 1360s in Spain, Turkey, and Morocco (GP 51–66). We may note too, to extend the geographic range, that the Wife of Bath has traveled to Jerusalem thrice (GP 463).

Among Lusignan's strongest proponents was Philippe de Mézières, former chancellor of the kingdom of Cyprus and, after the assassination of Lusignan in 1369, tutor to the young Charles VI of France. For four decades Mézières propagandized for the regaining of Jerusalem, founding the Order of the Passion of Jesus Christ Crucified to that end. He circulated documents calling for international support of the Order in 1368, 1384, and throughout the 1390s, winning twenty-two members from England.[5] Among them was Chaucer's friend and fellow-diplomat Lewis Clifford, who acted as intermediary between Chaucer and his admirer at the French court, Eustache Deschamps.

Another guest at the English court was Leo VI, king of Little Armenia (Cilicia). Expelled by the Mamelukes, who controlled Egypt and, intermittently, Palestine and Syria, Leo was in England in 1384–85; that is, just before the composition of the *Legend*. His aim was to forge a European alliance that would launch a crusade; hence Mézières writes, in his *Songe du vieux pelerin* (1389), of "ladicte paix . . . par le tresvaillant Lyon, roy d'Armenie diligemment traictee et poursuite" (1.78). Leo's visit provoked what May McKisack calls "a glaring example of royal recklessness," for Richard II bestowed on Leo "lavish gifts and entertainment and an annual pension of £1000." She adds that according to one chronicler, the king "was so liberal that he gave to all who asked him, dissipating the revenues of his crown so that he was forced to recoup himself by taxing his people" (441).

Following hard upon Leo's stay in England was the well-known Scrope-Grosvenor trial of 1385–86, in which Chaucer was called to testify. This was an armorial dispute over who had the right to display a certain heraldic figure. Tyerman observes that "at least fourteen individual crusaders either testified or were mentioned,

5. Coopland, *Philippe de Mézières: Letter*, Introduction, xxxiii–xxxiv. The letter in question, dated 1395, proposes peace between France and England as a necessary prerequisite to winning back the East. Another project of Mézières's, documented by William Coleman, was his campaign to have the Feast of Mary's Presentation in the Temple—long a major event in the Greek Church despite its apocryphal origin—included in the Latin liturgy. Coleman speculates that Mézières hoped to establish an ecumenical, then a military, alliance with the Byzantine Christians against the Turkish threat. The campaign included an anonymous sermon (dated about 1372) on Matt. 24:27: "Exit ab oriente et paret usque in occidentem" ("It [lightning] goes from the east and appears even in the west"), a scriptural citation enabling the preacher to expatiate on East-West relations on the theoretical rather than purely military level.

their exploits of the previous twenty-five years stretching from Egypt to Lithuania" (p. 259), and Maurice Keen has proposed this collective dossier as Chaucer's model for his Knight.

By and large, the official English policy toward the Crusades was not, in the 1380s, particularly supportive. Richard II was himself a crusade enthusiast, but his major plans in this area—an Anglo-French project to repel the Ottomans and recover Palestine—did not commence until the 1390s (that is, several years after the *Legend* was composed). In the late thirteenth and early fourteenth centuries, English kings had several times expropriated for their own use moneys raised by the papacy to fund crusades, and after 1336 no new mandatory crusade taxes were levied by the papacy in England (Tyerman, 253). It was consistent with the anti-papal and nationalistic policies of Edward III that, in contrast to the French, he declined to finance crusades, even though individuals were permitted to do so themselves; hence English crusaders of the fourteenth century were privately financed through loans, mortgages, or gifts, though by 1378 crusade bequests and legacies had virtually disappeared as a means of funding (Housley, 236). Indeed, Philippe de Mézières took the opportunity in his *Songe* (1.76–8) bitterly to denounce the English for (among other things) sabotaging French efforts to regain the Holy Land.

Yet despite the hands-off attitude of Edward III, and despite some criticism of the movement, recent scholars generally agree that both the theory and practice of crusade continued to enjoy a great deal of prestige in Chaucer's day:

> The crusade was very much in men's minds in England, and it was a live issue in political society, among the highest and most influential in the realm, in the late 1380s and 1390s. . . . Plenty of men went on crusade. (Keen, 57)

> Clearly it would be wrong to regard the crusade in the fourteenth century as an unpopular movement. There was a broadly based acceptance of the crusade . . . though criticism of what was happening in practice continued to be vociferous. (Housley, 239)

> Opposition to crusading was by no means widespread, and criticism of the ideal was even rarer. The crusade remained a practical and far-from-amateurish concern throughout the century. (Tyerman, 288)

Indeed, it was extremely practical. England may have taken a less active role in regaining the Holy Land than could satisfy Philippe de Mézières, but it did nonetheless plan and launch two crusades of its own between 1382 and 1386, just preceding the composition of the *Legend*. These were quite similar campaigns, both of them opportunistically exploiting the Great Schism in the Church for ends of foreign policy and personal profit, both of them designated "crusades"—equally opportunistically—by the Roman Pope Urban VI because they targeted opponents of his who professed loyalty to the rival antipope in Avignon, Clement VII.

It is important to remember the decisive and disruptive impact on public life at every level of the proclamation of a crusade: sermons being constantly preached for the crusade, a multi-pronged national fund-raising effort, new taxes and levies, the diversion of commercial shipping, and recruitment of armies.

One of these campaigns was the May 1383 invasion of Flanders: the crusade of Henry Despenser, bishop of Norwich. Nominally, its purpose was to ensure that the French did not force Flanders to support Clement. Richard Vaughan discerns an economic motive: to maintain free passage for English wool, which had been embargoed by the count of Flanders (28). J. J. N. Palmer sees instead a political motive: to use Flanders as a wedge against the French in the ongoing Hundred Years' War (21–22). A distinctive feature of this crusade was the gross abuse of plenary indulgence: in return for contributions to the crusade, Urban offered full remission of sins for both living and dead. This offer contributed to what McKisack calls "the prevailing mood of national hysteria"; she writes of "the avidity with which the credulous of all classes, men and more especially women, sought to buy the plenary remissions" (431). Paul Olson proposes that the abusive ecclesiastical practices of this campaign are reflected in the *Pardoner's Tale*; he notes too that Chaucer's Squire—who has learned chivalry in Flanders—has evidently participated in it (203–7).

The campaign was a complete disaster, in which cowardice, indiscipline, and dysentery all played a part; Vaughan cites a chronicler who observed, "percussit eos Deus in posteriora" (29). Wyclif also fulminated against it in his polemic *De cruciata*. The commander, Bishop Despenser, was impeached by Parliament and several captains were tried for treasonous surrender.

The other crusade of the early 1380s was the political adventure in Castile planned for 1383 by John of Gaunt. It was not Lancaster's first attempt to intervene in the dynastic affairs of that region, for ten years earlier, in pursuit of his own claim to the Castilian throne, he had led a campaign there, which P. E. Russell describes "as one of the outstanding failures in Lancaster's chequered career as a military commander" (204). Lancaster's claim was based on his 1371 marriage to Costanza, daughter of Pedro I of Castile and Leon. Negotiations for settlement dragged on through the 1370s, and by the early 1380s there was significant support in Parliament for peace, despite Lancaster's intention to mount another expedition against Castile in 1383. In March of that year, Urban appointed Lancaster "standard-bearer of the Church in the coming crusade against the Trastamaran schismatics" (Russell, 348), for the Trastamaran ruler of Castile supported the Avignon pope and was thus guilty of "the Clementist heresy." Although the plan failed, nonetheless some English troops were dispatched to Spain, and it is not difficult to believe that the cynically political deployment of crusade rhetoric would have been evident to many observers.

Yet this was not the end of the matter, for once again, in 1385, the "chemin d'Espaigne" was brought to Parliament. This time the project was unanimously accepted, and by February 1386 "vast and widely publicized preparations were being made" (Russell, 408). These included official propagation of crusade in England; fundraising; a tournament at Smithfield, at which Richard II presented John of Gaunt with a golden crown in anticipation of his coronation in Spain; and the arrest of commercial ships for diversion to military purposes. (One can imagine the indignation of an experienced customs officer like Chaucer, whose twelve years in that position ended in 1386.) This invasion took place in July 1386; it ended two years later when Lancaster abandoned his claim to the Castilian throne in exchange for a large compensatory payment and the betrothal of his daughter Catalina to his former enemy. "Nor," Russell remarks, "apparently, was his conscience greatly troubled by the thought that his daughter would be the bride of a heretic" (509), although the irritated pope did eventually revoke all acts performed under his sponsorship of the ill-fated "crusade."

Crusade was thus a rather complex phenomenon in England just before 1386, composed as it was of grandiose schemes proposed by foreigners against the infidel in distant Arabic lands, and cynical adventures against other European Christians, which had little effect besides draining the national treasury, already stressed by the war against France. That, at least, is how an ironically minded civil servant might have seen it, and I want to suggest that in the *Legends*, Orientalism becomes a rhetorical device enabling Chaucer to do two things: to create a moral structure in the poem and to offer a veiled commentary on some aspects of English foreign policy. It becomes his negative pole, for certain qualities associated with Easterners become paradigmatic of flaws and vices that, while not confined to Easterners, are nonetheless seen as most dramatically exemplified in them; certainly most memorably exemplified, inasmuch as these figures are the stuff of Western literary tradition.

As such, might not their presence in the *Legend* represent nothing more complicated than the poet's fidelity to his classical sources? Perhaps, but there are strong arguments to the contrary. Chaucer's freedom in altering his sources for political or other purposes is well known. Moreover, some of these stories—those of Dido, Cleopatra, and the Roman Lucretia—already had blatantly political purposes, whether colonial or domestic. Finally, the prominence of Orientalist and crusade concerns at the English court during the few years just preceding the composition of the *Legend*, and especially the "crusades" of the magnates Despenser and Lancaster, precludes, I believe, a merely innocent or coincidental choice of "Oriental" figures and themes.

As will be evident from what follows, the Oriental theme does not run consistently from start to finish of the work. I have not found it in the Prologue in any substantial way, for instance, even though some of the ladies named there in the balade—Helen, Lavinia, Cleopatra—did come to Chaucer from literary works heavily laden with colonialist intent. The theme tends rather to surface intermittently in several of the legends.

Cleopatra

To begin his series, as Chaucer does, with Cleopatra is, first, overtly to undercut his numenous sponsors' demand for "good" women. Second, it displaces the called-for theme of love with that of politics and the social order, specifically of colonialism gone soft. Antony,

the "senatour" who is sent "For to conqueren regnes and honour /
Unto . . . Rome" (584–85), scarcely advances the Roman values of
manly valor. The flaws in his character become all too obvious in
Egypt, where, after adultery and bigamy, all that remains to him as
a public person is his courage in battle. This will be lost with his
defeat at the sea battle of Actium—the "endlessly exemplary Actium," as Michel Foucault calls it (*Language*, 172)—after which he
commits suicide.

Of what is Actium here exemplary? Here and elsewhere in the
Legends, it is the debilitating or depoliticizing effect of foreigners,
Orientals, that I want to notice: their ability to distract a hero from
his (in this case explicitly colonial) mission, generally through sen-
sual and erotic pleasures. This sensuality could even corrode em-
pires, according to Augustine, for just when "the Romans lived
with greatest virtue and concord," the proconsul Manlius "introduced into Rome the luxury of Asia, more destructive than all
hostile armies. It was then that iron bedsteads and expensive car-
pets were first used; then, too, that female singers were admitted at
banquets, and other licentious abominations were introduced"
(*City of God* 3.21). The image of an enervating, effeminizing Eastern
sensuality set against a properly masculine Western energy, already
ancient by the high Middle Ages, was reinforced when the Crusaders encountered Eastern habits such as frequent bathing, the wear-
ing of perfumes and makeup by men, the heavy use of spices in
cooking, and an abundance of jewelry worn by both men and
women (Prawer, "Roots").

The story of Cleopatra is thus the other side of the coin to the
romantic exoticism represented in the *Squire's Tale*. The Orient is no
longer a realm of fantasy fulfilled, but one of hope and ambition
undone, for the Chaucerian version is a cautionary tale if ever there
was one. But what does it caution against, or for?

Different possibilities exist. Terry Jones argues, correctly, that
crusade was not officially approved of in England despite the participation of English knights in exotic campaigns. The reason, he
suggests, is that the major focus of English foreign policy was the
war against France, and then the defense of England's Scottish
border. Perhaps, then, the Knight's adventures abroad show a less
than patriotic commitment. Similarly, Alison's gadding about, even

to holy places, might be suspect: need one go so far to show one's faith? It is a question the Wycliffites posed continually in their critique of pilgrimage. By this token, Antony might be considered a negative exemplum in deserting his country for sybaritic pleasures and self-serving exploits abroad. His sad story might provide a very timely and distinctively English admonition against costly military adventure abroad—adventures such as those exhorted in the name of faith by Philippe de Mézières or undertaken for profit by John of Gaunt. Even the reference in the *Monk's Tale* to "worthy Petro," Mézières's old patron, could be ironic, for Lusignan was "notoriously immoral," had committed "deeds of the grossest cruelty," had incurred papal and episcopal censure, and had broken feudal contract with his barons (Coopland, *Songe*, 64). It seems, then, that both concrete results and historical personnel left much to be desired.

On the other hand, official—that is, royal and parliamentary— approval is not the whole story. If Maurice Keen is right in asserting that the number and status of persons taking up the banner in Chaucer's day made it impossible for the crusade to look obsolete or disreputable, then the Orientalism shown in this and other legends might tend to affirm British or European aspirations abroad. Antony would still be a negative exemplum, of course, but the tactic would be to show the Eastern adversary at its most alluring and therefore most dangerous. Thus the story might encourage, not total abandonment of the crusading ideal, but rather the proper firmness abroad: a "Desert Storm" type of strategy.

Deciding between these positions is not easy. Nor does Hatton's hypothesis—that the *Knight's Tale* reflects Mézières's ultimately unachieved program of reconquest—necessarily imply a positive attitude toward Orientalist projects. If Chaucer thought Mézières's plans unrealistic or fanatical (as some did), then the ironic or negative reading, for which there is ample textual and historical grounding, would be appropriate. The lawman John Gower, Chaucer's good friend and fellow poet, certainly pulled no punches in allowing his characters to debate and denounce crusading. A strong anti-crusade current runs through *Confessio Amantis*, of which two instances will have to suffice. Book 4 addresses the vice of sloth, and Genius explicitly identifies derring-do abroad with lovers' egotisti-

cal efforts to improve their status in their ladies' eyes. This is a form
of labor that Amans has not practiced—and, he says, for good
reason, one of which is that

> A Sarazin if I sle schal,
> I sle the Soule forth withal,
> And that was nevere Christes lore.
> (4.1679–81)

Earlier, in their discussion of war as a manifestation of Ire, Amans
has explicitly posed the question:

> I prei you tell me nay or yee,
> To passe over the grete See
> To werre and sle the Sarazin,
> Is that the lawe?
> (3.2487–89)

Genius can only admit that gospel urges us to preach and suffer for
faith, but not to kill; indeed, abandoning the word for the sword has
proved an inefficacious tactic, as witness the loss of parts once
Christian but now "miswent" (2513): obviously a reference to the
failure of the crusading movement.

As a rule of thumb, we might say that what Gower deplores,
Chaucer represents. In the present case, perhaps the Chaucerian
point is that Easterners are not so very different from ourselves,
because there is an "Oriental" tendency in all of us, which must be
tamed if it cannot be rooted out. (Surely Augustine himself, a North
African latecomer to Christianity, was a prime example of this
effort.) Yet to say as much is to acknowledge a very deep-rooted
Orientalism: Said's second definition. For if "European culture
gained in strength and identity by setting itself off against the
Orient as a sort of surrogate and even underground self" (Said,
Orientalism, 3), then the Oriental seducer or villain is an exter-
nalized aspect of the (European) self, and the East-West dynamic, in
its literary representation, becomes a form of self-exploration in the
interest of self-control. But not, after all, only *self*-control, for to be
able to represent the unruly or the transgressive as Oriental is
already to imply the desire to control the real Orient, a desire
expressed not only in literary texts but, as indicated above, in social
institutions.

THISBE

Chaucer's second legend is also an Oriental tale, as Ovid reminds us in the opening of his version (*Met.* 4.55–58), the main source of Chaucer's. The setting is Babylon, specified in both texts as the city whose baked-brick walls were built by Queen Semiramis. The Eastern location is important to the ideological structure of the *Metamorphoses*, which, we recall, super-patriotically ends with the apotheosis and stellification of Caesar. Although there may well be irony in this ending, nonetheless the ebb and flow of Oriental ideas is very much at stake in the Thisbe portion of the text. The tale occurs in a series narrated by the daughters of Minyas. They, worshippers of Athena, are boycotting the festival of Asian Bacchus, which has taken all the other women away from their proper domestic duties and off into the streets and woods. The Minyades stay indoors and spin, meanwhile telling cautionary tales of Oriental sensuality and excessive passion. Thus the narrators demonstrate the virtuous gender-behavior that their female character will fatally flout when she wanders into the woods to meet her lover. If Ovid has the Minyades transformed into bats because of their failure to acknowledge the power of Bacchus, this is his indirect critique of the repressive Augustan morality the tale itself overtly supports. The metamorphosis does not, in any case, alter the East-West conflict of values.

Babylon can scarcely portend any good to an author steeped, as Chaucer was, in the scriptural-Augustinian tradition. There Babylon is an enemy of the chosen people and predecessor of Rome as archetypal city of man (cf. *City of God* 18). Irene Samuel's formidably thorough study shows that it is in the patristic tradition too that Semiramis, formerly a much-honored military leader, becomes a prototype of feminine erotic evil: usurping man's prerogative to rule, murdering her husband to do so, committing incest with her son, and, in some texts, inventing trousers as female attire. In the *Man of Law's Tale*, Chaucer gives us a closer view of such a figure: the Sultan's mother, who so far transgresses the bounds of femininity that she no longer qualifies as a woman. She is "feyned womman . . . serpent under femynynytee . . . Virago"—and "Semyrame the secounde" (359–63). The polarities of Occident versus Orient and Christian law versus pagan law make up a basic structural principle in the *Man of Law's Tale,* and I think we may see it as developing ideas latent in the *Legend.*[6]

Although there is no Western pole in the legend of Thisbe, the tale is already sufficiently defined by its context to make its point about the hazards of unbridled eroticism and unnecessary adventure abroad. Where "Cleopatra" makes that point in the arena of international politics, "Thisbe" domesticates it: she neither gives up a kingdom nor crosses the sea, but she disobeys her parents to wander from home at night. So, of course, does Piramus: again there is no victim, no disloyalty, but a double death freely chosen on both sides. The republican and humanist Boccaccio had already interpreted this medieval Romeo-and-Juliet as a warning against parental interference in adolescent love in his *De claris mulieribus*:

> Wicked Fortune sinned, as perhaps did their wretched parents. Certainly the ardor of the young should be curbed slowly, lest by wishing to oppose them with sudden impediments we drive them to despair and perdition. The passion of desire is without temperance, and it is almost a pestilence and fury in youth. We should tolerate it patiently. (*Concerning Famous Women*, trans. Guarini, 27)

For the courtier Chaucer, though—who held the lucrative wardship of two young men's marriages and had three offspring of his own— the pathetic Oriental tale maintains its original Ovidian purpose. The outcome affirms, after all, the wisdom of parents who protect their daughters "lest they diden som folye" (723). In Chaucer's hands, humor or obscenity may neutralize pathos but not morality or prudence. If the story—however amusing or sentimental— suggests that adventures far from home rarely turn out well, this is a sentiment with international as well as strictly domestic weight.

Dido and Aeneas

Another aspect of medieval Orientalism was the sexual immorality and "unnatural" behavior often attached to societies of the ancient Near and Middle East. Said gives several instances from Flaubert (*Orientalism,* 103) and other modern writers. For the Middle Ages, this immorality was a stock theme, carried in numerous ways.

---

6. See S. Delany, "Womanliness in the *Man of Law's Tale*" in *Writing Woman,* and " 'Loi' and 'Foi.' "

Some writers claimed that Muhammad devised a "plan of general sexual license as an instrument for the destruction of Christendom" (Southern, 30). Some scholars glossed Mecca as "Mecha, id est adultera," playing on the Latin word *moecha* (Alverny and Vajda, 261); others explained the Islamic Friday holy day as owing to the Muslims' worship of Venus, whose day Friday is (Daniel, 145). Numerous lives of Muhammad carried the theme: in popular French poems, in chronicles of Spain or the Holy Land, in crusade histories, Dante commentaries, world histories, and a *Roman de Mahomet*, they portrayed the founder of Islam as a sensualist, a lecher, an adulterer with eleven or twelve wives, innumerable mistresses, and the virility of thirty men. For others the offense lay in the ancient royal institution of dynastic incest, said by various authorities to have characterized Persian, Armenian, and Egyptian society.[7] While incest plays no specific role in any of Chaucer's Oriental tales, he does have the Man of Law cite incest as the poet's reason for refusing to tell the stories of Canace or Antiochus. Though rejecting "swiche unkynde abhomynacions" (*MLT* 88) as narrative material, Chaucer shows us that it was part of his general frame of reference about the Orient.

Some authorities believed that the Qur'an authorized anal intercourse with women and intercourse during menstruation (Daniel, app. E). Moreover, the actual Islamic sanction of polygyny, of divorce or repudiating of wives, of extramarital relations with slaves, and of prostitution ("temporary marriage" with a fee for the middleman, a practice continuing into the present) contributed to Western perceptions of "the special lubricity of Muslims" (Daniel, 145). Nor were these perceptions limited to Muslims; they were generalized as "Oriental" attitudes.

In Chaucer's third legend, the hero and the heroine are two of a kind: both of them worthy people with an impressive history, yet both of them deeply flawed, intensely self-indulgent, manipulative—and Oriental.

---

7. The authorities include St. Jerome, Clement of Alexandria, Diogenes Laertius, Quintus Curtius; cf. Krappe. John Fyler relates incest to the romance rhetorical tropes of doubling and repetition, via their shared analogous concern with same and other, as well as their effect of forcing decisions about identity and discrimination. He argues that the tale shows that "reintegration—the quest of romance—is not fully achievable, that the other finally resists integration with the self" ("Domesticating the Exotic," 12).

The figure of Aeneas came to Chaucer compromised in several ways. One is the conflict between the Virgilian and the Ovidian version of his behavior toward Dido. Chaucer had already confronted this disjunction in the *House of Fame*. Another is the Orientalist tradition about his culture, for Phrygia (Troy) was often represented as the site of debilitating sensuality and, more particularly, of effeminacy. This is adumbrated in the *Aeneid* when Dido's suitor Iarbus refers contemptuously to "Paris, with his semi-male retinue, oily-haired" ("Paris, cum semiviro comitatu . . . crinemque madentem" [4.215–16]), or Turnus dismisses Aeneas as "half-male Trojan" ("semiviris Phrygis" [12.99]). The idea persisted in medieval poetry and scholarship. When Ovid calls Paris a "Phrygian man" ("Phrygio viro" [*Ars* 1.54]), this is glossed by a commentator as "Frigio. Troiana. vel debili. vel effeminatio" (Hexter, 75 n. 197), and one notes further that Ganymede, the passive homosexual boy butler of the gods, was Phrygian. In the *Roman d'Enéas* the accusation of homosexuality is used by Lavinia's mother to dissuade her daughter from the match with Aeneas. It is a long passage (8565–8621) full of explicit terminology ("traïtor," "sodomite") and obscene puns ("il n'aime pas poil de conin": rabbit fur / cunt hair); it uses cultural slander ("an ce sont Troïen nourri") and invokes the law of nature ("contre nature," "la natural cople"). In a non-literary context, the association of Oriental societies with homosexuality was helped along by papal propaganda justifying a Christian presence in Muslim lands with the story of Sodom and Gomorrah (Gen. 19). This well-known biblical locus, usually interpreted as punishment for the sin of sodomy, was used by Pope Innocent IV as a model for Christian intervention against infidels, who inevitably violated natural law (Muldoon, 11, 165 n. 34).

Although the Chaucerian Aeneas is not shown to be homosexual, he is somewhat "effeminate" in spirit: far from sturdy in adversity. On arriving in Carthage, Aeneas is devastated to discover the fate of his people portrayed on a temple wall. He weeps aloud, wishing himself dead: "Allas, that I was born! . . . No lenger for to lyven I ne kepe" (1027–32). This is already unlike the Virgilian hero, who weeps at the pictures but, like a proper leader, exhorts his companion Achates to "be free of fear; this story will bring you some good yet" ("solve metus: feret haec aliquam tibi fama salutem" [1.463]). Later, overwhelmed by Dido's generosity, Aeneas thinks he has "come to paradys" (1103), and, with its spicery and wines, its music and "amorous lokyng," its "riche beddes and . . . ornementes," it certainly seems to be an Islamic paradise he has in mind. In Chapter 5, I shall analyze the economic motif in this legend to suggest that Dido's hospitality is overgenerous, but in keeping with the theme of Orientalism, it is relevant to note that such an instance of lavish giving had been recently displayed—and criticized—when Richard II welcomed Leo of Armenia at the English court.

The despair felt by Aeneas at the beginning is acted upon by Dido at the end. Less committed than Antony and Cleopatra, less innocent than Piramus and Thisbe, Dido and Aeneas do not acquit themselves admirably. Between these two Oriental figures there is little to choose, trapped as they are in their "own" subjectivity: that is, in traditions incarnating the subjectivity of authors.

HYPSIPYLE, MEDEA, AND JASON

Jason is a questing hero from northern Greece who encounters two women on islands near Turkey. The actual distances throughout the Aegean Sea are not extremely great, but they sufficed to enable many authors to construct a typical Oriental motif: the hero from a relatively civilized (often Western) place and with a mission, detained by a woman in a less civilized (often Eastern) place. For when the *Argo* arrives from Greece, the women of Lemnos (according to tradition) couple with the treasure-seekers. Some accounts claim that Hercules had to force his shipmates back to their duty: the Tegernsee commentary on Ovid's Epistle of Hypsipyle (*Heroides* 6) says that Jason dallied and had frequently to be reminded of his mission (Hexter, 252). As for Medea, her primitivism and provinciality are usually stressed: she is a sorceress in an outlying island. In *Heroides*, Hypsipyle scornfully describes Medea as a barbarian (6.19, 81), and Medea herself deplores the fact that Jason considers her a barbarian (12.105).

The Oriental women we have seen in the *Legend* so far—Cleopatra, Thisbe, and Dido—all commit suicide. Unlike them, the two represented here turn their violence outward, and not merely in disappointment, for both of them are associated with distinctively gory events. The women of Lemnos "withdrew their untamed necks from the yoke of men" (as Boccaccio puts it [*Concerning Famous Women*, trans. Guarini, 33]) and massacred all the men on the island. They excepted only King Thoas, whose life was spared by his daughter Hypsipyle before she took the throne. Boccaccio duly praises Hypsipyle for her filial piety, but there is no comment about her complicity in the massacre or her failure to intervene against it—indeed, true to his project of rewriting woman good, or at least better, he exonerates Hypsipyle from the mysterious death of her ward Archemorus. These events, however, are firmly associated with Hypsipyle in accounts by Statius and Guido delle Colonne (Chaucer's primary source); Ovid's Hypsipyle refers to the massacre also (*Her.* 6.50), and it is likely that any version of the *Heroides* known to Chaucer would annotate the reference. Accordingly, Chaucer inserts a genuine viciousness into Hypsipyle's prayer that the woman who has stolen Jason from her may lose him, kill her children by him, and also kill any other woman who loves him (1571–75). As for Medea, she does, of course, fulfill this prayer; but even before being abandoned by Jason, she had embezzled her father's wealth and dismembered her brother in order to assist Jason's escape. Afterward she conspires against her father-in-law and attempts to poison the king of Athens: events related by Boccaccio in *De mulieribus claris*, in the Ovid scholia, and elsewhere.

Greek Jason is no gentleman, to be sure; greedy, ambitious, and manipulative he is. But what he learns of barbarism is taught him by two Oriental women.

PHILOMELA

With the legend of Philomela, seventh in his series of nine, Chaucer reverses the usual alignment of sex and place of origin. Rather than a Western or highly civilized hero and a barbarian or marginally located temptress, we are given two Athenian princesses, the sisters Procne and Philomela, and a villain, Tereus, who is not exactly Greek. Tereus is lord of Thrace, a territory to the extreme north and east of Greece, just below the Balkans and including the Bosphorus and Constantinople. Chaucer's Tereus is thus very nearly a Turk, and when he travels to Athens he is said to go "into Grece." Much is made of the sisters' dangerous distance from home and, implicitly, from civilized norms of behavior. As indicated above, this part of

the world was fairly close to European concerns in the late fourteenth century, for in 1361 the capital city of Thrace, Adrianople,
was captured by the Turks. It became a new capital of the Islamic
Ottoman Empire and a base for its expansion into Europe via the
Balkans. In this sense Tereus is, of all the fools and villains in the
Legend, the one most easily associated with contemporary events
and the Turkish threat.

Certainly Tereus is the worst of them all: incestuous adulterer,
liar, rapist, and mutilator—cannibal too, if we look at the Ovidian
ending, which Chaucer omits. So terrible is he that his story offers
an opportunity for Chaucer's Narrator to contemplate the problem
of evil in the world, in the form of a prayer for theodicy:

> Thow yevere of the formes, that hast wrought
> This fayre world and bar it in thy thought
> Eternally er thow thy werk began,
> Why madest thow, unto the slaunder of man,
> Or, al be that it was nat thy doing,
> As for that fyn, to make swych a thyng,
> Whi sufferest thow that Tereus was bore . . . ?
> (2228–34)

There is not much explicit Christian reference in the *Legend*, so this
prayer stands out. Full discussion of this and related passages is
reserved to Chapter 5, but I want here to observe that the introduction of a classic theme in Christian apologetics can scarcely be
coincidental at a point where Chaucer's traditional material most
nearly recalls the present threat from an alien ideology, its geography a reminder of the military penetration of Islam into Europe.

Not everything medieval Europe or medieval England knew about
the Orient was legendary and stereotypical. Peter Alfons—a Span-
ish Jew who converted to Christianity in 1106, and who lived briefly
in England as physician to King Henry I—produced a fairly balanced portrait of Islam in his *Conversations*. About 1120, William of
Malmesbury emphasized "against all popular thought" the monotheistic character of Islam, while the English monk Matthew Paris
discussed Islam in his *Chronica majora* to the effect that, as J. J.
Saunders writes, "we are surprised more by the accuracy than by
the distortions of his picture" (116). Other efforts of serious scholarly documentation featured major contributions by English schol-

ars, as Dorothée Metlitzki and others note. One of these was Robert Ketton, who, in the twelfth century, translated the Qur'an into Latin. Ketton's heavily annotated translation was widely diffused throughout scholarly Europe and England. It was used by the thirteenth-century Oxford Franciscan Roger Bacon, who denounced crusading in favor of preaching in the language of those to be converted. Toward the middle of the fourteenth century, both Richard Fitzralph and Ranulf Higden relied upon Ketton's translation of Qur'an, and despite its flaws the work continued in missionary use throughout the seventeenth century.

Ketton's work was sponsored by Peter the Venerable, abbot of Cluny, starting in 1141. The latter's purpose was defensive and polemical, to be sure, but his tactic was to understand the enemy so as to convert him: an "intellectual crusade," as Alverny put it. The premise was that this enemy offered no bizarre gallimaufry of deities (such as is represented in the *Chanson de Roland*, where the pagans worship Apollo, Tervagan, Mahomet, Jupiter, and many other figures) but rather a monotheistic faith with an ethics and a high intellectual tradition of its own, a faith that could, for just those reasons, pose a genuinely attractive alternative to Christianity. It is telling that in his *Summa totius heresis ac diabolicae sectae Sarracenorum*, Peter refers to Islam not as heathen worship but as a "heresy," indeed as a compendium of all previous heresies: like the Sabellian it denies the Trinity, like the Nestorian it denies the divinity of Jesus, like Manichaeism it denies Jesus's death. In so describing Islam, Peter implied that it was a deviation from truth but nonetheless in the same family, as it were, with Christianity. Mark of Toledo, who translated the Qur'an some decades after Ketton, wrote of Muhammad as a man learned in mathematics and Holy Scripture, deeply committed to converting the masses to monotheism. He considered Islam a *legem tertiam*, blending features of Judaism and Christianity. The famous debate of 1254 in Karakorum, Mongolia, between the Flemish Franciscan William of Rubroek and representatives of three Asian religions—Nestorian Christians, Buddhists, and Muslims— was predicated on an assumption of rationality, and indeed William won the debate with the Muslims as his allies at many points (Komroff). In Chaucer's century, *Mandeville's Travels* offered an extensive and surprisingly sympathetic view of Islam, opining that "be cause that thei gon so ny oure feyth thei ben lyghtly converted

to cristene lawe whan man preche hem And schewen hem dis-
tynctly the lawe of Ihesu crist & whan men tellen hem of the
prophecyes" (ch. 16). The similarities, beyond monotheism, are
that Islam too is a revealed religion dependent on a sacred book, it
too respects Moses and Jesus, it too has angels and saints and
prophets.

The scholarly approach was as determined as any other to extir-
pate Islam, although preferably by persuasion rather than by force
of arms. "I do not attack you," wrote Peter the Venerable to an
Islamic audience, "as some of us often do, by arms, but by words;
not by force but by reason; not in hatred but in love. . . . [Man,]
endowed with reason, which no other species has, . . . is known to
love what is like himself, led by reason. . . . [Hence] I love you;
loving, I write to you; writing, I invite you to salvation" (Kritzeck,
161–62). To this end, while no liberal or tolerant program, an effort
like Peter's did recognize the need for accuracy and for respect of the
considerable virtues of Islam. It acknowledged the sophistication of
a system whose adherents had, as Maria Menocal stresses, created
in Spain (al-Andalus) a tolerant, multicultural, intellectually advanced civilization that would last some seven centuries and decisively change the face of European literary and intellectual culture. Indeed, Peter had to go to Spain to hire his translators!

The twelfth-century scholarly impulse was repeated in later generations by both ecclesiastical and lay critics of crusade (Throop,
chs. 5 and 6). The question of whether force is a permissible tactic of
conversion had long been on the agenda. Those arguing the negative side included Alcuin during the Carolingian period, (Saint)
Peter Damian in the eleventh century, secular poets of various
nationalities, the thirteenth-century Dominican missionary William
of Tripoli (who traveled a short way with the Polo brothers), and
many other Dominican and Franciscan "missionary pacifists" who
believed in the principle that God is not pleased by forced worship.
Accepting the rationality and, evidently, the reasonableness, of
their opponent, these men insisted on the importance of refuting
Islam point by point, and, as we have seen above, Gower challenged the concept of crusading on the same grounds.

This is not the tradition Chaucer seems to have chosen to em-
body in his work, at least as I read it. To say so is not necessarily to
imply that the poet is a raving warmonger. On the contrary, my

reading suggests that he probably thought that England's resources could be more usefully disbursed domestically than in military adventures abroad. In any case, Chaucer did not write political treatises but poems—not even political treatises in verse, but poems. The rational-scholarly approach to the Orient is far less useful poetically than the mythic one. It lends itself less readily to moral drama, particularly when moral drama is embodied in stories of sexual desire, about which old-fashioned patristic-popular Orientalism has so much to say. The Oriental theme was particularly available to Chaucer in the few years just preceding the composition of the *Legend* because of a confluence of episodes and of demands being made on English finances and foreign policy: parliamentary debate in the early 1380s about the Despenser crusade and about John of Gaunt's crusade to Castile; the mobilization of resources for these campaigns through 1386; the presence at court of Leo of Armenia in 1384–85; the 1384 propaganda campaign of Mézières; the Scrope-Grosvenor trial of 1385–86; the glamorous appeal of crusading to many English knights and nobles. Chaucerian Orientalism seems to depend for its moral and literary thrust on older attitudes than the rationalistic one that had developed since the twelfth century. It partakes, albeit relatively subtly, of a patristic and popular Orientalism that maintained the idea of a sinister, immoral, insidious Orient and was therefore a useful mythos in the polarized moral world Chaucer sometimes liked to shape into his poems.

Chaucer was able to deconstruct gender difference sub specie aeternitatis: Christianity gave him a way to do so. The same possibility did not exist for an alien ideology embodied in Orientals who, although exposed to Christian truth, rejected it. The Christian woman is not *eternally* Other; the conscious infidel is.

5

A Gallery of Women

Exit in inmensum fecunda licentia vatum,
   obligat historica nec sua verba fide.
et mea debuerat falso lauda videri
   femina; credulitas nunc mihi vestra nocet.
                              Ovid, *Amores* 3.12.41–44

Boundless emerges the poet's fertile license,
historical fidelity does not constrain his words.
Even my lady ought to have been seen as falsely praised;
now your credulity damages me. (My trans.)

In the Chaucerian text, then, denial and affirmation of gender difference come as closely bound as true and false tidings from the House
of Rumor when they "compounded / Togeder fle for oo tydynge"
(*HF* 2108–9). It is sometimes tempting to see Chaucer as an outright
misogynist, especially when we recall his implication in the *raptus*
of Cecily Chaumpaigne (which the legal historian P. R. Watts says
can only have been a sexual offense) and notice the prominent role
assigned to rape in his work: Lucrece and Philomela in the *Legend*,
Malyn and her mother in the *Reeve's Tale*, the anonymous peasant
girl in Alison's tale, the wedding night of May and January as narrated by the Merchant, and the planned rape of Virginia (averted by
murder) in the *Physician's Tale*. Murders of women occur in three of
the *Tales*: the Physician's, the Manciple's, and the Second Nun's.
After a list like this, one would prefer to rest the case; on the
psychoanalytic level I would do so, and have done so in discussing
the *Manciple's Tale* (cf. *Writing Woman*).

Two things are minimized in this position, though. One is the
immense creative power the poet has invested in many of his
female characters, with such persuasive effect that Carolyn Dinshaw claims that "Chaucer writes like a woman." The other is the
substantial integration of women into English economic and social

life: visitors from Spain and Italy called England "a paradise for women" compared to their own countries. As a Londoner, a courtier, a traveler, a government bureaucrat, Chaucer was well aware of women's real social roles and capabilities, and that awareness is part of his sensibility. It matters aesthetically and historically, therefore, to grasp the ambivalent and multiply nuanced Chaucerian attitude toward women, its distance from a simplistic or essentialist misogyny that would portray women—"Woman"—as inherently passive or inherently wicked.

Proceeding once more through the series, I shall look at its explorations of sex and gender: how sexuality, mediated by language, subjectivity, money, or literary tradition, becomes gender; how it may relate to political power; where art enters the picture.

CLEOPATRA

King, governing, reigning queen, senator, conquering realms and honor, custom, having the world at their obedience: such is the cluster of images and concepts with which, in its first eight lines, the first legend opens. After this overture setting a political theme, the hero is introduced. Antony does everything wrong—or, as the Chaucerian Narrator obtusely puts it, "Fortune hym oughte a shame" (589). As a member of the ruling elite, he becomes "Rebel unto the toun of Rome" (591); as a husband, he abandons his wife "or that she was war" (593); as a tactician, he mortally offends Caesar, whose sister his wife is (592); as a moral being, he becomes, or wishes to become, a bigamist (594). In statesmanship and in marriage, Antony subverts the proper order, and we are soon shown the subjective operation of this subversion, as Antony allows passion to overwhelm reason.

There is only one thing the man does right, and that is being a lover. Antony is so absolutely committed to his beloved that "al the world he sette at no value" (602). His only desire is to love and serve her; he is quite willing to die in her defense (605–6). He is, in short, a very perfect gentle courtly lover, and, best of all, the dependency bond is reciprocated (607). This is so despite the fact that the pair are a wedded couple: Antony wishes to "han another wyf," Cleopatra "wax his wif," and the Narrator declines to describe "the weddynge and the feste" (616). Although the *Riverside Chaucer* remarks that they are married "only in the accounts of Vincent of Beauvais and Boccaccio," in fact there is a much nearer source for this detail: Higden's *Polychronicon*, where the monk writes, "Antonius repudiata sorore Caesaris quam duxerat, Cleopatram reginam Ægypti superduxit, cui et Arabiam dedit" (3.44). The same verb, *duco*, is used of both partnerships. Trevisa, displacing Cleopatra's name into the wrong clause, nonetheless preserves the relationship in translating, "Antonius putte from hym his wif Cleopatra, Cesar his suster, and wedded the quene of Egipt, and yaf hir Arabia." Whether the poet considered this unsanctioned marriage (and others in the *Legend*) to be morally and legally binding is debatable; the question is discussed below in connection with Dido. Clearly the characters and the narrator consider it so. Nonetheless Chaucer lightly underscores the erotic intensity of this marriage by inserting several tried and true phrases from the courtly lyric and romance tradition: "desert... chyvalrye... gentilesse... discrecioun and hardynesse.... And she was fayr as is the rose in May" (608–13). (This last phrase describing a North African queen must have evoked some little sense of irony in the keenly color-conscious medieval reader.)[1]

One can be an excellent lover, we see, and a terrible everything else. It is not, I believe, that Antony "is not the ideal courtly lover" (Frank, 41) but rather that he is precisely that—and a rebel, adulterer, traitor, and bigamist beside. The problem is that erotic intensity certifies nothing else at all. It can coexist with a wide range of

---

1. On medieval color-consciousness, see the collection *Les Couleurs au Moyen-Age* (Aix-en-Provence: University of Provence, 1988) and the bibliography on color in Kaske, 172–81.

Outstanding as an instance of high-medieval color-consciousness linked with Orientalism is the remarkable Gahmuret-prologue to Wolfram von Eschenbach's *Parzival* (1198–1212). The Angevin knight Gahmuret (the hero's father) marries a beautiful and virtuous black Moorish queen, Belacane. Much is made of the color difference, as in this description: "If there is anything brighter than daylight—the queen in no way resembled it. A woman's manner she did have, and was on other counts worthy of a knight, but she was unlike a dewy rose: her complexion was black of hue" (*Parzival*, trans. Mustard and Passage, bk. 1, p. 14). Belacane bears a son, Feirefiz Angevin, who is dappled black and white "like a magpie."

In the *Chanson de Roland*, it is only when he sees the Ethiopian troops—*La neire gent* from *une tere maldite* (*laisse* 143), blacker than ink, and with nothing white about them except their teeth—only then does Roland admit: "Now I know truly that today we shall die" (*laisse* 144).

moral deficiencies or even crimes, because the standard of erotic desire excludes too much. It can be fully met by immoral people. Nor is it a question of "the world well lost for love" (ibid., 40) but on the contrary, of the world ill lost for love. Nor is this simply a version of the "exotic temptress" topos (or ideologeme). While making use of the idea, Chaucer does not leave it at this, for if Cleopatra tempts Antony to abandon his country and his family, she is tempted equally by him. She too is a ruler, she too abdicates her social responsibility in sheer subjective self-indulgence, she too is far from lacking courage. This is a story, then, without a victim. The parties are true and devoted lovers, equal in passion and in irresponsibility. To represent shared and equal folly allows Chaucer to accomplish the same sort of simultaneous maneuver he performed in the balade: to collapse gender and political distinctions on the ethical level, while illustrating the disastrous consequences of such leveling in the world of social action.

Even in its erotic dimension, then, the legend of Cleopatra is in a sense about politics: that is, about the ultimate vacuity, sterility, and antisocial consequences of sheer eroticism. Chaucer was not alone in asserting this theme, not even in poetry. Chrétien's *Erec et Enide* is devoted to it, and not coincidentally Chrétien's romance employs the arch-Orientalist story of Dido and Aeneas as a metaphor for itself (5289–5300). Yet the legendary reference plays a minor part in Chrétien's narrative, occurring only toward the end of the work; indeed, part of the affective power of *Erec et Enide* is precisely that it de-exoticizes the issue in three ways. First, the setting is Britain, the characters French and British. Second, heroism is shared equally by the male and female protagonists, who are a married couple. Third, the poem locates the problem of duty versus pleasure squarely within normal masculine consciousness rather than projecting it onto the seductive ways of a temptress. It is not, I think, a vision Chaucer would necessarily contradict, but neither is it one he was able in his own work fully to express. I mean by this that his sensibility tends rather toward the negative than the positive in love: toward the failure of eroticism rather than the success of stable love. If there is a work that might qualify as Chaucer's *Erec et Enide*, it would be his *Franklin's Tale*, but the difference in scope suggests that this is the exception that proves the rule.

THISBE

The potential pathos of the Thisbe story is allayed in several ways: by obscene wordplay, as shown in Chapter 3, and by the heavily laden Oriental references with which the tale opens (Chapter 4). Another antisentimental tactic is a farcical narrative style, which surfaces in two places, both connected with the death of Piramus:

> And with that word he smot hym to the herte.
> The blod out of the wounde as brode sterte
> As water, whan the condit broken is.
>   (850–52)

> And at the laste hire love thanne hath she founde,
> Betynge with his heles on the grounde . . .
>   (862–63)

The first, the image of blood spurting out of a wound like water from broken plumbing, occurs in Ovid (*Met.* 4.121–24). Indeed, it is (by Ovidian standards) considerably overdone there. Clearly, it parodies Homeric extended simile, yet with the narrative justification that Piramus's blood must spurt high enough from the ground where he lies to dye the (hitherto white) fruit of the mulberry tree and thus accomplish metamorphosis. In Ovid and the *Ovide moralisé*, the wound is to the lower abdomen, while Boccaccio and Chaucer make it a cut to the breast or heart, and both omit the metamorphosis.

The second locus, however, the farcical detail of the hero beating with his heels on the ground, occurs neither in Ovid, the *Ovide moralisé*, nor Boccaccio. It comes from an author mentioned in the *House of Fame* as "Englyssh Gaufride" (1470) and cited as a source for certain details in the *Franklin's Tale*: Geoffrey of Monmouth's twelfth-century *Historia regum Britanniae*. Narrating the death of the tribune Frollo at Arthur's hands, Geoffrey writes, "Quo vulnere cecidit Frollo, tellurem calcaneis pulsans, et spiritum in auras emisit" ("With this wound Frollo fell, beating the ground with his heels, and sent his spirit out to the winds" [9.11]). Is the detail absurd in the original too? It might well be argued that the Frollo section is a deliberate study in anti-heroism, intended to glorify Arthur at the expense of his enemies. Although its narrative inconsistencies and rhetorical extravagances are not quite so blatant as those in Chaucer's *Thopas*, the effect is a humor that, even if unconscious, sometimes resembles that of the Chaucerian burlesque.

Although I do not want to suggest that Chaucer used this material simply for patriotic reasons, his distinctive ethico-literary vision is not unaffected by its English setting. Perhaps he felt a kindred spirit at work in his countryman's *Historia*, for his own engagement with the Latin literary classics parallels that of Geoffrey of Monmouth with British history. In a sense, the two Geoffries confronted a similar task: to integrate British experience with classical legend, to make contemporary English sense of the heterogeneous past. Geoffrey of Monmouth sought to graft British history onto the cycle of Troy and Rome, as represented in the *Aeneid*; Chaucer to retell classical tales for a courtly and urban English audience. Like the later Geoffrey, the earlier one produced a text that at once transmits and problematizes tradition; that is why, from the start, its reception was mixed. The nature of his project is ambiguous, for his history includes fantasy (e.g., the Merlin chapters), rhetorical exaggeration, contradiction, and authorial interjection. And, like the later Geoffrey, the earlier one is intensely self-aware, meditating in his Dedication on the problems of historical tradition and its modes of transmission.

For Chaucer, the *Historia* would be one of those books "That tellen of these olde appreved stories" (F 21), a book whose testimony we can neither prove nor disprove. This would be true of Chaucer's own recension of the classics too—and, as he was all too well aware, of the classics themselves. Yet to give "feyth and ful credence" to such a document as the *Historia* would strain anyone's credulity. I do not doubt that Chaucer, like many readers before him, encountered Geoffrey's *Historia* with a healthy skepticism. The line he stole from it to insert into his version of Piramus and Thisbe tells us something about how he read Geoffrey and Ovid—quite accurately, I think, and in a spirit he brought to his own *translatio*.

If Chaucer's version of Thisbe, with its absurdities and obscenities, is subversive of sentiment, its ending is equally subversive of Alceste's instructions. Here, as in the first legend, there is no victimization, for, as Edgar Finley Shannon remarked, Piramus "is not faithless, he merely failed to arrive on time" (193). The lovers are equal in passion, equal in self-sacrifice, with this improvement:

whereas Antony killed himself not for Cleopatra but for shame at losing the sea battle, Piramus does kill himself for Thisbe's sake. "Lat see now what man that lover be, / Wol doon so strong a peyne for love as she" (F 568–69), says Alceste with reference to Cleopatra's suicide. The Narrator has taken her literally, shown her just such a man. Likewise, the Narrator's apparent skepticism at the end of "Cleopatra"—"or I fynde a man thus trewe and stable, / And wol for love his deth so frely take" (703–4)—is gratifyingly negated by Piramus. Of course, the Narrator tactfully adds, with an eye to his sponsors Eros and Alceste, there are not many such (917–18); yet the last seven lines of the tale are about men. The Narrator intrudes in the first person to remind us that his writing is gender-marked:

> And therfore have I spoken of hym thus.
> For it is deynte to us men to fynde
> A man that can in love been trewe and kynde.
> (919–21)

He finishes by backhandedly reasserting masculinity as norm, which woman strives to equal, for

> Here may ye se, what lovere so he be,
> A woman dar and can as wel as he.

The material escapes the frame that has been set up for it by its sponsors; so does the narrative voice. The disruptive forces of tradition and of utterance break through again and again in the legends, swamping the simplistic demands of Eros and Alceste.

DIDO

The Scots poet Gavin Douglas would chide his master Chaucer for failing to keep the promise Chaucer made in the first lines of this life: "I shal, as I can, / Folwe thy lanterne, as thow gost byforn" (926). In the Prologue to the first book of his translation of the *Aeneid*, Douglas specifies this place in Chaucer's "legeand of notable ladyis." It is not through inadequacy of translation, Douglas writes, that Chaucer "greitlie Virgile offendit," for Latin is a difficult language and must often be translated for general meaning rather than word for word. The offense is rather to have "greitlie the prince of poets grevit" by saying that "Eneas to Dido was forsworne." This,

Douglas rightly observes, is alien to the Virgilian portrayal; but this lapse can be excused in Chaucer, "For he was ever, God wait, wemenis frend." In this generous manner does Douglas exculpate his great predecessor, who not only fails to follow Virgil scrupulously, but, in substituting Ovidian material (*Heroides* 7), replaces the epic-heroic viewpoint with a contradictory lyric-erotic scenario from the seduced-and-abandoned female's point of view.

But it is worse than Douglas acknowledges, for Virgil himself was what some medieval rigorists might consider a liar. It was Virgil who invented the Dido who comes down to us thereafter, the Dido whom Aeneas met and loved and abandoned, the amorous Dido characterized in medieval *Heroides* commentaries as *stultus amans*, because she loved a stranger, was overhospitable, and fought against (the hero's) fate.[2] Before Virgil there was no connection between the two figures; indeed, they were thought to have lived three centuries apart, so there could have been no meeting. Before Virgil, Dido was an emblem of faith in love. Married to Sychaeus and widowed, she killed herself in order to avoid the advances of a second suitor, Iarbus. Macrobius criticized Virgil for portraying an amorous Dido (*Saturnalia* 5.17.4–6); Ausonius has an epigram in which Dido blames not Aeneas but Virgil for destroying her virtue. Among the Church fathers, Tertullian was especially proud of the chaste Dido; he refers to her often and "spared no effort in promoting the fame of the heroine of his native Carthage," as Mary L. Lord observes in her thorough review of the chaste-Dido tradition (to which most of my comments here are indebted). The tradition was sustained by various grammarians, Virgil commentators, and medieval authors including Servius, Macrobius, Priscian, Petrarch, and early Dante commentators; indeed, the question seems to have attained the status of a fairly significant debate in fourteenth-century Italian letters. A modern text readily available to Chaucer was Boccaccio's *De mulieribus claris*, which Chaucer used for his Monk's account of Zenobia. Boccaccio's extended version of the Dido material argues that although Dido's death took place during Aeneas's visit, its oc-

---

2. Hexter, 256, and Shaner, 48–57. Shaner's work came to my attention when this manuscript was completed, and I was delighted that our conclusions were quite congruent (despite some interpretive differences). I am very grateful to the author for her generosity in sending me a copy of the thesis, and to Alastair Minnis for mentioning it to me.

currence had already been determined as a gesture of fidelity to her dead husband Sichaeus. Boccaccio retains the meeting with Aeneas, but, following the lead of the historian Justin's *Historiae Philippicae*, makes every effort to rehabilitate the queen's good name and to remove "the infamy undeservedly cast on the honor of her widowhood."[3] Higden aligns himself firmly with the anti-Virgilians, pointing out that on chronological grounds, "it may nought stonde that Virgilius and Phrygius Dares in his storie of the bataille of Troye seith, that Eneas sih that womman Dido, for Eneas was dede thre hundred yere and more or Cartage was i-founded" (1.21, and cf. also 2.26). As Lord observes (225), Chaucer must have been aware of this tradition, for Dorigen's complaint in the *Franklin's Tale* (V.1367–1456) draws heavily on the list of exempla in Jerome's *Adversus Jovinianum*, and this set includes the chaste Dido (although she is not used in the Chaucerian passage).

Chaucer's program differs, I suggest, from that of the defenders of Dido, for had he wanted to portray an unequivocally "good" and chaste Dido, in accordance with Eros's command, he need only have drawn on the tradition that shows her true to her dead husband, Sychaeus. In terms of plot, Chaucer is firmly on the Virgilian bandwagon by virtue of narrating Dido's affair with Aeneas—even Ovid did that much. Tonally, though, he will, like Ovid, deflate the epic-heroic dimension of the story, along with its lyric-sentimental version: that is, he will side with neither lover. Chaucer does not show Dido as unequivocally virtuous, merely as decent, human, and flawed—like Aeneas. His treatment of both characters subtly but strongly implies that they must each take responsibility for their fates. The resultant ambiguity of character and tone receives linguistic expression in an egregious pun strategically placed near the beginning of the tale: "And fyr, so wod it myghte nat been steered" ([935] wood: made of wood / crazy) in recounting the fall of Troy. This is a favorite Chaucerian pun, perhaps *the* favorite Chaucerian pun. It occurs twice in the *Knight's Tale* (1299–1302, 2950) and in the legends of Thisbe (736) and Phyllis (2419–20) as well as here. Even the description of Troilus's dismay after the decision to trade

3. Boccaccio, *Concerning Famous Women*, trans. Guarini, 86. There is very little direct borrowing from this text in the *Legend*, for Boccaccio's sincere and ardent humanism was not what Chaucer was aiming at.

Criseyde reaches after this pun, comparing the "wood" (crazed) Troilus to a bare tree and then giving a homonymic play on "bark" (tree bark/boat [*TC* 4.225–31]).

The moral equivalency of the sexes is suggested in the opening movement, which, as in the first legend, is about history and the hero's place in it. The story is not of Dido only but "of hym and of Dido" (956): both of them of heroic stature, both of honorable history (hers summarized by Venus but not by the Narrator: 994–97), and with faults. In the *Aeneid*, the Oriental Dido accuses the Trojan hero of savagery and barbarism because of his Asian origins: he was begotten on jagged cliffs and suckled by Hyrcanian tigers (4.366–67). Lee Patterson observes of this locus that "her accusation reveals both the deep kinship between her lover and herself and, more profoundly, her own fate as the stigmatized other in the thematic economy of imperial historiography. She must be banished from Virgil's narrative because she too closely expresses those aspects of the hero's own personality that are discontinuous with the ideology of his mission" (168). In the late-medieval English treatment, the similarity is much plainer than in the Roman national epic: Chaucer represents the pair as two of a kind—and, as noted of the two preceding legends, not only this pair. If Virgil invented (or appropriated) Dido as a figure for what the hero must divest, Chaucer retains her in the Virgilian mode to show the impossibility of such auto-amputation.

I have already noted Aeneas's suicidal despair when confronted with his own story. The picture begins to show a few more cracks when the hero and heroine are brought together. Rhetorically, the anaphoric "and" (eight out of eleven lines, 1061–71) suggests—as it did with Criseyde (*Troilus and Criseyde* 2.449–69, 2.1300ff.)—the search for "an heep of weyes" of justification. Dido likes Aeneas not only for his story (as Desdemona liked Othello) but for his looks as well; moreover, "for he was a straunger, somwhat she / Likede hym the bet, as, God do bote, / To som folk ofte newe thyng is sote" (1075–77). She is, we see, vulnerable to appearance and to new-fangledness. Later, to her sister Anne, she will describe her motives this way: "For that me thynketh he is so wel ywrought, / And ek so likly for to ben a man" (1173–74): motives scarcely more elevated than those of a present-day adolescent.

At first, the queen's provisioning of Aeneas's fleet is no more than the generous hospitality one would expect of a monarch (1090–99). Even here, though, the telltale anaphoric "And" (five times in eight lines: 1090–97) duplicates the piling up of goods and the piling up of reasons or motives. In the next section, eight lines running begin with "ne" (1115–22), listing all the gifts Dido bestows upon Aeneas: not only hospitality but horses, jewels, falcons, hounds, sacks of gold, cups of gold, and a great deal of money. The money is a particularly distasteful and discordant note, for it signals that Dido is engaging in a game of sexual and material power, in an attempt to buy the man she desires. Aeneas is her kept man: "And al is payed, what that he hath spent" (1125). She is giving too much materially, as she will shortly give too much of herself both physically and emotionally. Chaucer has Aeneas acknowledge the economic dimension in the Narrator's comment, just before his long apostrophe to victimized women, that

> Now laugheth Eneas and is in joye
> And more richesse than evere he was in Troye.
> (1252–53)

But this sexual economics will backfire, for paradoxically Dido sets herself up as victim by this too-generous giving, allowing herself to be used, representing herself as "easy." The passivity that lies at the heart of her aggressive giving comes clear in Dido's interview with her sister. Twice she hands over her life to Aeneas (1176, 1181), and she begs her sister to make a decision for her: "if that ye rede it me, / I wolde fayn to hym ywedded be" (1178–79). The moral abdication apparent here becomes generalized at the end, when Dido abdicates her social responsibility as governor of Carthage in order to indulge her personal disappointment. Like Cleopatra, she is a queen whose private life has overwhelmed her public obligation.

And so, victim to her own subjectivity, Dido believes she is wedded to Aeneas, although the Narrator's pointed deliberate mystification about the lack of a witness makes it clear that socially their union has no validity at all. "I not, with hem if there wente any mo [into the cave to consummate their desire]; / The autour maketh of it no mencioun" (1227–28). But the author does make mention; indeed, both authors do. Virgil has rather a lot of stage business around the cave scene, which parodies the traditional Roman ceremony so decisively reinforced by Augustan marriage and morality legislation. Instead of the marriage torch, there is lightning; instead of the ceremonial chants, there is the howling of nymphs; instead of attendants, there are Tellus and Juno. In short, instead of civil society, there are the forces of nature—scarcely, for Virgil, or for Chaucer, an adequate substitute. As for human witness, Virgil is quite clear that only "Dido and the Trojan leader came to the cave" (4.165–66). When we turn to Ovid, Dido's letter in *Heroides* (7.93–94) specifies *nos*—we: herself and Aeneas—in connection with the cave scene. Chaucerian disingenuity thus creates a reader response: it is not something the reader would normally wonder about, until reminded by the Narrator to do so. Once we do think about it, and realize that there was no witness, we understand that this is no marriage in the generally accepted sense of the term, but only in the imagination of the fictional speaker, whose subjectivity is so prominently at stake throughout the narrative. This perspective is confirmed when Virgil summarizes the episode this way: "conjugium vocat; hoc praetexit nomine culpam" ("she called it marriage, and with this word concealed her guilt" [4.172]). Henry Ansgar Kelly insists on the validity of clandestine marriage, particularly in his analysis of the story of Dido in the *Legend*; he nonetheless admits that "clandestine marriage was declared illegitimate by papal law" (210). It is important to note, furthermore, that Kelly's view of the relationship between Dido and Aeneas is part of an overall interpretation of the *Legend* as a poem in which "Chaucer strove to portray his lovers as sympathetically as possible, and therefore made them as moral as possible" (59). A different interpretation of the poem would require a different view of the "marriage," and I agree here with V. A. Kolve, who, in another context, observes that "pagan marriage does not normally carry sacramental value for a medieval poet" (173). Yet however ambiguous medieval attitudes toward clandestine marriage may have been, it seems to me that Chaucer stakes out a rigorist and conservative position here, and not—as observed elsewhere in this study—for the first or only time. A short generation after Chaucer's death, such rigor would be strongly enforced: in the Norwich heresy trial of 1428, one Margery Baxter, wife of William Baxter, wright, was accused, among other things, of having said that a vow of mutual love between man and woman sufficed to the sacrament of marriage, without any other words or ecclesiastical solemnization (Tanner, 46).

As for Aeneas, his behavior is nothing short of sleazy. Chaucer does not directly depict the apparition of Mercury that provokes the hero's departure in the epic. Instead, we are given this episode only in the hero's verbal account of it (1295–1300), which may or may not be true. Coming as it does between the Narrator's assurances of Aeneas's dishonesty, the passage virtually presents itself as a lie. Its rhetoric, moreover, is not such as to inspire confidence. We hear not only of one but of two nocturnal visions—surely a little overdone; and the hero's assertion of misery is interrupted by the distancing phrase "me thynketh" (1300). Even if the appearance of Mercury were to be interpreted not as a lie but as a real dream, it would remain equally an expression of the hero's subjectivity.

This puts Aeneas's assertion of his dream in the same category as Dido's assertion of pregnancy (1323): possibly true, possibly a hope, or a mistake, or a lie and desperate last resort. The detail of the pregnancy is imitated from Ovid, where it is equally ambiguous. *Forsitan*, Ovid begins his sentence about the pregnancy (*Her.* 7.133): perhaps. But this hint, this possibility, creates a moral double bind. If it is untrue, Dido is a liar; if true, a double murderer—of herself and the unborn child. Like Ovid, Chaucer questions not only a heroine's and a hero's motives but, more important, the tradition through which such personae survive, the *fama* and its inherent contradictions, the conventions according to which we read: in short, their subjectivity and ours.

HYPSIPYLE AND MEDEA

It has been noticed before that this tale is really about Jason: the women are paired because they share him. He has, in fact, a little prologue all his own: formal recognition of a tendency, already pronounced in the openings of the first three legends, to concentrate on the anti-hero. This mini-prologue makes no bones about its subject: Jason is clearly the exemplary figure here, albeit in negativity. For Jason is a hunter, a "devourere . . . of gentil wemen" (1369–70). In fact, he is a fowler, whose appearance, words, and pretended emotions are his "recleymyng and . . . [his] lures" (1371). It is the imagery of falconry; Chaucer uses it elsewhere both without sexual implication (*Manciple's Tale* IX.72), and with (*Friar's Tale* III.1340). To reclaim is to call back the hawk, usually after it has taken its prey;

the lure is a contraption made of leather and feathers that can be shaken to imitate a bird and attract the falcon or hawk. This picks up the memorable image of birds and fowler from the Prologue, recalling the network of values and attitudes represented there.

But the birds in question here are not those of the Prologue: no chirping songbirds, but rather themselves hunters of lesser prey. And, while the falconer is a superior and controlling figure, the relation of hawk to falconer is not that of prey or victim, but of trained partner in a hunting team. Given what Chaucer chooses to omit from his accounts of these two ladies, the predatory imagery is fully justified, for both women have participated in particularly grisly and violent events (see Chapter 4 above on Hypsipyle). Toward the end of Chaucer's version of this legend, the reader is left dangling uncomfortably with the Narrator's remark that Jason "with hire [Medea] lafte his yonge children two" (1657). Although the slaughter of her children is clearly the one thing Medea is best known for, the material is resolutely excluded as narrative event, to be as conspicuous in absence as it could be in presence, surely a deliberate cliff-hanger. Once again, as with Antony and Cleopatra or with Dido, we see that one can be a passionate and faithful lover, yet entirely inadequate on the ethical or social level. "Trewe of love, for oght that may byfalle" (F 561) does not suffice for much. The deconstruction of desire is well under way, and of gender stereotypes. Violence and brutality are not exclusively masculine behavior, nor is being victimized an exclusively feminine fate.

Animal imagery continues a few lines further on in the mini-prologue, with the rather inept comparison of Jason to a fox stealing the farmer's tender capons at night. The image is inept in several ways, not least because a capon is a castrated cock. However, let us grant that the tenderness, not the gender, of the stolen flesh is the salient point here. Beyond this, however, the little allegory does not work because Jason does not steal another man's wife. Since he is married, he may be an adulterer, but he fornicates with a single woman. It is a curiously uncontrolled scenario, with its enigmatic "good-man that therfore hath payed" (1391), whose point is perhaps less to speculate on real-life candidates than to call attention to its own procedures.

At the beginning of the Jason and Medea legend, there occurs another odd gender-shift, another curious apparent ineptitude.

Jason, passing from woman to woman, is likened to "mater" that "apetiteth forme alwey / and from forme into forme it passen may" (1582–83). The reversal here is that while the gender-linkage of matter and form is a classical and medieval commonplace, matter is conventionally identified with woman, form with man. Chaucer seems to suggest once again that gender does not matter in sexual ethics, because the demands of morality are the same for either sex. It is, I suppose, to Medea's credit that she takes responsibility for her choice: "Whi lykede me thy yelwe her to se / More than the boundes of myn honeste?" (1672–73). Perhaps this is why she does not kill herself: having articulated her fault, she is able to express anger at Jason rather than turn it against herself: she does, in her letter, more or less wish him dead (1676–77), and the conspicuously missing murder of the children is a gesture of revenge against him, undoing the marriage that he has already undone by betrayal. In her aggressive behavior, Medea leaves behind the socially defined "feminine" role of passive suffering, so that the myth itself, even apart from Chaucer's representation of it, already incorporates a gender-shift.

A third animal image, with a third gender-role reversal, comes at the beginning of the Medea portion of the story: Jason is "of love devourer and dragoun" (1581). But the dragon is distinctively Medea's beast: she was able to tame dragons (she boasts of this in her Ovidian letter), and in the *Ovide moralisé* (7.1358–9), as in Bersuire's earlier version of *Ovidius moralizatus*,[4] she is borne away triumphant in a dragon-drawn chariot. Yet though she could tame dragons and bulls, she writes, she was unable to tame Jason (*Her.* 12.163–64, 195–97). By using the dragon for similarity with Jason rather than contrast, Chaucer accomplishes another ambivalence. Is Jason, like the dragon, tamable (through sensuality), or is Medea's boast of power revealed as hollow? In either case, the dragon is a traditional Chris-

4. *Ovidius moralizatus*, ed. Engels, bk. 7, fol. 55, p. 111. This, the so-called "A" version (for Avignon, where the work was completed before Bersuire went to Paris and produced the revised "P" version), was printed under the name of Thomas Walleys in 1509 and several subsequent editions. The "P" version, which adds material from the *Ovide moralisé* and other sources, has not yet been printed in entirety, although it has circulated in manuscript form and its introduction ("De formis figurisque deorum") to chapter 15 was edited by Joseph Engels in 1966. The dragon-borne chariot does not appear in Guido's *Historia destructionis Troiae* (although much else does that Chaucer used here and in *Troilus*).

tian emblem of the devil, and if the she-devil is now transformed into a he-devil, we are reminded once again that neither sex has a monopoly on malfeasance.

LUCRECE

The Narrator opens this legend by acknowledging a different purpose from that of the original. His first line ("Now mot I seyn the exilynge of kynges") translates the first line of the section of *Fasti* in which Ovid relates the story of Lucrece ("Nunc mihi dicenda est regis fuga" [2, sec. 24]), but his own aim, the Chaucerian Narrator asserts, is not to narrate the events of Roman history, as Ovid and Livy did, but rather "to preyse and drawe to memorye / The verray wif, the verray trewe Lucresse" (1685–86). Both Latin texts use the story to motivate a rebellion against the tyrannical Tarquins, the result of which was the abolition of kingship in Rome. The two classical versions, written during the reign of Augustus, "when Rome is going through one of its fits of public morality" (Bryson, 163), are patriotic accounts of the evolution of Roman republicanism, in which Lucretia "is the figure of violated Rome" (Ian Donaldson, 9). As we might expect, Ovid shifts the weight of the episode, considerably amplifying its dramatic and pathetic aspects beyond Livy's relatively terse account and thus paving the way for its future depoliticization. Jean de Meun's version (*RR* 8578–8620) is inserted into an attack by the Jealous Husband on marital infidelity; and although he maintains the political consequence of the story, the Husband's summary treats Lucretia, along with Penelope, as exceptions who prove the rule about women:

> Si n'est il mes nule Lucrece,
> ne Penelope nule en Grece,
> ne preude fame nule an terre,
> se l'en les savoit bien requerre . . .
>   (8621–24)

> But there is no more Lucrece
> nor Penelope in Greece
> nor prudent woman on earth
> if one knows how to woo them.

Even Boccaccio, the ardent republican, stresses the personal and pathetic elements of the story (*De mulieribus claris* 46).

The tale comes to Chaucer, then, already contaminated by concerns other than political: even more so than the structurally similar story of Virginia and Virginius, which also originates in Livy as an anecdote motivating rebellion and which Chaucer, in the *Physician's Tale*, also revises into a commentary on sexual morality. (Aside from his Ovid commentary, Pierre Bersuire produced a translation of Livy, which could have served Chaucer for both stories.) Yet despite its medieval lapse into sexual moralism, the tale would revive, at least briefly, as a political anecdote when, in *The Serpent of Division* (written about 1422), John Lydgate used it to introduce his cautionary prose treatise about factionalism in Rome and, by analogy, at home. Because of the "outragious offence doone unto Lucresse wife of the worthy Senatour Collatyne . . . the name of king is ceased in the citie of Rome for evur more." Most of Lydgate's text focuses on Julius Caesar, and English barons are exhorted: "maketh a merowre" of Roman instability.

The Chaucerian narrator pushes the personal-pathetic tendency as far as he can with his emphasis on the triply true Lucrece ("verray . . . verray trewe"). Does he protest too much with this hyperbole? And what exactly does "true" (*vrai*) mean here: the faithful Lucrece, or the real Lucrece? The structure of the Chaucerian rendition allows us to attend to the latter meaning, the one more interesting to writers or readers concerned with textual authority and textual interpretation.

The Lucrece material was not compromised only by the sexual-pathetic emphasis of its medieval literary incarnations, but also and more seriously by the authoritative literary-theological controversy in which it figured, similar to the one surrounding Dido. On the one hand, Jerome praises Lucretia as a paragon of chastity (*Adversus Jovinianum* 1.46); many medieval commentators follow him in doing so, as Götz Schmitz points out (*Fall*, 17–20). On the other hand, Augustine offers a detailed and damning critique, and Aquinas excludes from martyrdom women who chose suicide over dishonor (*Summa theologica* 2a–e, Q. 123–40). It is to the Augustinian critique that the Narrator refers in mentioning "the grete Austyn" who "hath gret compassioun / Of this Lucresse" (1690–91).

What are we to make of this obtuse assertion by the Narrator? For to see Augustine's interpretation of the episode as sympathetic is to stretch our credulity to the breaking point. Here is Augustine's account, rhetorically framed as a lawyer's brief for the prosecution and occurring in the context of his defense of Christian martyrs charged with immorality because they have been raped:

> While the sanctity of the soul remains even when the body is violated, the sanctity of the body is not lost; . . . in like manner, the sanctity of the body is lost when the sanctity of the soul is violated, though the body itself remain intact. And therefore a woman who has been violated by the sin of another, and without any consent of her own, has no cause to put herself to death; much less has she cause to commit suicide in order to avoid such violation, for in that case she commits certain homicide to prevent a crime which is uncertain as yet, and not her own.
>
> To you I appeal, ye laws and judges of Rome. . . . If one were to bring to your bar this case, and were to prove to you that a woman not only untried, but chaste and innocent, had been killed, would you not visit the murderer with punishment proportionately severe? This crime was committed by Lucretia; that Lucretia so celebrated and lauded slew the innocent, chaste, outraged Lucretia. Pronounce sentence. But if you cannot . . . why do you extol with such unmeasured laudation her who slew an innocent and chaste woman? . . . Perhaps . . . she slew herself conscious of guilt, not of innocence? She herself alone knows her reasons; but what if she was betrayed by the pleasure of the act, and gave some consent to Sextus, though so violently abusing her, and then was so affected with remorse, that she thought death alone could expiate her sin? Even though this were the case, she ought still to have held her hand from suicide. . . .
>
> She was ashamed that so foul a crime had been perpetrated upon her . . . ; this matron, with the Roman love of glory in her veins, was seized with a proud dread that, if she continued to live, it would be supposed she willingly did not resent the wrong done her. . . . she burned with shame. . . . Not such was the decision of the Christian women who suffered as she did, and yet survive. They declined to avenge upon themselves the guilt of others, and so add crimes of their own to those crimes in which they had no share. . . . It suffices them to have the opportunity of doing good, and they decline to evade the distress of human suspicion, lest they thereby deviate from the divine law. (1.18–19)

There is no way this diatribe, with its imputation of motives and its forceful denunciation of a crime, can be convincingly construed as sympathetic or compassionate. Either Chaucer did not know the material he alludes to, or he deliberately characterized it falsely. Frank (97 n. 7) plausibly suggests the former: that Chaucer found a reference to Augustine's treatment of Lucrece in the *Gesta Romanorum*. Clearly this is one of those questions that cannot be unequivocally resolved, but I would like to entertain the possibility of deliberate falsification. This would not be out of keeping with other distortions already noted: the omission, for instance, of "what every schoolboy knows" about Medea, the assertion of fidelity to Virgil in narrating Dido, or even the nomination of Cleopatra and Medea as "good" women. We are dealing here with an unreliable Narrator, one who constantly brings his, and others', subjectivity into play. To hypothesize knowledge of at least portions of *The City of God* is also consistent with Chaucer's deep familiarity with many of the doctrinal discussions there. But even without firsthand knowledge of Augustine's argument about Lucretia, he could have found a two-sentence précis of it, with attribution, in Higden:

> Wise men here telleth that Lucrecia slough nought hire self for no vertu, but for schame and for anger, for nother man ne womman schulde be punsched with oute gilt, nother with gilt with oute juge. But for the Romayns coveyteth most preysynge of men and world-eliche worschepe, this Lucrecia . . . wolde nought lese hire good loos nother be despised [and] sche wolde no lenger lyve. Of this happe speketh . . . Seint Austyn de Civitate, libro primo, capitulo 19˙ etc. (3.6)

I am going to assume, therefore, that Chaucer did understand the Augustinian position on Lucrece; in any case he correctly duplicates its import in his Narrator's advice to the Black Knight (*Book of the Duchess* 714–37; see Chapter 2 above).

The interrelated issues of subjectivity, self-presentation, and interpretation surface early on in the tale when Lucrece is first glimpsed by the hidden husband Collatine and his friend Tarquinius. Lamenting the war, Lucrece

> mekely she let hyre eyen falle;
> And thilke semblaunt sat hire wel withalle.
> And eek hire teres, ful of honeste,
> Embelished hire wifly chastite;
> Hyre contenaunce is to hir herte dygne,
> For they acorde bothe in dede and sygne.
> (1734–39)

A few lines later the reassurance of Lucrece's sincerity is reiterated: "(And by no craft hire beaute nas nat feyned)" (1749). This double assurance is already somewhat suspicious, given Chaucer's habit of raising awkward doubts under pretext of laying them to rest. Although the ambiguous "semblaunt," together with the later lines about Lucrece's covering her feet (1858–59), might warrant some suspicion of excessive concern for self-presentation, my aim here is not to accuse the victim of hypocrisy. Rather, it is to suggest her participation, witting or not, in a system of signs in which she is interpreted. For the male observer, her tears are a "sygne" of virtually rhetorical status: they "embellish" her chastity. She becomes, precisely through the visible virtue of her behavior, a topos for the voyeur, who "Conceyved hath hire beaute and hyre cheere" (1746). Tarquinius spends the next day "Th'ymage of hire recordynge alwey newe" (1760) until the woman is reduced to "this conseit," which "hys herte hath newe ytake" (1764). Despite her absence, he experiences both the presence and "the plesaunce of hire forme" (1769) or image until he determines on rape. This passage is closely imitated from *Fasti* (2.761–83), but it evidently struck a genuinely Chaucerian chord. We know, from January's wallowing in subjective self-indulgence (*MerchT* 1577–1616), how unsympathetically Chaucer viewed the masculine subject's creation of a feminine object according to its own desires; the difference is that January's rape of May is legally and socially sanctioned. Yet the evidence of Lucrece's complicity in the reduction of herself to a sign is surely the very action that ensures her fame: her suicide. It is a story of semiotics, because she kills herself as the irrefutable sign of her real feelings, which might not otherwise be believed by the public at large (1843–44). Unwilling to risk a wrong interpretation of herself, Lucrece forces the issue. (She reckoned, of course, without the Christian exegete Augustine.)

Of Tarquin, Lucrece might well say, as a later raped heroine says, "I am but a *cypher*, to give *him* significance, and *myself* pain." As Terry Castle observes of Clarissa Harlowe and the rapist Lovelace, it is "she the text, he the exegete. . . . She remains the subject of his interpretation, without pleasure or power as such: a hermeneutic casualty" (15–16). This formulation, applicable to an extent, nonetheless omits two further dimensions of Chaucer's concern. One is the victim's unnecessary self-punishment, another is the authors who have written about her. As sign, "Lucrece" is subject to many interpreters, as the juxtaposition of Livy and Augustine at the start of the tale suffices to show. "She" is bent to authorial will, like any material. Tarquin may wish to see Lucrece as his "leman" (1772), but others have chosen to see her instead as "a seynte" (1871). Skeat proposed that this canonization was suggested by the calendrical structure of *Fasti*, so that Lucrece "seemed to have her own day, like a saint" (176). Shannon (227) adds the influence of Brutus's statement that Lucretia's spirit will always be a divinity ("numen") to him. Whatever its origin, the idea introduces an alternate view of Lucrece as extreme and reductive in one direction as Tarquin's is in the other. For Chaucer, I suggest, neither is adequate.

The ending of the tale seems to support my interpretation. It is a peculiar ending, containing the only reference to Jesus in the poem:

> For wel I wot that Crist himselve telleth
> That in Israel, as wyd as is the lond,
> That so gret feyth in al that he ne fond
> As in a woman; and this is no lye.
>   (1879–82)

Does the Narrator protest too much? For it is either a lie or another mistake: the statement about faith in Israel occurs in Matthew 8:10—but not about a woman; while in Matthew 15:28 Jesus does praise a woman for her faith—but not in the phrase cited here. We have, therefore, two highly authoritative Christian sources framing this classical tale: Augustine and gospel. Moreover, each reference gives an incorrect version of its source. The structural neatness here seems to deny sheer coincidence, and so do the last three lines of the tale:

> And as of men, loke ye which tirannye
> They doon alday; assay hem whoso lyste,
> The trewest ys ful brotel for to triste.

As we saw at the conclusion to Thisbe, gender is a significant component of the Narrator's subjectivity, expressed in his treatment of material. We are, therefore, already warned: the Narrator is a writing man who warns us in his writing, both explicitly and by exemplum, about the chances we take in trusting too completely the utterances of men. Here, the utterance is a bland assurance that women are good, men bad: kindness and stability always to be found in women (1876–78), treachery in men. Surely this is what Eros and Alceste require, but in how many ways has this requirement not already been undercut? As the cases already narrated illustrate, erotic intensity does not certify general morality, and neither does men's malfeasance certify women's virtue.

We are again in the presence of a double bind, one that works on behalf of the interpretation offered above. If we believe the Narrator's final words about untrustworthy utterances by men, then we must hesitate to trust his representation. If we do not believe his concluding essentialist claim, then we have already withdrawn credulity from his utterances and must hesitate again to trust his representation. It is something like the "Cretan liar" conundrum—a well-known sophism in Chaucer's day as in Ovid's[5] and our own—alerting us, through its self-referentiality and its infinite regress, to the pitfalls of the relationship we enter when we take up a book.

ARIADNE

The legend of Ariadne opens with another first-person narratorial intrusion, an apostrophe to Minos; rather perversely it asserts the Narrator's intention not to write about Minos mainly, but about Theseus. This villain of love is the same figure whom Chaucer had already included in a lost work about "the love of Palamon and Arcite" (F 420; G 408), probably the prototype of the *Knight's Tale,* whose hero Theseus is. He is thus as problematic a hero as Aeneas. As if to signal the shifty multiplicity of the Theseus tradition, Chaucer inserts a triple pun in the last line of his invocation. "Be red for shame! now I thy life begynne" (1893): "red" as colored with the blush of shame; "read" visually in the manner of a shameful example like the literary production about to be written; "red" as advised, in the matter of "synne" noted in the previous line, to avoid shame.

Despite the opening disclaimer, we are treated to a somewhat extended summary of Minos's past. This is perhaps justifiable because the Theseus story is set at the court of Minos in Crete (although line 1966 erroneously says "Athenes"). Thematically, though, the Minos prologue provides a warm-up story anticipating the main events: a story of filial treachery and a lover's cruelty. The deceitful

---

5. On Cretan liars, see Ovid, *Ars amatoria* 1.297–98; Titus 1:12; and Higden, *Polychronicon* 2.15.

girl is the daughter of Nysus, king of Alcathoe, with whom Minos is at war. She betrays the city to her father's enemy, whom she loves. He, however, "wikkedly . . . quitte hire kyndenesse / And let hire drenche in sorwe and distresse, / Nere that the goddes hadde of hire pite" (1918–20). Quite apart from the irony of describing an act of filial betrayal and treason as "kindness" (with its informing meaning of "behavior according to nature"), we see that the deception of Minos by his daughters Ariadne and Phaedra on behalf of Minos's prisoner Theseus is poetic justice indeed. Doubly so, since one of them, Ariadne, will be abandoned by her lover as Minos abandoned his benefactress. I think there is less here of a proprietarian "repayment" of Minos through his daughter (daughter-as-property) than of the perception of reiterated structures in history, and particularly family history: today we call them "scripts."

Ovid's rendering of the abandoned Ariadne is little short of farcical. The comedy derives largely from the series of violent but pointless physical motions in which the heroine engages: her frantic groping of the bed to be sure Theseus is not in it; her hair-tearing; her running back and forth along the shore screaming her lover's name; her screeching after the departed ship ("flecte ratum! numerum non habet illa suum!": "Turn the ship around! she doesn't have everyone aboard!" [36]); her angry reproach to the empty bed. Ariadne even hoists her veil on a stick as a signal, just in case Theseus has accidentally forgotten her (*Her.* 10:42). Chaucer's version, while somewhat moderated from Ovid's, nonetheless retains the salient comical points. Ariadne "gropeth in the bed" (2186), reminds the deserter that "Thy barge hath nat al his meyne inne!" (2201), sticks her kerchief on a pole for Theseus "that he shulde it wel yse, / And hym remembre that she was behynde" (2202–4), and blames the bed. Besides the sheer futility of these actions, the vocabulary hints at comedy, for her behavior seems distinctly plebeian, more appropriate to a village girl than to a princess.

Well may the reader wonder: what about Ariadne's sister, Phaedra, now sailing off to Athens with Theseus, the husband who was to have been her brother-in-law? Ariadne will be rescued from her desert island by Bacchus in his tiger-drawn chariot and end her days as a great lady. But we know all too well—anyone who has read the *Heroides* knows—what lies in store for Phaedra in Athens: incestuous passion for Theseus's son Hippolytus (to whom, ironically,

Ariadne had proposed Phaedra be wed: 2099–2100) and a tragic death for both of them. Like so much else that is omitted from the *Legend*, this aftermath is eloquent, if silent, testimony to the fatal potential of sheer stubborn passion.

The tales of Lucrece and Philomela can be linked as a pair of rape stories, and an equally important pairing is that of the adjoining Ariadne and Philomela. Both of these myths have been resurrected in contemporary criticism as metaphors of writing, particularly by feminists wishing to locate the female voice, and its suppression, in Western culture. "Ariadne" is important because its central image of thread winding through a labyrinth can be seen as a representation of narrative; "Philomela" because its tapestry that tells all maximizes the relationship with weaving inherent in the word "text" and therefore represents representation itself.[6] So the stories are linked by the common thread of thread—the thread that, carded, spun, and woven, was traditionally the stuff on which women worked, no less prominently in Chaucer's day than in any earlier one, for the textile industry that was England's boast in the high Middle Ages was largely staffed by women, both as employees and as masters in the industry. Indeed, it is another woman weaver, the Wife of Bath, who in the *Canterbury Tales* would be Chaucer's mouthpiece for posing outright the question of woman as producer of discourse. If Dame Alison's representations, her versions of authoritative texts and of her own biography, bear the mark of what Chaucer imagines as her subjectivity, then what can be said about Chaucer's Ariadne as unwinder of thread, as donor of a guide through the labyrinth, as generator of the narrative of herself and Theseus?

To begin, it is important to see the labyrinth or maze as no distant exoticism, but a fairly common medieval architectural artifact.[7] In

---

6. Naomi Schor writes of an "Ariadne complex, all readings that cling to the Ariadne's thread ('fil conducteur'), whether it be the 'synonymic chains' of Barthes, the 'chain of supplements' of Derrida, or the 'series' of Deleuze"; the thread is not only a metaphor for connection but "a metonym for femininity" (3–4). Also see J. Hillis Miller and Nancy K. Miller. On Philomela, see Marcus, "Still Practice" and "Liberty, Sorority, Misogyny," Hartman, and especially Joplin.

7. For information in this section, I have used Knight, Mathews, Bord, and Beal. In *Idea*, Howard discusses the labyrinth as an image of interlaced thematic structure, but without relating it to the *Legend* (ch. 5). I do not know how appropriate the image is, because, although medieval narrative structure may well be (loosely speaking)

France and Italy, mazes were built into the cathedral floors at Chartres, Poitiers, Rheims, Amiens, Arras, Sens, and other ecclesiastical buildings such as churches or chapter houses in Rome, Ravenna, Piacenza, Lucca, Pavia, Cremona, and elsewhere. In Britain, the west tower of Ely Cathedral has a pavement maze, as do several smaller churches, and some roof bosses represent a maze. Church mazes are rarer in England than on the continent, but even so England has numerous outdoor examples in earthenwork, stone, or turf in Winchester, Essex, Yorkshire, Lincolnshire, Cambridgeshire, Oxfordshire, Hampshire, and Dorset. Some of these structures are round, others square; some unicursal (without false turns), other multicursal (having dead ends or several routes to the exit). The church maze was often called the "chemin de Jérusalem," and to trace its convoluted course on one's knees was considered a substitute for pilgrimage. Or it might be considered a schematic representation of life itself (as, indeed, the pilgrimage was), with the central tile called "Le Ciel." Such Christian uses seem to have coexisted peacefully with explicit references sometimes made, in inscriptions alongside the labyrinth, as at Lucca, to the originary story of Theseus and Ariadne. But we have already seen this kind of Christian/classical coexistence in the tradition of medieval Ovid commentary: there the labyrinth is given doctrinal interpretation as world, flesh, and/or devil (e.g., *Ovide moralisé* 8.987–1082, 1395ff.). What we can derive from this real architectural and scholarly presence of the labyrinth, then, is that the episode did lend itself to contemporary moral application, that the labyrinth came to Chaucer already glossed as an image of life. Chaucer's earlier reference, in the *House of Fame*, to the House of Rumor as "Domus Dedaly, / That Laboryntus cleped ys" (1920–21) already links the labyrinth or maze to the image of (urban) life as a site of confused communication. I propose to extend these already-existing tendencies a short step further by adding the notion of narrative as another version of life, or conversely of one's version of life as itself a narrative.

The proleptic narrative that Ariadne unwinds to her sister is very

---

"labyrinthine," no labyrinth has two parallel or interlocking paths as is the case with *entrelacement*. The definitive work on the subject is now that of Doob, who presents persuasive evidence that "Chaucer knew both visual and verbal labyrinth traditions well" (308), but does very little with the *Legend*.

far from the one that actually comes to pass. Her firm expectation is nothing but good:

> This lady smyleth at his stedefastnesse,
> And at his hertely wordes and his chere,
> And to hyre sister seyde in this manere,
> Al softely: "Now, syster myn," quod she,
> "Now be we duchesses, bothe I and ye,
> And sekered to the regals of Athenes,
> And bothe hereafter likly to be quenes; . . . "
>
> (2123–29)

The *Ovide moralisé* makes the lady even more certain of the outcome of her scheme, allowing her to express herself at length in simple future tense: "Par mariage / Me prendra," "Cest avrai je," "il m'enmenra," "je serai dame clamee," (*OM* 8.1200–1228). Ariadne has worked hard for this ending—indeed, she has betrayed her father for it, but since her father's use of the Minotaur is clearly unjust, this is not a substantial objection. She has also conspired in the death of her half-brother, the Minotaur: a deed recalled in her epistle (*Her.* 10.77) but effaced in Chaucer's text. And she has, like Medea, made a quick, businesslike bargain: her life-saving help in return for marriage. Who could say no? There is, therefore, an element of not-so-subtle coercion to the "love" of Ariadne and Theseus, an element clearly recognized by the Ovid commentators and, I suggest, by Chaucer.

Ariadne is thus ambitious and manipulative, but these are neither sins nor crimes. She has, however, made the mistake of overvaluing her creative powers, seeing as merely a character in her own story someone who turns out to be its co-author. In the effort to shape one's life, one is rarely completely autonomous. To the very last, Ariadne refuses to credit the autonomy of Theseus, who has, after all, his own story. She assumes against all evidence that he has merely forgotten her, that he merely needs to be reminded of what he was supposed to do. Theseus, her own creation (in that she saved his life), escapes the neat script she has prepared; he acts, perversely, against his author, who had not written him as a villain. This is her true exemplarity in the *Legend*. As a message about texts, the tale of Ariadne reinforces the oft-made Chaucerian point about their independence of authorial intent (even assuming such intent is knowable). As a message about life, it reinforces the orthodox

Christian point about preparedness for the adversities of Fortune. As a message about women, it suggests that the harshest critic of their productions will be the same as is faced by men: contingency.

PHILOMELA

As I noted in Chapter 3, the tale of Philomela differs from the others in its lack of obscenity, wordplay, or other evidently ironic devices. It does omit from this already horrendous story of incestuous adultery, rape, and mutilation the further horrors of infanticide and cannibalism that are part of the complete version (in Ovid's *Metamorphoses* 6 and the *Ovide moralisé*), as well as the metamorphosis of the main characters into birds. Robert Frank remarks that the piece "suffers from overcutting": again, as I remarked of Donald Howard and Robert Burlin in Chapter 1, the critic seems to have contracted a tendency to wordplay from his material! Frank attributes the aesthetic failure of this legend to Chaucer's attempt to transform the material into "a tale of the pathetic." But it is really Chrétien de Troyes who rendered the tale pathetic by opening it up as fully as he did to detail, dialogue, internal monologue, family dynamics, and motivation. (Chrétien's *lai* of Philomela is incorporated into the *Ovide moralisé*, 6.2217ff.) Chrétien gives a remarkable portrait of the two sisters, Philomela and Procne, as independent, well-educated women, discreet, ingenious, capable of anger and force. His villainous Tereus is also very fully portrayed. Both the prelude to the rape and the mutilation scene are rendered in virtually novelistic amplification; both the rescue scene and the reunion of the two sisters are deeply moving. Chaucer does none of this, rendering the literary corpus as mutilated and as mute, in the affective sense noted by Frank, as its heroine. I believe that Chaucer had other fish to fry than pathos, and I see the legend as possessing an intellectual power and a creative energy of its own.

The tale is not unique in opening with an invocation—the lives of Ariadne, Hypsipyle, and Dido do the same—but this invocation is a prayer to a deity recognizably Platonic[8] and Christian in its eternity and creativity.

8. Karl Young shows that the material could have been known to Chaucer in an *accessus* to a commentary on the *Metamorphoses*, or in the *Ovide moralisé*.

> Thow yevere of the formes, that hast wrought
> This fayre world and bar it in thy thought
> Eternaly er thow thy werk began,
> Why madest thow, unto the slaunder of man,
> Or, al be that it was nat thy doing,
> As for that fyn, to make swich a thyng,
> Whi sufferest thow that Tereus was bore . . . ?
>   (2228–34)

The content of the prayer is a request for theodicy, for a justification of the ways of God to man, so that the passage resembles Dorigen's prayer in the *Franklin's Tale* (865–93). Whereas Dorigen challenges God's creation of "grisly feendly rokkes blake" (868) and their ability to destroy mankind, the Narrator of the *Legend* questions God's willingness to tolerate the existence of such a monster as Tereus, so vile that the utterance of his very name corrupts "this world up to the firste hevene" (2234). Why does evil exist?

It is not in either case a merely rhetorical question, but one with answers amply provided over the centuries by Catholic theology. In Chaucer's more leisurely exploration of this problem in the *Franklin's Tale*, Dorigen learns the answer experientially through her attempt to revise the postlapsarian institution of marriage. She learns that nature is such, and human nature is such, that some coercive authority—including husbandly marital authority—is required. That is the human condition, and by reminding us of it here, Chaucer deftly reintroduces the orthodox Augustinian perspective, which, as I have argued in Chapters 1 and 2, provides the backdrop to the *Legend* as a whole.

The opening prayer also restates the theme of narratorial subjectivity. The Narrator asserts that Tereus

> is in love so fals and so forswore,
> That fro this world up to the firste hevene
> Corrumpeth, whan that folk his name nevene[.]
>   (2235–37)

Yet this is clearly incorrect. We know full well that nothing changes in the world because of the existence of false lovers or even monstrously criminal individuals; still less is anything changed by the naming of such individuals. The Narrator's assertion contains a vastly inflated notion, not only of the power of evil, but also of the power of utterance, for nature is simply not so responsive to our behavior or our words. Why, then, would the Narrator think it is? Clearly because his own reaction to this horrifying material is so strong:

> And, as to me, so grisely was his dede
> That, whan that I his foule storye rede,
> Myne eyen wexe foule and sore also.
> Yit last the venom of so longe ago,
> That it enfecteth hym that wolde beholde
> The storye of Tereus, of which I tolde.
>
> (2238–43)

It is perhaps tempting to give an autobiographical-confessional cast to this passionate denunciation, connecting it (and also the untypical seriousness of tone in the tale as a whole) with the notorious episode of Cecily Chaumpaigne's *raptus*, from legal responsibility for which the lady released the poet in 1380.

But the passage probably elaborates the first line of *Heroides* 17, where Helen says that her eyes are already violated by reading Paris's letter, so that she might as well reply ("Nunc oculos tua cum violarit epistula nostros," etc.; I note for the sheer pleasure of doing so that the concentric structure of this clause mimes its content, "oculos . . . nostros" containing "tua . . . epistula" containing violation). Helen's choice of verb, of course, anticipates the greater *raptus* to come, the one that will result in the Trojan War. It also suggests a moral passivity to which Chaucer, or any Christian rigorist, could only retort with Jesus's remonstrance to the Pharisees that "not what goes into the mouth defiles a man, but what comes out of it" (Matt. 15:11)—or with Augustine's remarks on rape (cf. above, in "Lucrece"). Indeed, such a rejoinder might have been made to Philomela herself, whose Ovidian post-*raptus* invective against Tereus includes the suicidal wish that he had killed her before he wronged her, for then her shade would have been devoid of crime (*Met.* 6.539–41).

The existence of a likely (though hitherto unnoticed) literary source for the conceit about tainted eyes should give us some pause in the question of Chaucerian sincerity, much as Rosalie Colie's observation that Sidney's famous "Foole . . . look in thy heart and write" comes from Ronsard, emphasizes "the conventional nature of poetic honesty."[9] Whether its source be experience, authority, or both, the Chaucerian passage cited above is surely the ultimate in reader-response criticism: a story so disgusting that its poison, despite its age, putrefies the Narrator's eyes and infects every reader. But we know that this too is incorrect, for our eyes are not befouled by reading the Chaucerian (or any other) version of the story, and as to whether our will is infected by it, that is a moral choice. We would do ill to allow fiction such power. Once again, then, the Narrator's subjectivity is brought into play, to the point where he is compelled to make both theological and aesthetic errors. If we take the point here, we must apply it to the work at hand. The Narrator is (only) a poet; his work is necessarily the expression of a (particular and tainted) subjectivity; literature possesses neither the power the Narrator ascribes to it here, nor the power Eros ascribes to it in the Prologue; interpretation is a function of will.

Philomela is a woman without utterance, literally without a tongue. I find it curious that Chaucer should efface this tongue from his story, except for the bare mention of its removal (2334). It is curious, first, because in the *Manciple's Tale* (314–42), Chaucer would give (or had already given, depending on chronology) such close attention to that organ; second, because one would think the tongue important to a story about dismembering and remembering; third, because in the sources the tongue becomes virtually another character in the narrative, almost a separate entity from its possessor, even after being severed. In Ovid's account, Tereus's wrath and fear are provoked by Philomela's threats to tell the world about the rape. He whips out his sword (*vagina liberat:* frees it from its sheath [*Met.* 6.551]); then

> he seized her tongue with pincers, as it protested against the outrage, calling ever on the name of her father and struggling to speak, and cut it off with his merciless blade. The mangled root quivers, while

9. Colie, *Paradoxia*, 91. Also relevant to this question is Lowes's 1904 article on the *Legend* in its relation to the French marguerite tradition, for Lowes demonstrates that the powerful and intensely self-conscious passage celebrating the daisy (F 66–96) is close to being a pastiche of material from Boccaccio, Deschamps, and Machaut. To ignore artifice, Lowes comments, "is to commit the tempting anachronism of measuring [Chaucer] by the standards of the Preface to the *Lyrical Ballads*, instead of recognizing 'ever y-lyke newe' the consummate art involved in his treatment of the artistic conventions of his own time" (630–31). Unfortunately, Lowes ignores his own caveat later in the article in arguing for the priority of F text (cf. 663).

the severed tongue lies palpitating on the dark earth, faintly murmur-
ing; and, as the severed tail of a mangled snake is wont to writhe, it
twitches convulsively, and with its last dying movement it seeks its
mistress's feet. (Loeb trans.)

Later, when Procne receives the tapestry, she says nothing—
"mirum potuisse," remarks Ovid: a wonder that she could—and
words sufficiently indignant are absent to her seeking (or inquiring)
tongue (584). When the sisters are reunited, Procne threatens to cut
out Tereus's tongue and eyes and castrate him (616–17). Chrétien's
version omits the grotesquerie of the severed-but-animate tongue,
as well as Procne's threats, but adds a number of further developments of the tongue image such as

> ne poist, ce croi, sofire
> A totes ses granz biautez dire
> Li sans ne la langue Platon
> Ne la Omer ne la Caton.
> (OM 6.2345–48)

> I believe that to tell all her great beauty
> the judgment and the tongue/language of Plato
> or of Homer or of Cato
> could not suffice.

He also includes wordplay on the theme of silence and speech using
Tereus / se taire (e.g., 2992–93).

In French, the missing langue denotes language as well as
tongue. Philomela does not, however, lack ability to communicate,
indeed with powerfully effective consequences. This is not because,
as Roman Jakobson (12–13) observes, tonguelessness does not necessarily prevent speech (in any case, the classical and medieval
authors thought it did), but because Philomela finds other means of
expression. As Lisa Kiser observes, Philomela herself "enacts the
role of the giver of forms" (112) already adumbrated in the opening
lines of the legend. In this sense she is emblematic of women
generally who, although excluded from the means of cultural
production—in the Middle Ages this meant from university education or teaching; from taking orders and preaching; and from employment in law, government, and diplomacy—nonetheless managed to express themselves through other channels: whether with
the ready answer conferred by Proserpina in the Merchant's Tale, by

writing (like Marie de France or Christine de Pizan, both of them known to Chaucer), or in other professional arts, such as illumination or textiles, in which women worked. Indeed, for Chrétien, Philomela is already an artist, and not merely metaphorically: among her many talents, she is able to

> ovrer une porpre vermoille
> Qu'an tot le mont n'ot sa paroille.
> Un diaspre ou un baudequin
> Nes la Mesniee Hellequin
> Seüst ele an un drap portreire.
> Des autors sot et de gramaire
> Et sot bien feire vers et letre . . .
>   (2405–11)

> work [embroider] a scarlet cloth
> So that no one ever saw its like.
> On a silk brocade or wool cloth
> She could portray
> Even hell's assembly.
> She knew the *auctores* and grammar
> And could write and compose verses . . .

The importance of artistic and expressive media in this tale has led some recent critics to see it as exemplary of textual production, as noted above under "Ariadne." The question of media is prominent here, as it was in the *House of Fame* (see Chapter 1) and with similar confusion. Chaucer's Philomela knows how to weave tapestry as women usually do ("As it of wemen hath be woned yore" [2353]). She is able to read and also to compose poetry: "She coude eek rede, and wel ynow endyte" (2356)—a rather grudging concession, unlike Chrétien's glowing endorsement. Presumably her compositions are meant for oral delivery or dictation to a scribe, for unlike Chrétien's highly literate heroine, Chaucer's cannot write, even though she can weave letters as well as images into her tapestry, so that the story is both shown and told: "She waf it wel, and wrot the storye above" (2364). It is difficult for us to comprehend how someone might be able to read but not write, or to form letters in weaving but not with a pen. Historians of education inform us, however, that these distinctions were far more common in the Middle Ages than they are now: the Paston women, for example, could read but perhaps not write, and the same has been suggested about Juliana of Norwich.[10] M. T. Clanchy confirms that writing with a pen was a very specialized skill, often limited to copying of characters and not necessarily coupled with the ability to read (88, 218, 227). Although this situation does not apply to Philomela, who was not copying an already written text, it does provide social analogues. What remains a puzzle, though, is why Chaucer goes through all this: why not simply let the woman be thoroughly literate?

One reason is dramatic: were she able to write a letter, doubtless she would do so early on, sparing herself the year of waiting and the toil required to produce the tapestry that is so essential an object in the tradition. Another reason is source-related, for while Ovid is fairly clear that the story is written in letters (*notas*: signs/characters [*Met.* 6.577]), Chrétien has both *portreite* (3338) and *escrit* (3347) so that, as Lowes long ago observed, Chaucer's work agrees with the French in combining written and visual representation. In doing so it would be consistent not merely with a source but with a tradition, for the blurring and blending of media boundaries seems fairly common in medieval art. Jean Frappier, for instance (cited in Freeman, 880 n. 20), notes that *escrire* (to write) may also mean to draw, paint, or design, so that the phrase *brudé et escrit* predicated of a piece of fabric "constitutes a synonymous redundancy, considered moreover in the twelfth century as stylistically elegant," as when the lady in Marie de France's *Laustic* sends a dead bird to her lover wrapped "En une piece de samit / A or brusdé e tut escrit" ("in a piece of gold-embroidered samite scrolled [lit. 'written'] all over" [135–36]). Some churches of the period displayed paintings of *faux-tapis* in which an elaborately patterned and draped hanging is painted on the wall behind the altar; above it are painted niched statues of saints; above that the real ribbing proceeds to the crown of the vault. In the *Wife of Bath's Tale*, the old hag "rowned . . . a pistel" (literally, "whispered an epistle") in the young knight's ear (III.1021). There seems, in short, to be a certain equivalency among the various arts and crafts, so that any of them might be equivalent to literacy or substitute for it. None is epistemologically superior;

10. Paston, 1: xxxvi–viii, cited in Orme; Pelphrey, 20 (but see his notes for controversy on the question of Juliana's literacy).

they can be used as metaphors for one another (e.g., the Anglo-Saxon and later "web of words," the "entrelacement" in Celtic visual arts and in Old French romance).

Lastly, the Chaucerian Philomela's semi-literacy and lack of other accomplishments serves to intensify what Patricia Joplin calls "the power she discovered in exile" (47). Her weaving is not one of many forms of communication available to her, but a real transcendence of silence. Her effort is all the more heroic, and here I think we do have a concession to pathos, one recognizable from Chaucer's method elsewhere. Constance, too, had an elaborate education in Chaucer's French-language source for the *Man of Law's Tale* (the Anglo-Norman *Chronicle* of Nicholas Trevet), and Chaucer deprives her of it to render her the more helpless, the more dependent on no other resource than faith. Whereas the French authors seem to believe that a wronged heroine should start with as much as possible, to render her misfortune the more extreme, Chaucer on the contrary seems to aim at an image of depletion as extreme as possible, which means starting with fewer resources. For his particular purpose, "less is more"—or "the worse the better."

The ending of the story is lame, mutilated by its amputation of the tragic consequences. These are dismissed with:

> The remenaunt is no charge for to telle,
> For this is al and som: thus was she served,
> That nevere harm agilte ne deserved
> Unto this crewel man, that she of wiste.
> (2383–86)

But the evasion need not be heard as ironic trivialization in the vein of the Medea story. Its resemblance is rather to the Man of Law's Prologue with its rejection of such abominations as are recounted in the story of Canace (incest, infanticide, suicide; cf. *Heroides* 11): a distancing of seriously distasteful material. And in fact the terse summary is correct, for the heaping of horror upon horror can become sensationalistic after a point, and the point has been adequately made by the material already narrated. The real lameness occurs with the "moralization" that attempts to jam this narrative into the conceptual framework established by Eros and Alceste, that of the erotic battle of sexes:

Ye may be war of men, if that yow liste.
For al be it that he wol nat, for shame,
Don as Tereus, to lese his name,
Ne serve yow as a morderour or a knave,
Ful lytel while shal ye trewe hym have—
That wol I seyn, al were he now my brother—
But it so be that he may have non other.

(2387–93)

The cynicism and inadequacy of this framework stand exposed in contrast with the real evil just portrayed.

PHYLLIS

In medieval commentaries upon the *Heroides*, Phyllis "serves as the canonical example of 'amor stultus' " (Hexter, 174), or foolish love.[11] One of them explains that Phyllis's foolishness lay in her impatience, for Demophon had not betrayed her with another woman, and had she but waited, he would have returned. An alternate account is that she was foolish to love a man who was certain to leave her (en route either to or from the Trojan War). Another offers the rather cynically dismissive explanation that "quia viro indigebat ipsum adamavit. Unde, quia concumbere ei concessit, reprehenditur" ("because she lacked a man she fell for him. So, because she was willing to sleep with him, she is to be blamed" [Hexter, 223, 235]). Although there is no clear proof that Chaucer used or knew these commentaries, his Phyllis seems to echo this last idea in her self-reproachful "But I wot why ye come nat. . . . For I was of my love to yow to fre" (2520–21). To be sure, the concept is not so specialized as to require a particular source, but Chaucer's formulation is closer to the commentary than to Ovid's vague "non sapienter amavi" ("I didn't love wisely" [*Her.* 2.27]).

At the end of her tale, Phyllis expresses the wish (a curse, really) that her lover may go down in history as a proverbial flattering traitor:

11. A sample: "In hoc igitur opere ait Ovidius de amore secundum omnes species amoris, que sunt hee: legitimus, quem comendat in Penelope; stultus, quem redarguit in Phillide; illicitus, quem condemnat in Phedra et Canace" (Hexter, 223). See also Huygens, 30, 31.

> And whan thyne olde auncestres peynted be,
> In which men may here worthynesse se,
> Thanne preye I God thow peynted be also
> That folk may rede forby as they go,
> "Lo! this is he that with his flaterye
> Bytraised hath and don hire vilenye
> That was his trewe love in thought and dede!"
>
> (2536–42)

But, as with Ariadne, history turns the tables on Phyllis and her intention for the future: it is she who remains the more widely known, and less for a true than for a foolish love.

I have begun with an ending; now for the beginning. The tale opens with a line—"By preve as wel as by autorite"—that invokes both the Wife of Bath's Prologue, and the opening of the Prologue to the *Legend* with its meditation on empiricism. Here, however, the lesson of experience and authority is "That wiked fruit cometh of a wiked tre" (2395), an image recalling not contemporary interest in philosophical matters but the Christian myth of humanity's creation and fall: the Original Sin that was a consequence of Adam's and Eve's partaking of the forbidden fruit (Gen. 3). This is not to suggest that the scriptural tree was wicked, or its fruit; simply that the juxtaposition of tree, fruit, wickedness, and generational transmission of the disposition to evil can only, for a Christian audience, call to mind the story of Original Sin. Insofar as it does so, it also reminds its audience that such is the inheritance of every man, and of every woman as well.

Chaucer would have found inspiration for this theme in his Ovidian source (*Her.* 2.75–78); yet the enthusiasm with which he expanded it is distinctly his own, for the Christian motif continues to surface through the tale. In the next lines occurs a prayer for God's grace:

> "God, for his grace, fro swich oon kepe us!"
> Thus may these women preyen that it [the story] here.
>
> (2401–2)

The point about sinful nature is restated a few lines further on when Demophon is said to be like his father in looks and height and infidelity: "it com hym of nature" (2447). And, if we have lost sight of the subtle Christian reference of the opening movement, it too is restated here:

As doth the fox Renard, the foxes sone,
Of kynde he coude his olde faders wone. . . .
(2448–49)

The fox is a common medieval emblem of Satan, whose influence is in the realm "of kynde" (nature). In this context, the adjective "olde" evokes the old law / new law dichotomy: the contrast between pre-Christian or non-Christian doctrines (old law) and Christianity (new law) that structures the relation of nature and diabolical influence. There follows another prayer for God's grace, this time on behalf of the Narrator himself ("Which to performe God me grace sende" [2457]), then the natural sin motif again with another reference to the devil, this one explicit:

Me lyste nat vouche-sauf on hym to swynke,
Ne spende on hym a penne ful of inke,
For fals in love was he, ryght as his syre.
The devil sette here soules bothe afyre!
(2490–93)

The notion of sin is kept before our eyes (and ears) in the syllabic wordplay in line 2550 ("But syn thus synfully . . . "). In six lines in this section (2545–50), the word "begile" occurs twice and "subtilte" once, words very commonly used in a doctrinal context in connection with the temptations of world, flesh, and devil. Finally, Phyllis is said to commit suicide out of despair—"She for dispeyr fordide hyreself, allas" (2557)—the worst of all sins in a Christian context, because it denies the hope of salvation. Although she is certainly not the only heroine—or hero—in the *Legend* to commit suicide, she is the only one whose motive is specified as despair.

What is one to make of this orthodox doctrinal subtext supporting an Ovidian tale? In no way do I wish to propose that Chaucer intends an allegory as such, notwithstanding that the allegorical habit was deeply familiar to him from his reading of the *Ovide moralisé* and many other exegetical texts. What I would propose is something closer to what Erich Auerbach has called a figural approach: one that, while maintaining the historicity of an event, sees it as representing or figuring (whether before or after) another event, also historical, but with spiritual significance as well. One convenience of this approach is that it eliminates anachronism, for the repetitive, patterned figural history knows no linear-sequential or causal absolute. This is one reason why figures from the distant past can be genuinely exemplary. Phyllis is no Christian, but she enacts patterns that only a Christian can fully comprehend. The figuralism of the classical ladies in Chaucer's *Legend* tends, however, to resemble that of Virgil in Dante's *Commedia* rather than that of Beatrice. By this I mean that, like Virgil, they—their lives—may assist the reader to approach spiritual truths, but that none of them is what Auerbach calls "an incarnation of divine truth . . . incarnate revelation" ("Figura," 74–75). Here Chaucer draws the line.

A doctrinal perspective surfaces once again in the advice to women with which the tale approaches its conclusion:

> Be war, ye wemen, of youre subtyl fo,
> Syn yit this day men may ensaumple se. . . .
> (2559–60)

Because, to this day, the examples may be seen, therefore beware of your subtle foe. The referent of "subtle foe" is not specified, and there are several choices. We might jump ahead to "men" as a gender-specific term, tempting because of its neat opposition to "wemen," even though it is not syntactically part of the previous clause. Or, taking "men" as "people" we might follow the ear rather than the eye, accept the hint offered by "Syn" and hear "sin" as the referent—an easier choice in an unpunctuated manuscript or in one read aloud. Or we might think of the traditional characterization of Satan as humanity's subtle (tricky) foe (see *MED* s.v. "fo") and take the doctrinal message. The choice, as usual, is ours.

On the other hand, there can be no doubt that "man" in the last line does denote sex: "And trusteth, as in love, no man but me." The specification of love as the field of concern makes the denotation inevitable. The Narrator has already specified his sex in previous legends, and he has distorted the literary corpus. By this point in the *Legend* we can scarcely take this line as anything but authorial irony (however sincere we might believe the Narrator to be), for there seems little reason to trust either the Narrator or his sponsor Eros, who has also revised "woman" according to his masculine desire. If Eros does violence to women in assimilating them to an unrealistic concept of their nature, so does the Narrator do violence to his sources, and so may he do to the reader who, in granting the Narrator's plea for trust, assumes a passive, "feminized" position. To carry the analogy further, though, is to see that—as Peter Allen observes (420)—just as the women in the tales do not have to be victims, or at least do not have to despair and die because they are abandoned, or because their love is unreciprocated, so the reader does not have to believe everything he or she is told. The reader can and must assume responsibility for what "happens" to him or her while reading. We can be active in the production of meaning, certainly in the moral conclusions we draw from literary sources and in the behavior we choose to base upon exemplary literary characters. Interpretation is a necessity, for there is always more than meets the eye.

HYPERMNESTRA

At the beginning of this tale, Chaucer engages in a bit of euhemerism, rationally explaining the fifty sons of Danao and the fifty daughters of Egiste as bastards, products of illicit love. (Chaucer reverses the fathers' names, not without precedent.) Danao spawns offspring "As swiche false lovers ofte conne" (2565), while Egiste "was of love as fals as evere hym liste" (2571), so that of his many daughters only one is "gat upon his ryghte wyf" (2573): the youngest, Hypermnestra. This legitimate child is beloved of the gods, "That of the shef she sholde be the corn" (2579). In the Prologue, the Narrator had asserted that his aim in making poetry is to praise neither flower against leaf nor corn against sheaf (F 188–90), so that there is perhaps a reminder here of the earlier locus, a reminder that is reinforced by another line describing how "The flour, the lef" is torn up to make wedding garlands for the young couple (2613). Further on, the natural/botanical imagery continues when Hypermnestra is compared with "the lef of aspe grene" as to quaking, with "an ash" as to pallor (2648–49), and again to "the braunche that Zepherus shaketh" (2681) for trembling. She is, we see, a natural woman—and more evidently good than some of the other heroines. As Mary Shaner points out (109–11), the *Heroides* scholia do not describe Hypermnestra as "stultus." On the contrary, she is commended for marrying dutifully, for mercy, and for wedded chastity. Moreover, she does not regret her generosity (as do Medea and Ariadne), and neither is she betrayed.

Yet I suggest that even this portrait participates in the general strategy of the series, albeit in somewhat subtler ways. To begin with, the Narrator does take the trouble to point out that the mar-

riage of Linus and Hypermnestra is incestuous (they are first cous-
ins, hence within the officially forbidden degrees of consanguinity):

> To Danao and Egistes also
> Althogh so be that they were brethren two—
> For thilke tyme was spared no lynage—
> It lykede hem to make a maryage
> Bytwixen Ypermystre and hym Lyno . . .
>   (2600–2604)

The marriage is thus already compromised, and, in view of medieval and particularly Chaucerian attitudes toward the violation of
natural law (see above, "Cleopatra" and "Dido"), so is the bland
excuse the Narrator gives here.

   If the preceding tale of Phyllis reveals an orthodox Christian
subtext, the ideological orientation of Hypermnestra is, on the contrary, destiny and stellar fatalism. "The Wirdes, that we clepen
Destine" (2580) determine the heroine's virtues: Venus, Jupiter, and
the waning power of Mars decree that she will be beautiful, pru-
dent, and unable to handle a knife (2584–95). In much the same
way, the Wife of Bath would account for her particular temperament by referring to her natal stellar influences (609–20). If the effect
is different, the methodology is identical—and, to a Christian rigorist, deplorable. These "Oriental" attitudes, which came to the medieval West through Arab translations of Greek and Latin philosophers, would be further exploited by Chaucer in the *Man of Law's
Tale*, where they form a counterpoint to the proper Christian understanding of Providence and the exercise of free will. Here, there is
no explicit counterpoint, so that interpretation of this theme is left
to the reader—a valorization of interpretive activity quite consistent
with what has come before in the *Legend*. Hypermnestra's father,
Egiste, continues the theme when he asserts the influence of "the
fatal systren" on his "dom" (2630). If we have taken the point of all
that precedes in the *Legend*, we shall, I believe, be able to see the
stellar account of Hypermnestra's virtue, or of Egiste's vice, as
having very limited explanatory power indeed.

   The young woman does give her own reasons for not following
her father's inhumane command, and they are terribly superficial.
At no point does she penetrate to the heart of the matter and say, or
think, that murder is wrong. Instead, we have protracted tergiver-
sation: she is afraid to incur her father's threat of death; she is a

virgin (the marriage has apparently not been consummated on the wedding night); her hands are not made for a knife (2684–95) or for murder. (One notes parenthetically that this last appears to be an Ovidian formula, for in *Heroides*, beside Hypermnestra's "quid mihi cum ferro?" [14.65], Canace also says that the knife is not fit for her womanly hand [11.19–20]). Nonetheless, despite its lack of moral dignity, the monologue does rise to the occasion and the heroine manages to do the right thing:

> "yit is it bet for me
> For to be ded in wifly honeste
> Than ben a traytour lyvynge in my shame."
> (2700–2702)

If Hypermnestra's monologue lacks dignity, so does the treatment as a whole. Chaucer's rhetoric, in the second part of the story, includes a number of words that seem to trivialize the narrative in their colloquialism, to be more appropriate in context of village than of court. The heroine's father coyly says that they will have a "biker" (quarrel [2661]) if she refuses his demand; this is also a masterpiece of understatement, since he has threatened to have her killed if she disobeys. He offers her a "costret," or flask ("In the Craven dialect, a costril is the little wooden barrel carried by reapers" [Skeat, 196]). The princess swears by the "devel" (2694); belittles her decision with the rather cynical line "Be as be may, for ernest or for game" (2703); determines to send Linus away "Out at this goter" (2705), and "roggeth" her husband awake (2708).

It has been proposed that the present ending is all that was ever intended; it has also been suggested that the ending has been lost. The very debate shows that the ending must minimally be acknowledged as what Barbara Herrnstein Smith has called "weak poetic closure," if indeed it is closure at all. Following Smith's terminology (34, 210, 221), we might at best consider it "closural failure" or "disappointment," and if it fits any of her types, it might be "cheap closure" or, more charitably, open-ended or an anti-closural ending. Yet if closure "creates in the reader the expectation of nothing," that is, nothing more, nothing to follow, then this seems a good reason not to see the end of the *Legend* as closure, for it seems to end in a colon. On the other hand, that may have been the intention. On the other hand again, Beverly Boyd has suggested that the conditions of production and consumption of the Chaucerian book may account for the fact that "Chaucer's store of unfinished works is very large for a poet of his reputation" (115). She adduces two possibilities: first, that oral presentation of a work before a live audience would remove pressure to bring the work to a final state; second, that presentation of a portion of a larger work to an individual friend or patron would have the same effect.

As with the *House of Fame*, the lack of an explicit or at least an obvious conclusion to the *Legend* does not hamper, in the main, the work of interpretation. Incompleteness, not necessarily at the end, is a condition Chaucerians are accustomed to, for the *Canterbury Tales*, which has a very powerful ending, nonetheless remains a work in progress. Beside the "missing" tales, the *Cook's Tale* is unfinished, and the Squire and Narrator (and perhaps Monk) are interrupted in theirs. *Troilus* also has a strong and wonderfully orchestrated ending, although critics endlessly debate its tone and suitability. Even the beautifully finished *Parliament of Fowls* defers the conclusion of its narrative to outside the poem, and falls deliberately one line short of its perfect seven hundred. The two prose treatises—the *Astrolabe* and the *Equatorie*—are evidently incomplete, or not, at least, completed according to plan. Beginnings seem to be less problematic with Chaucer than endings, whether deliberately or not. But if art imitates life despite its best intentions toward fictionality, then I suppose that is what we might fairly expect. Indeed, through the idea of the book of judgment, in which one's good and bad deeds are recorded against the day of doom, the Middle Ages had a very firm sense of life-as-text, and as uncompleted text. A variant, based on Apocalypse 20:12, is developed by the London preacher Thomas Wimbledon, in a sermon composed in 1387. Here, a book of individual conscience and a book of Jesus's teachings will be opened:

> In the first bok schal be write al that we have do; in the tother book schal be write that we schulde have do. And than shulle dede men be demed of thilke thyngis that beth writen in the bookis. . . . For the dom schal be yove aftir oure werkis. (122–23)

By comparison with the exemplar, most copies will be imperfect: what we should have done will remain always unwritten.

Semi-Polemical Conclusion

Among the pleasures of writing is that of discovery, and to the extent that interpretation is a kind of allegorical projection upon the text, to that extent it is self-discovery. To borrow E. M. Forster's epigram, how do I know what I think till I see what I say? Or, more contemporaneously, this from Foucault: "If you knew when you began a book what you would say at the end, do you think you would have the courage to write it? . . . The game is worthwhile in so far as we don't know what will be the end" (*Technologies*, 9). The conclusions of this study were far from foregone, even though some portions of it were published separately. One might say this was the case precisely because some portions were published separately, and even though I think of it as a long-deferred sequel to my 1972 book on the *House of Fame*, which includes some observations about the *Legend*. I do not regret this deferral, because it has enabled me to write the book I wanted to: my own work and that of others during the interval has permitted me to translate intuition into scholarship. This is why the eclecticism deployed here is not inappropriate but, on the contrary, well serves a densely layered and intensely meaningful Middle English poem. This too is why I have chosen for my title Chaucer's own phrase "the naked text"; for its polysemous reference to body and gender, tradition and rhetorical play, interpretation and translation seems perfectly suited to the critical versatility demanded by the poem. I trust that the elucidation of meanings and separation of layers—with the surprises that sometimes accompany these processes—is not mistaken for incoherence at one extreme or, at the other, for an attempt to impose a phantasmic unity.

One such surprise was the Englishness that pervades this classically derived and French-influenced poem. Some of it is quite deliberately tactical; in other respects, it is simply (or not so simply) part of the sensibility created by immersion in a specific environment.

There is the presence of Wycliffism helping to focus Chaucer's concern for translation and interpretation: a presence that brings, as a side effect, as strong an argument for the priority of the G text as has yet been proposed. There is the continuing relevance of the distinctively English philosophical project to the poet's epistemological anxieties, already vented in the *House of Fame*. There are the assimilated or naturalized English queens whose names crown the historical progression in stanza 1 of the balade; the detail from Geoffrey of Monmouth in "Thisbe" revealing the poet's attention to others' efforts to reconcile English and classical histories; the striking similarity between some of Chaucer's formulations on tradition and those of the monk of Chester, Ranulf Higden. There is the Englishness not only of daisies but of relics, of women weavers and of voyages to the Orient and other, closer, territories.

The "Orientalism" theme doubtless represents a generally European attitude, but its Chaucerian manifestation, I have argued, points to distinctively English uses. Moreover, it suggests another important aspect of the Chaucerian frame of mind: not only a national-patriotic but a conservative slant. For it is not the rationalist-scholarly tradition about Islam that Chaucer chose to incorporate into his own work. Rather, he availed himself, for reasons doctrinal, political, and poetic, of the much older patristic/popular mythos of the ever-threatening Orient—much as he chose an old-fashioned patristic historical scheme as the structural skeleton for part of his balade. For Augustine, Platonism was the most difficult enemy of all, because of its similarities to Christianity (*City of God* 8.1–13); for the high Middle Ages, Islam filled that role.

The effort represented in the *Legend*, then, is both to medievalize the ancient and the foreign and to anglicize them: to domesticate them locally as well as temporally. No one will quarrel with Elizabeth Salter's claims about "Chaucer and internationalism," for the paradox is that if Chaucer became what generations of masculinist critics have metaphorized as "the father of English poesy," it was only and precisely by being open to the power of continental and classical literatures. Nor is this situation entirely paradoxical when we recall Beryl Smalley's reminder that "Antiquity . . . came to Englishmen as part of their own history" (*English Friars*, 23–24): the legendary history of Britain.

Hence it seems to me that the only way the paternal image can possibly make sense is for it to recognize the existence of numerous "fathers" of English poetry—all of them Italian and French. Their names are Virgil, Ovid, Boccaccio, Deschamps, and Machaut (to name only the most obvious candidates for paternity). Indeed, the critic who insists on parental-originary imagery might more suitably represent Chaucer as the "mother" of English poetry: the receptive vessel or linguistic matrix in which developed the seminal influence of earlier authors. To be sure, the maternal matrix was not without its own distinct inseminating contribution, as medieval and Renaissance medical lore allowed. Perhaps this is why Sir Philip Sidney was so often pleased to represent himself in prose and verse in the maternal-authorial role.

However, recent concern for the politics of critical language may be expected to render obsolete the notion of paternal and paternalistic absolute origins, surely one of the hardest-dying metaphysical constructs still informing some literary scholarship. The bureaucrat-poet Thomas Hoccleve, who launched this tradition within a few years of Chaucer's death, had an agenda at once semiotic and political, as Joseph Hornsby has perceptively argued. John Fisher has enabled us to see Hoccleve's effort as one prong in a royal campaign both political and linguistic. Chaucer became, conveniently, "the cynosure for this movement" ("A Language Policy," 1174), whose aims were to stir nationalist feeling in time of war, to mobilize popular opinion against the threat of Wycliffism, and to legitimate a usurper's dynasty. The last becomes particularly relevant to our paternal metaphor when we recall that the Lancastrian claim to the throne relied on an entirely male descent from Edward III, while the claim of its strongest rival, the House of York, was transmitted at more than one point through a female. The paternal image of Chaucer was thus meant to codify—and not merely metaphorically—an interrelated set of values and positions we are well able to do without.

The poet's general conservatism was not a surprise, for I have always seen Pauline-Augustinian orthodoxy as fundamental to the Chaucerian sensibility. Its depth and extent, particularly around the woman question, were new, although confirming the larger pattern. What I noticed about the poet's attitude toward marriage (in "Dido"), about the structure of the balade in the Prologue, and especially about the ambiguous role of Alceste reinforced once again my sense of the limits to Chaucerian ideological openness or "friendliness" to women. If one takes the hortatory ending of *Troilus* at face value (as I do), then the *Legend* makes sense as an extension of its otherworldly "sentence" by other means. Nature is the key concept here: nature in its orthodox plenitude of meaning as the site of complexity rather than simplicity, nature as that which we constantly struggle to overcome.

This is why, as some readers will have noticed, the name of Dante is so infrequently invoked in these pages. Dante's work is committed to the redemptive possibility of human love, and for that reason it is, I believe, deeply incompatible with the Chaucerian sensibility on the ideological level. I would maintain this to be the case despite certain specific verbal echoes or borrowings in various of Chaucer's works as documented by numerous scholars. Even Lisa Kiser, whose new book is devoted to showing the Dantean influence on Chaucer, constantly stresses that Chaucer must inevitably reject Dante's ideas, must use his great predecessor as contrast or foil (*Truth and Textuality*, 36, 112, etc.). Ideologically, *Troilus* could well be read as an anti–*Vita nuova*. There is for Chaucer no Beatrice—not even, as Chapter 2 aims to show, Alceste. For Chaucer there is a clear distinction between nature and eternity: therefore it seems to me that the title of Donald Rowe's recent study of the *Legend*—*Through Nature to Eternity*—gets the relationship exactly wrong. "The goal of Chaucer's poetry is to undo the fall," Rowe writes (140), but as I have argued at several points, this would be, in Chaucerian terms, a utopian and potentially heretical program. Nature may exemplify principles of divine order, but those principles are constantly and necessarily subverted by fallen human perceptions and behavior. In communication, we have confusion; in love, *cupiditas*; in society and in sexual relations, power.

It is a deeply Augustinian agenda, nowhere more so than in its staging of that distinctively Augustinian contribution to Christian theology, Original Sin (cf. Pagels). This ideological stance does not lie, as D. W. Robertson, Jr., argued over thirty years ago, in reducing all meaning to the notion of *caritas*; rather it infuses the work at a far deeper level. The *Legend*'s real links in the *Tales* are not, therefore, to episodes of courtly love or lament such as narrated by Knight or Squire but rather to the theodicy of the *Franklin's Tale*, the historical patterns of the *Monk's Tale*, the *Merchant's Tale*'s investigation of perception and subjectivity, and the East-West polarities of the *Man of Law's Tale*. When the *Legend*'s allusions and structures are explored, what emerges is an agenda that is surprisingly serious and profoundly historical.

The extent of Ovidian influence can be no surprise to anyone who has studied the *Legend*, but the multiplicity of formats constituting "Chaucer's Ovid" might be. The *Ovide moralisé* is a work whose rich potential usefulness to Chaucer—along with scholastic Ovid commentaries and the work of Pierre Bersuire—has not yet been fully explored. In looking at the history of Chaucer criticism, one senses a certain reluctance to do so among scholars of a previous generation, despite the early work of Lowes arguing Chaucer's indebtedness to the French text for details in his version of Philomela. When Sanford Meech extended Lowes's research to include "Ariadne," he assured his audience that these two legends "are the only productions of Chaucer's pen in which the impress of the moralized Ovid can be positively established," and further that "there is no satisfactory evidence of an employment of the *Ovide moralisé* in other legends or in any production of Chaucer before the *Legend of Good Women*." This premature closing off of possibility was odd and inaccurate, but even odder is the strenuous resistance to the French text displayed in a slightly earlier study of Chaucer and the classics. E. F. Shannon attempted to refute Lowes's hypothesis, but not very convincingly. His tenacity seems somewhat perverse until one understands what view of the classics, and of Chaucer, it advances:

> Chaucer's mood and spirit as well as methods of narration are more closely akin to the Latin with its unity of thought and precision of expression than to the psychologizing habits of the Old French writers. His interest is in human relationships realistically and dramatically portrayed. It is apparent that the Old French translations and allegorizations of the Classics weighed virtually nothing either in the extent of Chaucer's knowledge or the shaping of his art. . . . Chaucer's [verse] evinces simplicity and manly vigor. (283, 372)

Here, Chaucer and the classics are linked by standards of unity, simplicity, and virility that the *Ovide moralisé* lacks, for it is a quirky, bizarre, grotesque sort of text. It is, in short, too Gothic and too Gallic; indeed, were one to pursue the implications of "manly vigor," it is seen as effeminate or even feminine because of its "psychologizing habits" and its allegorizations, its fantasy and multiplicity of interpretation. As for the feminine, when we read Shannon's opinion that the Wife of Bath is "frankly animal in her nature" (373), we may wonder whether there is indeed any place for femininity at all in his scheme of things.

"Vigorous, manly and English": from the mid nineteenth century on, this formula was, as Philip Dodd points out, the conventional collocation of qualities defining the national character and the national style. Repeated in educational and ecclesiastical institutions, it participated in the construction of masculinity (and therefore, by exclusion, of feminity). Much like their medieval or ancient predecessors, generations of English-speaking scholars—I do not intend to exclude Americans here—have "licensed to other groups and to other nationalities those 'female' qualities which [they] did not acknowledge [themselves] to possess" (Dodd, 6), although in this particular modern instance the target is French rather than, as in earlier times, Oriental.

In this connection I am reminded of Frederick Ahl's recent analysis of still-prevalent attitudes toward Latin literature, attitudes that continue to define classicism in exactly the same terms Shannon used: unity and simplicity. Ahl's work, with that of other classicists cited in this study (and many I regret being unable to cite for reasons of space), helps to correct this distortion, which is after all not merely the personal taste of particular classically educated scholars but rather a deep-rooted cultural premise or even prejudice, the kind for which, in Chapter 2, I have used the Bakhtinian term "ideologeme." This one affects not only a critic's approach to the question of Chaucer's French versus Latin sources, nor indeed only the question of Chaucer's latinity in general (on this last I am in agreement with Götz Schmitz's assertion of the "limited and secondhand" knowledge of the classics on the part of many late medieval authors and the consequent importance of florilegia and commentaries ["Gower, Chaucer, and the Classics," 95]). The same notion of classicism as unity and simplicity has also blinded many literary scholars to the perception of wordplay, an important dimension in my study of Chaucerian rhetoric in the *Legend*, and one that has yet to be fully restored to medieval poetry.

The *Ovide moralisé* is no longer under quite the shadow it once was, although it receives grudgingly scant attention in the *Riverside Chaucer*, and many scholars continue to want to see it as a source for a few details or a handy trot. It was both of these—and more; for beside verbal borrowing it evoked, I believe, a profound response from the English poet because of its interpretive tactics. In this sense the exploration of what Charles Muscatine called "Chaucer and the French tradition" has not been exhausted; but the tradition I mean is not that of romance and fabliau but that of ecclesiastical and scholarly compendia.

Given the changes that Chaucer is able to ring on the "abandoned woman" theme—to make it a vehicle for positions on sex, gender, religion, politics, history, interpretation, and writing—I think we need to be skeptical about any approach to the *Legend* that takes for granted some simplistic "lack of ambiguity" or "the conclusive purpose of speaking well of women" or "the single-minded didactic impulse that propels the legends." These are the phrases of Larry Sklute, who compares the poem to "a set of Hail Marys . . . : it mesmerizes others who hear it but who are not caught in the same state of feeling" (86, 88). In the same vein, Carolyn Dinshaw dismisses the poem as "downright boring . . . dull, a formula . . . insisting on reducing complexity to produce a whole, monolithic structure" (74, 86, 87). I hope to have shown that the *Legend* is not about feeling per se—that it is not a sentimental work mainly—but rather about structures of feeling, a very different thing: ways to understand feeling, to place it systematically and therefore to develop a perspective on it. The narrative model may be repetitive, but within it the rest, the *writing*, is unsettling, playful, subversive of easy assumptions. Surely recent developments in art—the work of John Cage, say, or Philip Glass or Steve Reich—have something to tell us about boredom being in the eye or ear of the beholder, and about the paradoxically rich possibilities of minimalism and repetition. The Indonesian gamelan ensemble makes the same point. These kinds of music are not the same as a Beethoven symphony, but they are not trying to be: they are premised on a different aesthetic. Or—by analogy to another art—one might as well call abstract expressionism or constructivism boring because they offer sheer form, depriving us of representations that we can quickly cathect. They simply do not employ an aesthetic of realism. Neither does the *Legend of Good Women*, a *writerly* poem, a poet's poem offering little comfort to cling to (such as narrative, character, or dialogue) and requiring a good deal of work to excavate. Far from being "a colossal blunder" that "may already have seemed so in the poet's lifetime" (Burlin, 34), the *Legend* is a document of serious moral-instructional value and sophisticated poetic craft, acknowledged as such by discriminating readers of Chaucer's own and the next generations. The earnest Lydgate echoed it often: not only in the lines I have quoted in Chapter 1, but in his long, royally commissioned *Life of Our Lady* (1421–22), where the "Absolon" balade is twice imitated (1.302–9 and 5.407–13) in praising the Virgin Mary; clearly Lydgate had the book before him.

If the *Legend* is "conclusive"—if, as Sklute writes, it "resolves the problems it raises" (85)—this is not, I suggest, because of the seduced-and-abandoned plot, but because its interest is doctrinal, and doctrine is closed. It might be said that Chaucer is always doctrinal; nonetheless we notice a movement of advance and recession in the proportional emphasis. The *Book of the Duchess* is closed: it offers a fairly specific and "correct" sort of comfort in urging moderation of sorrow. The *Parliament* and the *House of Fame* are open: open, that is, to alternatives to a rigorous orthodox line, open to pluralism. *Boece* is closed. *Troilus* is open (to multiplicity of experience and of language), but with a closed ending. The *Legend*—as if to extend the import of that ending—is doctrinally closed despite its verbal play. The *Tales* is open but again with a closed ending: the *Parson's Tale* and Retraction. Chaucer thus plays with open structures, with their attractive but potentially dangerous and misleading pluralisms and ambiguities, but he retains and returns to the safety net of reassuring Augustinian certainties.

The sorts of aesthetic comment I have made here and throughout must necessarily broach the question of audience. For whom can a work of such intellectual depth and formal play have been intended? It is, after all, a poem that looks very much like a charming courtly-classical divertissement, and that in one of its two extant versions commends itself to Queen Anne. "Goo now thy wey," says Alceste,

> "this penaunce ys but lyte.
> And whan this book ys maad, yive it the quene,
> On my byhalf, at Eltham or at Sheene."
>
> (F 495–97)

How might we reconcile the recondite themes I have noticed in the *Legend* with this audience: royal, courtly, female—and, for that matter, foreign (for Anne was from Bohemia)?

The most responsible answer I can give to this entirely legitimate concern is that it does not seem to me that the question of audience was posed in the late Middle Ages identically to the way we pose it now. Let me illustrate what I mean with the example of an art form that receives little attention today despite its importance in the medieval period: the roof bosses found on church, priory, and abbey ceilings throughout England (and elsewhere) dating from the twelfth through the fifteenth centuries.

These decorative medallions—a foot or more across—provided a channel for free artistic expression; what surprises is the variety of subject matter and treatment. Besides the expected narrative or emblematic material from Old and New Testaments, hagiography, liturgy, and doctrine, there is a wealth of imagery that seems to express the sheer joy of form and invention as well as the darker side of the human personality. We find, for instance, portraits (including one of a black man, at Ely); naturalistic social, athletic, or work scenes; a variety of animals (bat, owl, elephant, caterpillar, ape, pig, etc.); formal designs in foliage and in pure line; fantastic or mythical creatures (mermaid, centaur); astrological signs; grotesques, including deformed or phallic creatures and the "sheila-na-gig," an Irish-derived female fertility image; and Picasso-esque double heads with shared middle eye or quadruple head with shared mouth. At the church of St. Mary in Redcliffe, Bristol (which has over 1,100 roof bosses, surpassing even the 1,000 or so in Norwich Cathedral), one finds a quite astonishing level of formal and representational play, including a maze, a *mise-en-abîme* that is actually a model of the church's transept roof, and a man at stool. Some motifs are drawn from secular literature such as the *Roman de Renard* and the *Gesta Romanorum*. There are coats of arms and name-rebuses (e.g., for Bishops Walter Lyhart and William Goldwell at Norwich Cathedral: a hart lying on wa(l)ter; a golden well).

Besides the motifs, the detail in execution is often astoundingly minute. C. J. P. Cave observes:

> In the transepts at Norwich there are several compositions in which figures are represented with books in their hands, and on the pages of the books lines and dots represent writing.

> In the south transept of St Mary, Redcliffe, the Three Persons are represented. . . . The head of an aged man with long hair and beard in the centre of the third bay can only be meant for the Holy Ghost. . . . In the long hair at the side and on the beard below the face are four small figures . . . It is difficult to know why such figures, one of them definitely grotesque, should be thus represented hidden in the hair and beard of the figure of the Holy Ghost. . . . I almost feel that they were put there by some craftsman in a spirit of mischief, if not even in a spirit of actual disrespect for images. (3, 25)

The point of all this is that roof bosses were not meant to be seen, at least not by many and not up close. Indeed, this is why, as Cave points out (1), so many of them survived periods of iconoclasm (such as the Reformation and the Civil War). They are carved and painted in all their superb variety fifty or eighty feet above the church floor, and even today can only be fully appreciated by telephoto lens.

What can have been the conception of audience at work here? I can think of four possibilities, not mutually exclusive. The artist's love of formal play and experimentation is one: it proceeds independent of audience, as many a medieval artist's sketchbook or manuscript margin reveals. Another is the medieval notion of art as a form of tribute, or even analogue, to divine creativity as manifested in the world's multifariousness. To this form of worship no human audience is necessary: God sees all. On the other hand, my third possibility, a few people do perambulate the heights of a church clerestory; they are the ecclesiastical personnel who staff the establishment and who would derive edification and amusement from the designs. Lastly, there might well be individuals willing to risk a sprained neck in order to see and perhaps even enjoy the art over their heads. The distance was not only a challenge but an obstacle to screen out those who lack "eyes to see or ears to hear" (Deut. 29:4): a fairly common exclusivist position in medieval aesthetics.

Coming back to Chaucer, then, I do not see that a dedication to Queen Anne, or the possibility of a female readership, or any other considerations of audience, need affect my (or any other) interpretation. On one level the *Legend of Good Women* is a charming courtly tribute to female fidelity. On other levels, depending on what one brings to it, it yields other meanings. It is, in this, fairly typically Chaucerian.

By sheer serendipity, I am able to end with Virginia Woolf, whose last work, *Between the Acts* (1941), I read while completing this book. I read it in part because one of the feminist essays I had used in connection with this study (a piece by Jane Marcus) suggested that the novel was a reworking of the Philomela motif, and I wanted to pursue this for obvious reasons. I differ from Marcus's hypothesis, but what I found in Woolf's novel was even more relevant to the present project: a massive deployment of classical myth in service of a vision of British history. Woolf asks us to see recognizable individuals—our neighbors, acquaintances, spouses, relatives—in their archetypal dimensions; and, conversely, classical legendary and mythic figures as, at some level, real individuals with the same passions as our own (albeit expressed in action—incest, murder, rape, etc.—where ours are likely to be suppressed). Her playwright is a Sappho; her heroine Isa a Medea manquée; the ancestress in a portrait is a Diana, "silver arrow in her hand and a feather in her hair"; even the butler Candish, who "loved flowers. . . . Queerly, he loved them," might be Ganymede in another time. Woolf's two-level work of art—a play within a novel—shows us art in the making, with the fictional artist, the playwright Miss La Trobe, confronting mixed reactions from an imperfectly comprehending audience to which, nonetheless, she remains (as La Trobe's manuscript note confesses) "always enslaved." What binds it together down the ages, for Woolf, is poetry, monument of feelings recurrent and transmitted, poetry as shaped by and as shaper of both individual psyche and national sensibility. The novel is a valiant effort at national and political and cultural self-definition, set "between the acts" of the two world wars, between the acts of a neighborhood pageant at a manorial house, between the acts of love and of violence that punctuate a difficult marriage. And it ends—or could end—with a colon: "Then the curtain rose. They spoke."

Most of these general statements could be made of the *Legend* as well. I find it interesting that two great English literary artists confronting the same strategy—to relate the disturbing English present to the supposedly glorious cultural/mythic/classical past—should come up with so many of the same tactics despite their difference in gender, religious attitude, politics, genre, and historical epoch. Both were trying to develop the sense of what it means to be English. Chaucer did so somewhat furtively, because he wrote at the start of the period when that concept began to mean something important internationally; Woolf did it perfectly overtly, writing near the end of the period when that concept could mean something important internationally. World War II, which Virginia so deeply feared, would give the idea of Englishness a new lease on life, for the English at least, but a short-lived one. There is an apothegm among social historians that all the oldest English traditions were invented in the last quarter of the nineteenth century—except, I would add, the habit of inventing traditions, which is as old as ideology itself and indeed probably the oldest form of ideology.

Was William Heale right, then—or, for that matter, Gavin Douglas in asserting that Chaucer was always woman's friend? Or, on the other hand, was Osbern Bokenham justified in correcting Chaucer's classical-courtly *Legend* with his own real hagiography? I hope to show in a work now in progress that Bokenham's more conventional legendary makes a statement finally quite similar to Chaucer's, albeit in very different generic and rhetorical clothing. Not to beat about the bush, though, I think that Bokenham mistook Chaucer's rhetoric for his "sentence." Perhaps he needed to do so in order to clear a space for himself as what Harold Bloom would call belated ephebe to a great and recent precursor.

My Prolocutory suggested that this study would clarify the ambivalence of Chaucer's attitude toward women, not resolve or eliminate it. It remains an ambivalent attitude: egalitarian sub specie aeternitatis, but by the same token recognizing and accepting the extent to which everything here falls short of that perspective. I cannot think of another writer of the period, of whatever politics—the republican Boccaccio, the conservative courtier Christine de Pizan, the Yorkist Austin friar Bokenham—who goes further than that. Our discomfort with such ambivalence is all to the good, provided we do not attempt to dispel it by rewriting the past, as they did. Better, as they were not able to do, to rewrite the future: not a merely literary task.

Works Cited

Adams, J. N. *The Latin Sexual Vocabulary*. London: Duckworth, 1982.

Ahl, Frederick. *Metaformations: Soundplay and Wordplay in Ovid and Other Classical Poets*. Ithaca, N.Y.: Cornell University Press, 1985.

Aigrain, René. *L'Hagiographie: Ses Sources, ses méthodes, son histoire*. Paris: Bloud & Gay, 1953.

Alanus de Insulis. *De planctu naturae*. Ed. N. M. Haring. *Studi Medievali* 19 (1978): 797–879.

——. *The Plaint of Nature*. Trans. James J. Sheridan. Toronto: PIMS, 1980.

Allen, Judson B. *The Ethical Poetic of the Later Middle Ages*. Toronto: University of Toronto Press, 1982.

Allen, Peter. "Reading Chaucer's Good Women." *ChR* 21 (1987): 419–34.

Alpers, Svetlana. *The Art of Describing: Dutch Art in the Seventeenth Century*. Chicago: University of Chicago Press, 1983.

Alverny, Marie-Thérèse d'. "Deux traductions latines du Coran au Moyen-Age." *Archives d'histoire doctrinaire et littéraire du Moyen-Age* 22–23 (1947–48): 69–131.

Alverny, Marie-Thérèse d', and Georges Vajda. "Marc de Tolède, traducteur d'Ibn Tumart." *Al-Andalus* 16 (1951): 99–140 and 259–307.

Amy, Ernest F. *The Text of Chaucer's Legend of Good Women*. 1918. Reprint, New York: Haskell, 1965.

Atiya, Aziz S. *Crusade, Commerce and Culture*. Bloomington: Indiana University Press, 1962.

Auerbach, Erich. "Figura." In id., *Scenes from the Drama of European Literature*, 11–76. New York: Meridian, 1959.

Augustine. *The City of God*. Trans. Marcus Dods. New York: Random House, 1950.

——. *On Christian Doctrine*. Trans. D. W. Robertson, Jr. New York: Liberal Arts Library, 1958.

Barthes, Roland. *Writing Degree Zero*. Paris: Editions du Seuil, 1953. Trans. Annette Lavers and Colin Smith. New York: Hill & Wang, 1968.

——. *Mythologies*. Paris: Editions du Seuil, 1957. Trans. Annette Lavers. New York: Hill & Wang, 1978.

Beal, Rebecca S. "Dante in the Labyrinth." Special issue of *Mediaevalia* 13 (1987): 227–45.

Berg, Stephen, and Robert Mezey. *Naked Poetry: Recent American Poetry in Open Forms*. Indianapolis: Bobbs-Merrill, 1969.

Bersuire, Pierre. *Ovidius moralizatus*. Ed. J. Engels. Utrecht, 1962.

———. *Petrus Berchorius De formis figurisque deorum*. Ed. J. Engels. Utrecht, 1966.

Bilderbeck, J. B. *Chaucer's Legend of Good Women*. London: Hazel, Watson & Viney, 1902.

Birney, Earle. "The Beginnings of Chaucerian Irony." *PMLA* 54 (1939): 637–55. Reprinted in *Essays on Chaucerian Irony*, ed. Beryl Rowland. Toronto: University of Toronto Press, 1985.

Boccaccio, Giovanni. *Concerning Famous Women*. Trans. Guido Guarini. New Brunswick, N.J.: Rutgers University Press, 1963.

———. *De mulieribus claris*. Vol. 10. Ed. Vittorio Zaccaria. In *Tutte le opere*, ed. Vittore Branca. Verona: Mondadori, 1967.

Bokenham, Osbern. *Legendys of Hooly Wummen*. Ed. Mary S. Serjeantson. EETS, o.s., 206 (1938).

Bord, Janet. *Mazes and Labyrinths of the World*. London: Latimer, 1976.

Boswell, John. *The Kindness of Strangers: The Abandonment of Children in Western Europe from Late Antiquity to the Renaissance*. New York: Pantheon Books, 1988.

Boyd, Beverly. *Chaucer and the Medieval Book*. San Marino, Calif.: Huntington Library, 1973.

Braddy, Haldeen. "Chaucer's Bawdy Tongue." *Southern Folklore Quarterly* 30 (1966): 214–22.

Branciforti, F., ed. *Piramus et Thisbe*. Florence: L. S. Olschki, 1959.

Braswell, Laurel. "Chaucer and the Legendaries: New Sources for Anti-Mendicant Satire." *English Studies in Canada* 2 (1976): 373–80.

———. "Chaucer and the Art of Hagiography." In *Chaucer in the Eighties*, ed. Julian Wasserman and Robert J. Blanch, 209–21. Syracuse, N.Y.: Syracuse University Press, 1986.

Braudel, Fernand. "La Longue Durée." *Annales: Economies, sociétés, civilisations* 4 (1958): 725–53. Reprinted in *Ecrits sur l'histoire*, 41–83. Paris: Flammarion, 1969.

Bronson, Bertrand H. "The *Book of the Duchess* Reopened." *PMLA* 67 (1952): 863–81. Reprinted in *Chaucer: Modern Essays in Criticism*, ed. Edward Wagenknecht, 271–94. New York: Oxford University Press, 1959.

Brown, Peter. *Relics and Social Status in the Age of Gregory of Tours*. Reading: University of Reading Press, 1977.

———. *The Cult of the Saints: Its Rise and Function in Latin Christianity*. Chicago: University of Chicago Press, 1981.

Brundage, James A. "Sexual Equality in Medieval Canon Law." In *Medieval Women and the Sources of Medieval History*, ed. Joel T. Rosenthal, 66–79. Athens, Ga.: University of Georgia Press, 1990.

Bryson, Norman. "Narratives of Rape in the Visual Arts." In *Rape*, ed. Sylvia Tomaselli and Roy Porter, 152–73. Oxford: Blackwell, 1986.

Buhler, Curt, ed. "A Lollard Tract: On Translating the Bible into English." *Medium Aevum* 7 (1938): 167–83.

Burlin, Robert. *Chaucerian Fiction*. Princeton: Princeton University Press, 1977.

Bynum, Caroline Walker. "Jesus as Mother and Abbot as Mother: Some Themes in Twelfth-Century Cistercian Writing." In *Jesus as Mother: Studies in the Spirituality of the High Middle Ages*. Berkeley and Los Angeles: University of California, 1982.

Campbell, P. G. C. *L'Epître d'Othéa: Etude sur les sources de Christine de Pisan*. Paris: E. Champion, 1924.

Carruthers, Mary. *The Book of Memory: A Study of Memory in Medieval Culture*. Cambridge: Cambridge University Press, 1990.

Castle, Terry. *Clarissa's Ciphers: Meaning and Disruption in Richardson's "Clarissa."* Ithaca, N.Y.: Cornell University Press, 1982.

Cave, C. J. P. *Roof Bosses in Medieval Churches: An Aspect of Gothic Sculpture*. Cambridge: Cambridge University Press, 1948.

Chaucer, Geoffrey. *The Riverside Chaucer*. Ed. Larry D. Benson. Boston: Houghton Mifflin, 1987.

———. *The Works of Geoffrey Chaucer*. Ed. F. N. Robinson. 2d ed. Boston: Houghton Mifflin, 1957.

Christine de Pizan. "The *Livre de la cité des dames*: A Critical Edition." Ed. Maureen Curnow. Ph.D. diss., Vanderbilt University, Nashville, Tenn., 1975.

Cixous, Hélène. "The Laugh of the Medusa." *Signs* 1 (1976): 875–93. Reprinted in *New French Feminisms*, ed. Elaine Marks and Isabelle de Courtivron. Amherst: University of Massachusetts Press, 1980.

Clanchy, M. T. *From Memory to Written Record: England, 1066–1307*. London: Arnold, 1979.

Cline, Ruth. "Four Chaucer Saints." *Modern Language Notes* 60 (1945): 480–82.

Coleman, William E., ed. *Philippe de Mézières' Campaign for the Feast of Mary's Presentation*. Toronto: PIMS, 1991.

Colette[, Sidonie-Gabrielle]. *Claudine at School*. In *The Complete Claudine*, trans. Antonia White. 1956. New York: Avenel, 1984.

Colie, Rosalie. *Paradoxia Epidemica: The Renaissance Tradition of Paradox*. Princeton: Princeton University Press, 1966.

Colish, Marcia. *The Mirror of Language: A Study in the Medieval Theory of Knowledge*. New Haven: Yale University Press, 1968.

Coopland, G. W., ed. *Le Songe du Vieil Pelerin*. Cambridge: Cambridge University Press, 1969.

———, ed. *Philippe de Mézières: Letter to King Richard II*. Liverpool: Liverpool University Press, 1975.

Courtenay, William. "The Reception of Ockham's Thought in Fourteenth-Century England." In *From Ockham to Wyclif*, ed. Anne Hudson and Michael Wilks, 89–107. Oxford: Blackwell, 1987.

Cowen, Janet M. "Chaucer's *Legend of Good Women*, Lines 2501–3." *Notes and Queries* 31 (1984): 298–99.

————. "Chaucer's *Legend of Good Women*: Structure and Tone." *Studies in Philology* 82 (1985): 416–36.

Curtius, E. R. *European Literature and the Latin Middle Ages.* New York: Pantheon Books, 1953.

Dahmus, Joseph. *The Prosecution of John Wyclif.* New Haven: Yale University Press, 1952.

Daniel, Norman. *Islam and the West: The Making of an Image.* Edinburgh: Edinburgh University Press, 1960.

David, Alfred. *The Strumpet Muse: Art and Morals in Chaucer's Poetry.* Bloomington: University of Indiana Press, 1976.

Deanesly, Margaret. *The Lollard Bible and Other Medieval Biblical Versions.* Cambridge: Cambridge University Press, 1920. Reprint, 1966.

————. *The Significance of the Lollard Bible.* London: Athlone, 1951.

Delany, Sheila. "Chaucer's *House of Fame* and the *Ovide moralisé.*" *Comparative Literature* 20 (1968): 254–64.

————. *Chaucer's House of Fame: The Poetics of Skeptical Fideism.* Chicago: University of Chicago Press, 1972.

————. "Techniques of Alienation in *Troilus and Criseyde.*" In *The Uses of Criticism*, ed. A. P. Foulkes, 77–95. Bern/Frankfurt: Lang, 1976. Reprinted in *Chaucer's Troilus . . . Current Essays in Criticism*, ed. R. A. Shoaf. Binghamton, N.Y.: Medieval & Renaissance Texts and Studies, 1992.

————. *Writing Woman: Women Writers and Women in Literature, Medieval to Modern.* New York: Schocken Books, 1983.

————. " 'Loi' and 'Foi' in the Man of Law's Introduction, Prologue and Tale." *Mediaevalia* 8 (1985 for 1982): 135–49.

————. "The Logic of Obscenity in Chaucer's *Legend of Good Women.*" *Florilegium* 7 (1987 for 1985): 189–205.

————. "The Naked Text: Chaucer's 'Thisbe', the *Ovide moralisé*, and the Problem of *translatio studii* in the *Legend of Good Women.*" Special issue of *Mediaevalia* 13 (1989 for 1987): 275–94.

————. *Medieval Literary Politics: Shapes of Ideology.* Manchester: Manchester University Press/New York: St. Martin's Press, 1990.

————. "Anatomy of the Resisting Reader: Some Implications of Resistance to Sexual Wordplay in Medieval Literature." *Exemplaria* 4 (1992): 7–34.

Demats, Paule. *Fabula: Trois études de mythographie antique et médiévale.* Geneva: Droz, 1973.

Desmond, Marilynn, ed. *Ovid in Medieval Culture.* Special issue of *Mediaevalia* 13 (1989 for 1987).

Dictionary of National Biography. Ed. Leslie Stephen and Sidney Lee. 21 vols. with supp. London: Oxford University Press.

Dinshaw, Carolyn. *Chaucer's Sexual Poetics.* Madison: University of Wisconsin Press, 1989.

Dodd, Philip. "Englishness and the National Culture." In *Englishness: Politics and Culture, 1880–1920*, ed. Robert Colls and Philip Dodd, 1–28. London: Croom Helm, 1987.

Doherty, Dennis. *The Sexual Doctrine of Cardinal Cajetan*. Regensburg: Pustet, 1966.

Donaldson, E. Talbot. *Speaking of Chaucer*. New York: Norton, 1970.

Donaldson, Ian. *The Rapes of Lucretia: A Myth and Its Transformations*. Oxford: Clarendon, 1982.

Doob, Penelope. *The Idea of the Labyrinth from Classical Antiquity through the Middle Ages*. Ithaca, N.Y.: Cornell University Press, 1990.

Dronke, Peter. *Poetic Individuality in the Middle Ages: New Departures in Poetry, 1000–1150*. Oxford: Clarendon, 1970.

du Bois, Page. "Sexual Difference: Ancient and Modern." *Pacific Coast Philology* 19 (November 1984): 43–49.

Duby, Georges. *The Three Orders: Feudal Society Imagined*. Paris: Gallimard, 1978. Trans. Arthur Goldhammer. Chicago: University of Chicago Press, 1980.

———. *The Knight, the Lady, and the Priest: The Making of Modern Marriage in Medieval France*. Trans. Barbara Bray. New York: Pantheon Books, 1983.

Engels, Joseph. *Etudes sur l'Ovide moralisé*. Groningen-Batavia: J. B. Wolters, 1945.

Erasmus[, Desiderius]. *Correspondence*. Ed. R. A. B. Mynors. Toronto: 1982.

Evelyn, Charlotte d', and Anna Mill, eds. *The South English Legendary*. EETS 235, 236 (1956; reprint, 1967).

Ferris, Sumner. "Chaucer, Richard II, Henry IV, and 13 October." In *Chaucer and Middle English Studies*, ed. Beryl Rowland, 210–17. London: Allen & Unwin, 1974.

Ferster, Judith. *Chaucer on Interpretation*. Cambridge: Cambridge University Press, 1985.

Fisher, John H. *John Gower. Moral Philosopher and Friend of Chaucer*. New York: New York University Press, 1964.

———. "The Revision of the Prologue to the *Legend of Good Women*: An Occasional Explanation." *South Atlantic Bulletin* 43 (1978): 75–84.

———. "A Language Policy for Lancastrian England." *PMLA* 107 (1992): 1168–80.

Fleming, John. "Hoccleve's 'Letter of Cupid' and the 'Quarrel' over the *Roman de la Rose*." *Medium Aevum* 40 (1971): 21–40.

Forsyth, Karen. *Ariadne auf Naxos by Hugo von Hofmannsthal and Richard Strauss: Its Genesis and Meaning*. Oxford: Oxford University Press, 1982.

Foucault, Michel. *Language, Counter-Memory, Practice*. Ed. Donald F. Bouchard. Ithaca, N.Y.: Cornell University Press, 1977.

———. *The Care of the Self*. New York: Random House, 1986.

———. *Technologies of the Self*. Ed. Luther H. Martin et al. Amherst: University of Massachusetts Press, 1988.

Frank, Robert W., Jr. *Chaucer and the Legend of Good Women*. Cambridge, Mass.: Harvard University Press, 1972.

Freeman, Michelle. "Marie de France's Poetics of Silence." *PMLA* 99 (1984): 860–83.

Fry, Donald K. "The Ending of the *Monk's Tale.*" *JEGP* 71 (1972): 355–68.

Fulgentius. *Mythologies.* Trans. Leslie G. Whitbread. In *Fulgentius the Mythographer.* Columbus: Ohio State University Press, 1971.

Furnivall, F. J., ed. *Political, Religious and Love Poems.* EETS, o.s., 15 (1866).

———, ed. *Jyl of Breyntford's Testament . . . and Other Short Pieces.* London: Taylor & Co., 1871.

———, ed. *Love-Poems and Humorous Ones.* Hertford: S. Austin & Sons for Ballad Society, 1874.

Fyler, John. *Chaucer and Ovid.* New Haven: Yale University Press, 1979.

———. "Domesticating the Exotic in the *Squire's Tale.*" *ELH* 55 (1989): 1–26.

Gaignebet, Claude, and J. D. Lajoux. *Art profane et religion populaire au Moyen-Age.* Vendôme: Presses universitaires de France, 1985.

Galinsky, G. Karl. *Ovid's Metamorphoses.* Berkeley and Los Angeles: University of California Press, 1975.

Gascoigne, Thomas. *"Loci e Libro veritatum": Passages Selected from Gascoigne's Theological Dictionary Illustrating the Condition of Church and State.* Ed. James E. Thorold Rogers. Oxford: Clarendon Press, 1881.

Geary, Patrick. *Furta Sacra: Thefts of Relics in the Central Middle Ages.* Princeton: Princeton University Press, 1978.

Gellrich, Jesse. *The Idea of the Book in the Middle Ages: Language Theory, Mythology and Fiction.* Ithaca, N.Y.: Cornell University Press, 1985.

Genette, Gérard. *Palimpsestes: La Littérature au second degré.* Paris: Editions du Seuil, 1982.

Gesta Romanorum. Ed. and trans. Charles Swan and Wynnard Hooper. 1876. Reprint, New York: Dover, 1959.

Ghisalberti, Fausto. *L'Ovidius Moralizatus di Pierre Bersuire.* Rome: Cuggiani, 1933.

Gies, Frances, and Joseph Gies. *Marriage and the Family in the Middle Ages.* New York: Harper & Row, 1987.

Gilbert, Neal W. "Richard de Bury and the 'Quires of Yesterday's Sophisms.'" In *Philosophy and Humanism: Renaissance Essays in Honor of Paul Oskar Kristeller,* ed. Edward P. Mahoney, 229–57. Leiden: Brill, 1976.

Gilson, Etienne. *The Unity of Philosophical Experience.* New York, 1937. Cited in Leo Donald Davis, S.J., "The Intuitive Knowledge of Non-Existents and the Problem of Late-Medieval Skepticism," *New Scholasticism* 49 (1975): 410–30.

Glendinning, Robert. "Pyramus and Thisbe in the Medieval Classroom." *Speculum* 61 (1986): 51–78.

Goddard, Harold C. "Chaucer's *Legend of Good Women.*" *JEGP* 7 (1908): 87–129; 8 (1909): 47–112.

Gower, John. *Confessio Amantis.* In *English Works,* ed. G. C. Macaulay. EETS, e.s., 81 (1900, reprint, 1957, 1969).

Griffith, D. D. "An Interpretation of Chaucer's *Legend of Good Women.*" In *The Manly Anniversary Studies in Language and Literature,* 32–41. Chicago: University of Chicago Press, 1923. Reprinted in *Chaucer: Modern Essays in*

Criticism, ed. Edward Wagenknecht, 396–404. New York: Oxford University Press, 1959.

Gubar, Susan. "'The Blank Page' and Female Creativity." In *Writing and Sexual Difference*, ed. Elizabeth Abel, 73–93. Chicago: University of Chicago Press, 1982.

Hardyng, John. *John Hardyng's Chronicle.* Ed. Henry Ellis. London: Woodfall, 1812.

Hartman, Geoffrey. "The Voice of the Shuttle: Language from the Point of View of Literature." In id., *Beyond Formalism*, 337–55. New Haven: Yale University Press, 1970.

Haskell, Ann S. *Essays on Chaucer's Saints.* Hague: Mouton, 1976.

Hatton, Thomas J. "Chaucer's Crusading Knight: A Slanted Ideal." *ChR* 3 (1968): 77–87.

Hawkins, Peter. "Virtuosity and Virtue: Poetic Self-Reflection in the Commedia." *Dante Studies* 98 (1980): 1–18.

Heale, William. *An Apologie for Women. Or an opposition to Mr. Dr. Gager in his assertion. Who held in the Act at Oxforde. Anno 1608, That it was lawfull for husbands to beate their wives.* Oxford: Joseph Barnes Printer to the Universitie, 1609.

Heffernan, Thomas J. *Sacred Biography: Saints and Their Biographies in the Middle Ages.* New York: Oxford University Press, 1988.

Helmholz, R. H. "Infanticide in the Province of Canterbury during the Fifteenth Century." *HCQ* 2 (1974): 379–90.

Henderson, Jeffrey. *The Maculate Muse: Obscene Language in Attic Comedy.* 2d ed. Oxford: Oxford University Press, 1991.

Hermand-Mascard, Nicole. *Les Reliques des saints.* Paris: Klincksieck, 1975.

Hexter, Ralph J. *Ovid and Medieval Schooling: Studies in the Medieval School Commentaries.* Munich: Arbeo-Gesellschaft, 1986.

Higden, Ranulf. *Polychronicon.* Trans. John Trevisa. Rolls Series Rerum Britannicarum Medii Aevi Scriptores, no. 41, ed. Churchill Babington. 9 vols. London, 1865.

Hill, Archibald A. "Chaucer and the Pun-Hunters: Some Points of Caution." In *On Language . . . A Festschrift for Robert P. Stockwell*, ed. Caroline Duncan-Rose and Theo Venneman, 66–78. London: Routledge, 1988.

Hoccleve, Thomas. *Works.* Vol. 1, ed. F. J. Furnivall, EETS, e.s., 61 (1892); vol. 2, ed. Israel Gollancz, EETS, e.s., 73 (1925).

Hornsby, Joseph. "Resurrecting the Vernacular: Hoccleve's Chaucer and the dead 'honour of Englyssch tong.'" Paper given at New Chaucer Society Congress, 1992.

Housley, Norman. *The Avignon Papacy and the Crusades, 1305–1378.* Oxford: Clarendon Press, 1978.

Howard, Donald R. "Chaucer the Man." In *Chaucer's Mind and Art*, ed. A. C. Cawley, 31–45. Edinburgh: Oliver & Boyd, 1969.

———. *The Idea of the Canterbury Tales.* Berkeley and Los Angeles: University of California Press, 1976.

———. *Chaucer: His Life, His Works, His World.* New York: Dutton, 1987.

Hudson, Anne, ed. *Selections from English Wycliffite Writings.* Cambridge: Cambridge University Press, 1978.

———. *Lollards and Their Books.* London: Hambledon, 1985.

———. *The Premature Reformation: Wycliffite Texts and Lollard History.* Oxford: Clarendon Press, 1988.

Hulme, Hilda M. *Explorations in Shakespeare's Language: Some Problems of Word Meaning in the Dramatic Text.* London: Longmans Green, 1962.

Huppé, Bernard F., and D. W. Robertson, Jr. *Fruyt and Chaf: Studies in Chaucer's Allegories.* Princeton: Princeton University Press, 1963.

Hutcheon, Linda. *A Theory of Parody: The Teachings of Twentieth-Century Art Forms.* New York: Methuen, 1985.

Huygens, R. B. C., ed. *Accessus ad auctores.* Leiden: Brill, 1970.

Hyman, Arthur, and James J. Walsh, eds. *Philosophy in the Middle Ages.* Indianapolis: Hackett, 1973.

Isidore of Seville. *Etymologiarum.* Ed. W. M. Lindsay. 2 vols. Oxford: Clarendon Press, 1911.

Jacobson, Howard. *Ovid's Heroides.* Princeton: Princeton University Press, 1974.

Jacquart, Danielle, and Claude Thomasset. *Sexuality and Medicine in the Middle Ages.* Paris: Presses universitaires françaises, 1985. Trans. Matthew Adamson. Cambridge: Polity Press; Princeton: Princeton University Press, 1988.

Jakobson, Roman. *Six Lectures on Sound and Meaning.* Hassocks: Harvester Press, 1978.

Janssen, J. P. M. *The Suffolk Poems: An Edition of the Love Lyrics in Fairfax 16 Attributed to William de la Pole.* Groningen: Universiteitsdrukkerij, 1989.

Jeffrey, David L. "Chaucer and Wyclif: Biblical Hermeneutic and Literary Theory in the XIVth Century." In *Chaucer and Scriptural Tradition,* ed. D. L. Jeffrey, 109–40. Ottawa: University of Ottawa Press, 1984.

John of Salisbury, bishop of Chartres. *The Metalogicon: A Twelfth-Century Defense of the Verbal and Logical Arts of the Trivium.* Trans. Daniel D. McGarry. Berkeley and Los Angeles: University of California Press, 1962.

Jones, Charles W. *Saints' Lives and Chronicles in Early England.* Ithaca, N.Y.: Cornell University Press, 1947.

Jones, Terry. *Chaucer's Knight: The Portrait of a Medieval Mercenary.* London: Weidenfeld & Nicolson, 1983.

Joplin, Patricia K. "The Voice of the Shuttle Is Ours." *Stanford Literature Review* (1984): 25–53.

Jordan, Robert M. *Chaucer and the Shape of Creation: The Aesthetic Possibilities of Inorganic Structure.* Berkeley and Los Angeles: University of California Press, 1957.

Kane, George. *The Autobiographical Fallacy in Chaucer and Langland Studies.* London: H. K. Lewis, 1965.

———. "The Text of *The Legend of Good Women* in CUL MS Gg4.27." In

Middle English Studies Presented to Norman Davis, ed. Douglas Gray and E. G. Stanley, 39–58. Oxford: Clarendon Press, 1983.

Kaske, R. E., ed. *Medieval Christian Literary Imagery: A Guide to Interpretation.* Toronto: University of Toronto, 1988.

Keen, Maurice. "Chaucer's Knight, the English Aristocracy and the Crusade." In *English Court Culture in the Later Middle Ages,* ed. V. J. Scattergood and J. W. Sherborne, 45–61. London: Duckworth, 1983.

Kellum, Barbara. "Infanticide in England in the Middle Ages." *HCQ* 1 (1973): 367–88.

Kelly, Henry A. *Love and Marriage in the Age of Chaucer.* Ithaca, N.Y.: Cornell University Press, 1975.

Kiser, Lisa J. *Telling Classical Tales: Chaucer and the Legend of Good Women.* Ithaca, N.Y.: Cornell University Press, 1983.

———. *Truth and Textuality in Chaucer's Poetry.* Hanover, N.H.: University Press of New England, 1991.

Knight, W. F. J. "Maze Symbolism and the Trojan Game." *Antiquity* 6 (1932): 445–58.

Koch, John. *The Chronology of Chaucer's Writings.* London: Kegan Paul, Trench, Trübner, 1890.

Kolodny, Annette. *The Lay of the Land: Metaphor as Experience and History in American Life and Letters.* Chapel Hill: University of North Carolina Press, 1975.

Kolve, V. A. "From Cleopatra to Alceste. An Iconographic Study of the *Legend of Good Women.*" In *Signs and Symbols in Chaucer's Poetry,* ed. John P. Hermann and John J. Burke, Jr., 130–78. University, Ala.: University of Alabama Press, 1981.

Komroff, Manuel, ed. *Contemporaries of Marco Polo.* 1928. Reprint. New York: Dorset, 1989.

Koonce, B. J. "Satan the Fowler." *Mediaeval Studies* 21 (1959): 176–84.

Krappe, A. H. "La Belle Hélène de Constantinople." *Romania* 63 (1937): 324–83.

Krauss, Russell. "Chaucerian Problems." In *Three Chaucer Studies,* ed. Carleton Brown, 2–182. London: Oxford University Press, 1932.

Krieger, Murray. *Ekphrasis: The Illusion of the Natural Sign.* Baltimore: Johns Hopkins University Press, 1992.

Kritzeck, James. *Peter the Venerable and Islam.* Princeton: Princeton University Press, 1964.

Lanfranco of Milan. *Lanfrank's Science of Chirurgie.* Ed. R. von Fleischhacker. EETS, o.s., 102 (1894). Reprint, Millwood, N.Y.: Kraus, 1973.

Laqueur, Thomas Walter. *Making Sex: Body and Gender from the Greeks to Freud.* Cambridge, Mass.: Harvard University Press, 1990.

Lawton, David. *Chaucer's Narrators.* Woodbridge, Suffolk, and Dover, N.H.: D. S. Brewer, 1985.

Leach, Eleanor Winsor. "Ekphrasis and the Theme of Artistic Failure in Ovid's *Metamorphoses.*" *Ramus* 3 (1974): 102–42. [See also Winsor.]

Lévi-Strauss, Claude. *The Elementary Structures of Kinship.* Paris, 1949. Trans., Boston: Beacon Press, 1969.

Liebeschütz, Hans, ed. *Fulgentius Metaforalis.* Leipzig: Teubner, 1926.

Linder, Amnon. "The Myth of Constantine the Great in the West: Sources and Hagiographic Commemoration." *Studi Medievali* 16 (1975): 43–95.

Lopez, Robert S. and Irving Raymond. *Medieval Trade in the Mediterranean World.* New York: Columbia University Press, 1955.

Loraux, Nicole. *Tragic Ways of Killing a Woman.* Cambridge, Mass.: Harvard University Press, 1987.

Lord, Mary Louise. "Dido as an Example of Chastity: The Influence of Example Literature." *Harvard Library Bulletin* 17 (1969): 22–44, 216–32.

Lorris, Guillaume de, and Jean de Meun. *Le Roman de la Rose.* Ed. Felix Lecoy. 3 vols. Paris: Champion, 1970.

Lowes, John Livingston. "The Prologue to the *Legend of Good Women* as Related to the French *Marguerite* Poems and the *Filostrato.*" *PMLA* 19 (1904): 593–683.

———. "The Prologue to the *Legend of Good Women* Considered in Its Chronological Relations." *PMLA* 20 (1905): 749–864.

———. "Is Chaucer's *Legend of Good Women* a Travesty?" *JEGP* 8 (1909): 513–69.

———. "Chaucer and the *Ovide moralisé.*" *PMLA* 33 (1918): 302–25.

Lydgate, John. *The Serpent of Division.* Ed. Henry N. MacCracken. London: Frowde, 1911.

McCall, John P. "Chaucer and the Pseudo Origen *De Maria Magdalena*: A Preliminary Study." *Speculum* 46 (1971): 491–509.

———. *Chaucer among the Gods: The Poetics of Classical Myth.* University Park, Pa.: Pennsylvania State University Press, 1979.

McCarney, Joe. *The Real World of Ideology.* Brighton: Harvester Press; Atlantic Highlands, N.J.: Humanities Press, 1980.

MacCracken, H. N. "An English Friend of Charles of Orléans." *PMLA* 26 (1911): 142–80.

McFarlane, Kenneth B. *John Wyclif and the Beginnings of English Nonconformity.* London: English Universities Press, 1952. Reprint, 1972.

McGrade, Arthur Stephen. "Seeing Things: Ockham and Representation." *Philosophes médiévaux* 27 (1986): 591–97.

Mack, Francis, ed. *Seinte Marherete.* EETS, o.s., 193 (1934).

McKisack, May. *The Fourteenth Century, 1307–1390.* Oxford: Clarendon Press, 1959.

Malone, Kemp. "A Poet at Work: Chaucer Revising His Verses." *American Philosophical Society: Proceedings* 94 (1950): 317–20.

Mandeville, John [pseud.]. *Mandeville's Travels, Translated from the French of Jean d'Outremeuse.* Ed. P. Hamelius. EETS, o.s., 153 (1919; reprint, 1960), and o.s., 154 (1923; reprint, 1961).

Marcus, Jane. "Liberty, Sorority, Misogyny." In *The Representation of Women in Fiction,* ed. Carolyn Heilbrun and Margaret Higonnet, 60–97. Baltimore: Johns Hopkins University Press, 1982.

———. "Still Practice, A/Wrested Alphabet: Toward a Feminist Aesthetic." In *Feminist Issues in Literary Scholarship*, ed. Shari Benstock, 79–97. Bloomington: Indiana University Press, 1987.

Marin, Louis. *Le Récit est un piège*. Paris: Editions de minuit, 1978.

Mathews, W. H. *Mazes and Labyrinths: Their History and Development*. New York: Dover, 1970.

Medvedev, P. N., and Mikhail Bakhtin. *The Formal Method in Literary Scholarship*. Leningrad, 1928. Baltimore: Johns Hopkins University Press, 1978.

Meech, Sanford B. "Chaucer and the *Ovide moralisé*: A Further Study." *PMLA* 46 (1931): 182–204.

Menocal, Maria Rosa. *The Arabic Role in Medieval Literary History: A Forgotten Heritage*. Philadelphia: University of Pennsylvania Press, 1987.

Metlitzki, Dorothée. *The Matter of Araby in Medieval England*. New Haven: Yale University Press, 1977.

Michalski, Konstanty. "Le Problème de la volonté à Oxford et à Paris au XIVe siècle." In Michalski, *La Philosophie au XIVe siècle*, ed. Kurt Flasch, 279–415. Frankfurt: Minerva, 1969.

Miller, J. Hillis. "Ariadne's Thread: Repetition and the Narrative Line." In *Interpretation of Narrative*, ed. Mario J. Valdes and Owen J. Miller, 148–66. Toronto: University of Toronto Press, 1976.

———. "Ariachne's Broken Woof." *Georgia Review* 31 (1977): 44–60.

Miller, Nancy K. "Arachnologies." In *The Poetics of Gender*, ed. Nancy K. Miller, 270–95. New York: Columbia University Press, 1986.

Muldoon, James. *Popes, Lawyers and Infidels: The Church and the Non-Christian World, 1250–1550*. Philadelphia: University of Pennsylvania Press, 1979.

Mulligan, Winifred Joy. "The British Constantine: An English Historical Myth." *JMRS* 8 (1978): 257–79.

Munro, John. *Wool, Cloth and Gold: The Struggle for Bullion in Anglo-Burgundian Trade, 1340–1478*. Toronto: University of Toronto Press, 1972.

Murdoch, John E. "*Subtilitates Anglicanae* in Fourteenth-Century Paris: John of Mirecourt and Peter Ceffons." In *Machaut's World: Science and Art in the Fourteenth Century*, ed. Madeleine P. Cosman and Bruce Chandler, 51–86. New York: Academy of Sciences, 1978.

Myerowitz, Molly. *Ovid's Games of Love*. Detroit: Wayne State University Press, 1985.

Nichols, John. "Female Nudity and Sexuality in Medieval Art." In *New Images of Medieval Women*, ed. Edelgard E. DuBruck, 165–206. Lampeter: Edwin Mellen Press, 1989.

Noonan, John T., Jr. *Contraception: A History of Its Treatment by the Catholic Theologians and Canonists*. Cambridge, Mass.: Harvard University Press, 1965.

Norton-Smith, J. "Chaucer's *Anelida and Arcite*." In *Medieval Studies for J. A. W. Bennett*, ed. P. L. Heyworth, 81–99. Oxford: Clarendon Press, 1981.

Olson, Paul. *The Canterbury Tales and the Good Society.* Princeton: Princeton University Press, 1986.

Orme, Nicholas. *English Schools in the Middle Ages.* London: Methuen, 1973.

Ormrod, W. M. "The Personal Religion of Edward III." *Speculum* 64 (1989): 849–77.

Ortner, Sherry. "Is Female to Male as Nature Is to Culture?" In *Women, Culture and Society,* ed. Michelle Z. Rosaldo and Louise Lamphere, 165–206. Stanford: Stanford University Press, 1974.

Ovid. *"Heroides" and "Amores."* Trans. Grant Showerman. Loeb Classical Library. Cambridge, Mass.: Harvard University Press, 1914. 2d ed., revised by G. P. Gould, 1977.

———. *Metamorphoses.* Trans. Frank Justus Miller. 2 vols. Loeb Classical Library. Cambridge, Mass.: Harvard University Press, 1916. 3d ed., revised by G. P. Gould, 1977.

———. *The Art of Love and Other Poems.* Trans. J. H. Mozley. Loeb Classical Library. Cambridge, Mass.: Harvard University Press, 1929. 2d ed., revised by G. P. Gould, 1979.

Ovide moralisé: Poème du commencement du quatorzième siècle. Ed. Cornélis de Boer. 5 vols. Amsterdam: J. Müller, 1915–38.

Pagels, Elaine. *Adam, Eve, and the Serpent.* New York: Random House, 1988.

Palmer, J. J. N. *England, France and Christendom, 1377–99.* London: Routledge & Kegan Paul, 1972.

Parkes, M. B., and Richard Beagle, eds. *Poetical Works: Geoffrey Chaucer. A Facsimile of Cambridge University Library MS Gg 4.27.* 3 vols. Norman, Okla.: Pilgrim Books, 1980.

Partridge, Eric. *Shakespeare's Bawdy.* London: Routledge, 1947.

Paston. *The Paston Letters.* Ed. John Warrington. 2 vols. London: J. M. Dent & Sons, 1924. Rev. ed. 1956.

Patterson, Lee. *Negotiating the Past: The Historical Understanding of Medieval Literature.* Madison: University of Wisconsin Press, 1987.

Payne, Robert O. *The Key of Remembrance: A Study of Chaucer's Poetics.* New Haven: Yale University Press for University of Cincinnati, 1963.

Pelphrey, Brant. *Love Was His Meaning: The Theology and Mysticism of Julian of Norwich.* Salzburg: Institut für Anglistik und Amerikanistik, Universität Salzburg, 1982.

Petrarch. *Le familiari.* Trans. Aldo S. Bernardo. In *Francesco Petrarca Rerum familiarium libri I–VIII.* Albany, N.Y.: SUNY, 1975.

Pinborg, Jan. "The English Contribution to Logic before Ockham." *Synthèse* 40 (1979): 19–42.

Plato. *The Symposium.* Trans. Walter Hamilton. Harmondsworth: Penguin Books, 1951.

———. *The Sophist and the Statesman.* Trans. A. E. Taylor. London: Thomas Nelson, 1961.

Poirion, Daniel. "De la signification selon Jean de Meun." In *Archéologie du signe,* ed. Lucie Brind'amour and Eugene Vance, 165–85. Toronto: PIMS, 1983.

Pouchelle, Marie-Christine. *Corps et chirurgie à l'apogée du Moyen-Age*. Paris: Flammarion, 1983.

Prawer, Joshua. *The Latin Kingdom of Jerusalem: European Colonialism in the Middle Ages*. London: Weidenfeld & Nicolson, 1972.

———. "The Roots of Medieval Colonialism." In *The Meeting of Two Worlds: Cultural Exchange between East and West during the Period of the Crusades*, ed. Vladimir P. Goss and Christine V. Bornstein, 23–38. Kalamazoo: Western Michigan University Press, 1986.

Rashdall, Hastings. "Nicholas de Ultracuria, A Medieval Hume." *Proceedings of the Aristotelian Society*, n.s., 7 (1906–7): 1–27.

Rathbone, Eleanor. "Master Alberic of London, 'Mythographus Tertius Vaticanus.'" *Mediaeval and Renaissance Studies* 1 (1941–43): 35–38.

Reiss, Edmund. "Chaucer's Parodies of Love." In *Chaucer the Love Poet*, ed. Jerome Mitchell and William Provost, 27–44. Athens, Ga.: University of Georgia Press, 1973.

Reames, Sherry. "A Recent Discovery Concerning the Sources of Chaucer's 'Second Nun's Tale.'" *Modern Philology* 87 (1990): 337–61.

Rigg, A. G. "Some Notes on Trinity College, Cambridge, Ms. O.9.38." *Notes and Queries*, n.s., 13 (September 1966): 324–30.

Robbins, Rossell Hope, ed. *Secular Lyrics of the XIV and XV Centuries*. Oxford: Clarendon Press, 1952.

Robertson, D. W., Jr. *A Preface to Chaucer*. Princeton: Princeton University Press, 1962.

———. *Chaucer's London*. New York: John Wiley, 1968.

Rowe, Donald W. *Through Nature to Eternity: Chaucer's Legend of Good Women*. Lincoln: University of Nebraska Press, 1988.

Rowland, Beryl, ed. and trans. *Medieval Woman's Guide to Health: The First English Gynecological Handbook*. Kent, Ohio: Kent State University Press, 1981.

Russell, P. E. *The English Intervention in Spain and Portugal in the Time of Edward III and Richard II*. Oxford: Clarendon Press, 1955.

Ruths, Rudolf. *Die französischen Fassungen des Roman de la belle Helaine*. Griefswald: Kunicke, 1897.

Said, Edward W. *Orientalism*. New York: Pantheon Books, 1978.

———. *The World, the Text and the Critic*. Cambridge, Mass.: Harvard University Press, 1983.

Salutati, Coluccio. "Declamatio Lucretiae." Ed. and trans. Stephanie H. Jed. In *Chaste Thinking: The Rape of Lucretia and the Birth of Humanism*, 133–58. Bloomington: Indiana University Press, 1989.

Salverda de Grave, J.-J., ed. *Eneas: Roman du XIIe siècle*. 2 vols. Paris: Champion, 1964–68.

Samuel, Irene. "Semiramis in the Middle Ages: The History of a Legend." *Medievalia et humanistica* 2 (1943): 32–44.

Saunders, J. J. "Matthew Paris and the Mongols." In *Essays in Medieval History Presented to Bertie Wilkinson*, ed. T. A. Sandquist and M. R. Powicke, 116–32. Toronto: University of Toronto, 1969.

Saussure, F. de. *Course in General Linguistics.* From lecture notes of 1906–11. New York: Philosophical Library, 1959. Reprint, New York: McGraw-Hill, 1966.

Schapiro, Meyer. "The Bowman and the Bird on the Ruthwell Cross." *Art Bulletin* 45 (1963): 351–54.

Schmitz, Götz. "Gower, Chaucer, and the Classics: Back to the Textual Evidence." In *John Gower: Recent Readings,* ed. R. F. Yeager, 95–111. Kalamazoo: Western Michigan University, 1989.

———. *The Fall of Women in Early English Narrative Verse.* Cambridge: Cambridge University Press, 1990.

Schor, Naomi. *Breaking the Chain: Women, Theory and French Realist Criticism.* New York: Columbia University Press, 1985.

Schwartz, W. *Principles and Problems of Biblical Translation.* Cambridge: Cambridge University Press, 1955.

Searle, John. *Speech Acts.* London: Cambridge University Press, 1969.

Shaner, Mary C. E. "The Legend of Good Women and Medieval Commentaries on the *Heroides.*" B. Litt. diss., Oxford University, 1953.

Shannon, Edgar Finley. *Chaucer and the Roman Poets.* 1929. Reprint, New York: Russell & Russell, 1964.

Shapiro, Herman, ed. *Medieval Philosophy.* New York: Random House, 1964.

Shea, Virginia A. "Nat Every Vessel Al of Gold: Studies in Chaucer's *Legend of Good Women.*" Ph.D. diss., University of Connecticut, 1971.

Shoaf, R. A. *Dante, Chaucer and the Currency of the Word: Money, Images, and Reference in Late Medieval Poetry.* Norman, Okla.: Pilgrim Books, 1983.

Skeat, Walter W., ed. *Chaucer: The Legend of Good Women.* Oxford: Clarendon Press, 1889.

Sklute, Larry. *Virtue of Necessity: Inconclusiveness and Narrative Form in Chaucer's Poetry.* Columbus: Ohio State University, 1984.

Smalley, Beryl. *The Study of the Bible in the Middle Ages.* New York: Philosophical Library, 1952.

———. *English Friars and Antiquity in the Early Fourteenth Century.* Oxford: Blackwell, 1960.

Smith, Barbara Herrnstein. *Poetic Closure: A Study of How Poems End.* Chicago: University of Chicago Press, 1968.

Sneyd, Charlotte Augusta, ed. *A Relation . . . of the Island of England . . . about the Year 1500.* Translated from the Italian by Charlotte Augusta Sneyd. London: J. D. Nichols & Son for the Camden Society, 1847.

Southern, R. W. *Western Views of Islam in the Middle Ages.* Cambridge, Mass., Harvard University Press, 1962.

Spearing, A. C. *Criticism and Medieval Poetry.* London: Edward Arnold, 1964. Reprint, 1972.

———. "Chaucerian Authority and Inheritance." In *Literature in Fourteenth-Century England,* ed. P. Boitani, 185–202. Tübingen, 1983.

Spurgeon, Caroline. *Five Hundred Years of Chaucer Criticism and Allusion, 1357–1900.* 2 vols. Cambridge: Cambridge University Press, 1925.

Steadman, John. "Venus's *Citole* in Chaucer's *Knight's Tale* and Berchorius." *Speculum* 34 (1959): 620–24.

Strohm, Paul. "*Passioun, Lyf, Miracle, Legende*: Some Generic Terms in Middle English Hagiographical Narrative." *ChR* 10 (1975): 62–75, 154–71.

Tachau, Katherine H. *Vision and Certitude in the Age of Ockham: Optics, Epistemology and the Foundations of Semantics, 1250–1345.* Leiden: Brill, 1988.

Tanner, Norman P., ed. *Heresy Trials in the Diocese of Norwich, 1428–31.* London: Royal Historical Society, 1977.

Taylor, Beverly. "The Medieval Cleopatra: The Classical and Medieval Tradition of Chaucer's *Legend of Cleopatra*." *JMRS* 7 (1977): 249–69.

Terdiman, Richard. "Problematical Virtuosity: Dante's Depiction of the Thieves." *Dante Studies* 91 (1973): 27–45.

Thomas, Elizabeth. "Ovidian Echoes in Juvenal." In *Ovidiana: Recherches sur Ovide,* ed. Niculae I. Herescu. Paris: Les Belles Lettres, 1958.

Throop, Palmer A. *Criticism of the Crusade: A Study of Public Opinion and Crusade Propaganda.* Amsterdam: Swets & Zeitlinger, 1940. Reprint, Philadelphia: Porcupine, 1975.

Trexler, Richard C. "Infanticide in Florence: New Sources and First Results." *HCQ* 1 (1973): 98–116.

Tuchman, Barbara. *A Distant Mirror: The Calamitous Fourteenth Century.* New York: Knopf, 1978.

Twycross, Meg. *The Medieval Anadyomene: A Study in Chaucer's Mythography.* Oxford: Blackwell, 1972.

Tyerman, Christopher. *England and the Crusades, 1095–1588.* Chicago: University of Chicago Press, 1988.

Vance, Eugene. "Saint Augustine: Language as Temporality." In id., *Mervelous Signals: Poetics and Sign Theory in the Middle Ages,* 34–50. Lincoln: University of Nebraska Press, 1986.

van Emden, W. G. "Shakespeare and the French Pyramus and Thisbe Tradition." *Forum for Modern Language Studies* 2 (1975): 193–204.

Vauchez, André. *La Sainteté en occident aux derniers siècles du Moyen-Age.* Rome: Palais Farnèse, 1981.

Vaughan, Richard. *Philip the Bold: The Formation of the Burgundian State.* Cambridge, Mass., Harvard University Press, 1962.

Verducci, Florence. *Ovid's Toyshop of the Heart: Epistulae Heroidum.* Princeton: Princeton University Press, 1985.

Voragine, Jacob da. *Legenda aurea.* Ed. Th. Graesse. Dresden and Leipzig, 1846.

Wagenknecht, Edward, ed. *Chaucer: Modern Essays in Criticism.* New York: Oxford University Press, 1959.

Wallace, David. *Chaucer and the Early Writings of Boccaccio.* Woodbridge, Suffolk, and Dover, N.H.: Boydell & Brewer, 1985.

Wallis, Mieczyslaw. "Inscriptions in Paintings." *Semiotica* 9 (1973): 1–28.

Wasserman, Julian, and Robert J. Blanch, eds. *Chaucer in the Eighties.* Syracuse, N.Y.: Syracuse University Press, 1986.

Watts, P. R. "The Strange Case of Geoffrey Chaucer and Cecily Chaumpaigne." *Law Quarterly Review* 63 (1947): 491–515.

Wetherbee, Winthrop. *Chaucer and the Poets: An Essay on Troilus and Criseyde.* Ithaca, N.Y.: Cornell University Press, 1984.

Wieruszowski, Helene. "Arezzo as a Center of Learning and Letters in the Thirteenth Century." *Traditio* 9 (1953): 321–91.

Wilks, Michael. "Royal Priesthood: The Origins of Lollardy." In *The Church in a Changing World,* 63–70. Uppsala: Almqvist & Wiksell, 1978.

Wimbledon, Thomas. *Wimbledon's Sermon: Redde rationem villicationis tue; A Middle English Sermon of the Fourteenth Century.* Ed. Ione Kemp Knight. Pittsburgh: Duquesne University Press, 1967.

Wimsatt, James I. *The Marguerite Poetry of Guillaume de Machaut.* Chapel Hill: University of North Carolina Press, 1970.

Winsor, Eleanor J. "A Study in the Sources and Rhetoric of Chaucer's *Legend of Good Women* and Ovid's *Heroides.*" Ph.D. diss., Yale University, 1963. [See also Leach.]

Wolfram von Eschenbach. *Parzival,* trans. Helen Mustard and Charles Passage. New York: Random House, Vintage Books, 1961.

Wood, Anthony. *Athena Oxoniensis.* 1691–92. 5 vols. London. 1813.

Woolf, Virginia. *Between the Acts.* New York: Harcourt, Brace & World, 1941.

———. "The Leaning Tower." In *Collected Essays,* 2: 162–81. New York: Harcourt, Brace & World, 1967.

Young, Karl. "Chaucer's Appeal to the Platonic Deity." *Speculum* 19 (1944): 1–13.

Zacher, Christian. *Curiosity and Pilgrimage: The Literature of Discovery in Fourteenth-Century England.* Baltimore: Johns Hopkins University Press, 1976.

Index